Critical Studies in Fashion and Beauty

UNIVERSITY OF WOLVERHAMPTON
LEARNING & INFORMATION
SERVICES

ACC NO
2496219

CLASS

CONTROL NO

WITHDRAWN

DATE
-2 JUL 2012

SITE
Ul

CRI

intellect Bristol, UK / Chicago, USA

D1355539

First published in the UK in 2012 by
Intellect, The Mill, Parnall Road, Fishponds, Bristol, BS16 3JG, UK

First published in the USA in 2012 by
Intellect, The University of Chicago Press, 1427 E. 60th Street, Chicago, IL 60637, USA

Copyright © 2012 Intellect Ltd

All rights reserved. No part of this publication may be reproduced, stored in a
retrieval system, or transmitted, in any form or by any means, electronic, mechanical,
photocopying, recording, or otherwise, without written permission.

A catalogue record for this book is available from the British Library.

Cover designer: Holly Rose
Cover image: 'Flower Bomb' outfit designed by Amy Rodgers, Lauren Crimes and
William Coma, School of Design University of Leeds
Copy-editor: Macmillan
Typesetting: Holly Rose

ISBN 978-1-84150-648-7

Printed and bound by Latimer Trend

CONTENTS

CSFB 1 (1) pp. 3–53 Intellect Limited 2010

Critical Studies in Fashion and Beauty
Volume 1 Number 1

© 2010 Intellect Ltd Editorial. English language. doi: 10.1386/csfb.1.1.3_2

EDITORIAL

EFRAT TSEËLON
University of Leeds

Outlining a fashion studies project

Part 1

Two decades ago when I finished my Ph.D. on 'Communication via clothing' the field of 'fashion studies' was non-existent as an independent enterprise, but inhabited the margins of scholarly pursuits and belonged mostly to costume and art history, anthropology and the frivolous end of the social sciences. My own work – however innovative in its methodological shift from observational to experiential approaches, and its theoretical shift from a focus on 'stereotypic clothing' to 'everyday dress' (wardrobe research) – was charting new ground at the periphery of my core discipline (experimental social psychology), which was oblivious to such trivial pursuits. So it is with genuine delight that I have been observing the field coming into its own.

When I mentioned to a number of people that I was going to edit this journal I got two types of responses. Some people responded with enthusiasm, others with 'what do we need another fashion journal for?' The responses were not random. They reflected a schism that exists in the field regarding what 'fashion studies' is about, and how to do it. Those ontological and epistemological differences run deeper than first appears. They represent a hegemonic struggle between two broad perspectives, which both regard themselves as 'the true voice' of the field.

Below, I propose a suggestive characterization of the two group-types that I will designate as *fashion natives* and *fashion migrants*. The *fashion natives* see themselves as guardians of the original and true spirit of the field. They come from a tradition of working with detailed fashion artefacts, either historical (museums, art, costume history) or contemporary (fashion design, fashion business, journalism). *Fashion migrants*, on the other hand, include people working within a social sciences

Group features	Fashion natives	Fashion migrants
Disciplines	Arts, humanities, museum curation, ethnography, journalism, fashion marketing	Sociology, psychology, philosophy, social and cultural theory
Level of research focus	Specific, concrete	Generic, abstract
Dimension of research focus	Visible, observable (e.g. style, craftsmanship)	Invisible, conceptual (attitudes, lived experience, perceptions, emotions, principles, patterns)
Object of research focus	*'Object'* of material culture, beauty procedures	*'Idea'* of a garment or appearance, analogy, metaphor, symbol
Aims of research	Chronicle, classify, categorize, describe uses	Explain meanings, functions, reasons
Method of research	Inductive, evidence based, systematic	Deductive, conceptual, eclectic
Research outcome	Detailed thematic or period account, typology, record keeping	Critical argument, reflexive account, set of meanings

Table 1: A schematic representation of the contours of fashion studies agendas.

framework, health science, philosophy, and social and cultural theory – who are interested in fashion and appearance as instances of social activity, and as a vehicle for exploring and understanding social processes and meanings.

Neither group is an accurate representation of reality: they are merely abstract idealizations constructed from a particular point of view (*ideal-types* in Weber's sense) to serve as analytical tools. And there is sufficient crossover between them at the level of individual researchers.

To illustrate the potential for conflicts of interest, the following examples will suffice. In reviewing the portfolios of candidates for a fashion studies chair (a position which required a multidisciplinary background with disciplinary roots in a whole range of fields, most of them social studies) two very well known fashion academics recommended the winning 'ideal candidate' on the grounds of expertise in 'both historical and contemporary fashion'. The fashion scholars with a social science background, on the other hand, were deemed to be lacking 'the specificity of detail and focus on fashion and its history'. Similarly, while reviewing a collection of essays on social science and the theoretical aspects of fashion entitled 'Through the wardrobe' for *Fashion Theory*, Wilson Trower recalls a conversation with a dress historian who did not know any of the contributors. This dress historian commented that the collection was 'not well enough informed for use in fashion retailing/ marketing studies, too broad a scope for comparative literature, too sociologically focused for fashion as consumption studies'. Interestingly, in a gesture that reads like an ethnographic interest in a rare and exotic tribe, she did recommend most of the chapters 'if only to increase one's understanding of fashion as seen through the eyes of sociologists' (Wilson Trower 2004: 351–354).

Incidentally, another costume historian commented in her book, *Feeding the Eye*

> There have never been writers trained in art history and fashion history who have steadily commented on its current condition for current publication. The result is that the largest body of serious writing on fashion has been the work of sociologists of one flavour or another.
>
> (Hollander 1999: 109)

Neither of these approaches is particularly helpful. Pluralism cannot speak in a single framework. If knowledge is a beneficiary then a synthesis, or synergy or cooperative co-existence is a more helpful strategy, better still a truly interdisciplinary approach – more on that later.

Real fashion in a society of hyper-mobility

Since the 1990s the landscape of 'real world' fashion had undergone a sea change, and this has been mirrored in 'academic fashion'. I would like to sketch the relevant developments in both spheres.

The processes of globalization changed not just the nature of production and retail but also ushered in new types of relationships between consumers and objects. The instantaneous availability of catwalk styles from around the globe and the speed with which 'fast fashion' retailers translated these into ready-to-wear, as well as the emergence of street fashion (championing a ground-up approach) signalled the end of trend as an industry dictate (Hedström and Ingesson 2008). The demise of trends coincided with a backlash against the mass market and a rise in nostalgia for 'objects with a story to tell' (either by virtue of their qualities, or the experiences woven into them).

Most theorists of consumer culture problematize the appeal to image or appearances over the appeal to substance or values – on conceptual and ethical grounds. The metaphors of Alvin Toffler's 'future shock' and Zygmunt Bauman's 'liquid modernity', which they have elaborated on in several books, capture the spirit of this approach. In 1970 Toffler envisaged that the shift from the industrial age to the information age would generate an accelerated rate of technological and social changes leaving people *disconnected* and *disoriented*. Zygmunt Bauman explains the dynamics of globalization, the loss of community and the gradual privatization of public life, as closely related to the nation-state's renunciation of its functions of security and stability (employment, finance, health). The hero of liquid modernity may not be *disconnected* and *disoriented* but he/she is still anxious: with only loosely connected and unstable communities online and offline, with no bonds but 'connections' of a transient and non-obliging nature. The consumerist habits of such a hero are likewise geared more to fun, conviviality and temporality than to duty, values, and rational choice behaviour. Even if they are not customers of the fast-fashion value chains, the heroes of liquid modernity participate in the throwaway society by virtue of shopping for pleasure, not necessity.

But objects are not the only way global consumers distinguish themselves. Bauman describes a new class of elite global consumers defined by the privilege of *increased mobility*. Unlike the *forced mobility* of the displaced, these globetrotters are truly 'citizens of the world'. This new breed is already the focus of new marketing thinking, as the following example shows.

The development of Les Boutiques d'Aeroport de Paris is mushrooming into veritable shopping precincts. The product range is not limited to cosmetics and alcoholic beverages alone, but also encompasses jewellery, fashion and food. In 2008 over 250 boutiques spread throughout the various terminals will offer passengers the very best in Parisian shopping – and the magic of its greatest brands – at duty free prices. The director of Chronos group explains the change in travel retail marketing strategies directed to meet the needs of 'consumers on the move': his research identified a new type of consumer '*hyper-mobile people* represent a third of the respondents. Fifty-eight per cent of them visit 26 different shops in the space of a year compared to 6% of geographically stable respondents. And they make multiple use of means of transport, media and digital technology'. To accommodate the needs of this growing market transit area operators have to invent new consumer trends. 'In addition to shopping, passengers must be able to communicate or work with the help of the latest technology, socialize in comfortable surroundings if they so choose or simply sit and daydream', Bruno Marzloff points out. A concept that's particularly true of airport terminals, potent vehicles for escapist fantasies is 'a vast exotic garden in Singapore airport where passengers can stroll leisurely away from the impressive Duty Free area into the park abounding in plant-life and bathed in light.' The needs of transit passengers also influence product forms with many food and cosmetics produced in mini form and single doses. 'In short, *everything is being done so that the consumer on the move can both purchase a modern lifestyle and save time'*.

(Paris Aéroports magazine 2007–2008, emphasis added)

'L'éphémère n'est pas une mode éphémère'

But what is there to indicate that the characteristics of the market that produced this type of consumer are not as transitory as the fashion they describe? In other words, how do we know that the current trends are here to stay? While the social, political and economic context where fashion operates needs to be taken into account, the meaning of that context is open to interpretations. Indeed, the French social theorist Gilles Lipovetsky has a different outlook on the meaning of the changes we are witnessing; in one of his books written in 1987, *L'empire de l'éphémère – La mode et son destin dans les sociétés modernes/ The Empire of Fashion* (1994), he analysed the meaning of the transitory nature of fashion. In particular he was keen to understand the origins of the *Me* generation that developed in France under a socialist regime. In the French intellectual tradition, the idea of indulgent and narcissistic individualism for the sake of personal gratification is disapproved of. Lipovetsky, however, viewed it in the context of the historical evolution of democratic modernity over the last two centuries. His conclusion was to consider fashion as an important tool of social renewal. He argued that it is the mechanism which freed people from the authority of the past, traditions and rigid class cultures. The very features that fashion is criticised for – an ephemeral quality, superficiality, instability and artifice – came to represent an almost subversive potential to resist 'ancestral laws' whose essential change and novelty are a counter force to tradition.

According to Lipovetsky, the idea of fashion as 'marginal to the social core of any society' has become the true ruler of post-industrial age, and contrary to normal expectations, has led to a time of true freedom for the individual (Lipovetsky [1987] 1994). Thus the slogan of our contemporaneity could be '*freedom through ephemeral fashion*' (Kritzman and Reill 2007). Lipovetsky is in no doubt that the trends we see now are not passing fads. In his mind constant change and novelty are unwitting consequences of the desire to avoid routine and boredom.

In an interview Lipovetsky gave in October 2009 to *Newzy* magazine he referred to the ubiquity of the pop-up and guerrilla shops, and he pointed out that the ephemeral has become a structural principle: market dynamics have taken over from tradition as source of authority – as the economic crisis has demonstrated only too well.[1] Another indication that *fashion is being upgraded* as a more serious subject (more art than craft) is in the fact that the last two decades saw many art museums give space to retrospective exhibitions (which are essentially free publicity) of iconic designers. Even this upgrade holds its own risks. Adrian Hamilton writing in *The Independent* recently observed that the last decade saw museums and galleries focus on 'blockbuster exhibitions' almost entirely neglecting their general core collections or reserve holdings.[2]

Why has 'academic fashion' changed?

Some changes are attributed to the different role fashion is increasingly playing as a global multi-billion pound business; other changes are the result of the growing perception of fashion as relevant to personal and company branding (an area of increasing importance in public and commercial life), and the corresponding shift of 'image' from the realm of 'frivolity' to the realm of 'serious business'. Other reasons for the improved standing of fashion in academe have to do with the academizing of vocational schools and the increasing requirement, due to government funding strategies, to engage in industrial collaborations: fashion has easy affinities with all types of players in this capacity. Finally, trends in academic thinking – from the rise of the *postmodern* and *poststructuralist* conversation, to the *cultural turn*, which saw fashion positioned as a 'cultural phenomenon', and the *methodological turn*, which saw the emergence of qualitative methodology as a respectable alternative or accompaniment to quantitative methods – combined to facilitate the legitimization of this new interdisciplinary field.

The interdependent developments of the field of *fashion as an industry* and *fashion as a discipline* highlight both the potential for collaboration and the potential risk of 'cosying' up to the industry in exchange for funding and star dust celebrity status. The benefits cannot be highlighted enough, but the risks cannot be underestimated. Fred Davis (1992) and Mark Tungate point out that unlike other creative fields (film, literature, theatre, plastic and performing arts) fashion has not produced a critical discourse. Referring to the press Tungate observes that 'the vast percentage of fashion journalism is at best effervescent, at worst fawning' (Tungate 2005). In the same way that commercial considerations may lead cash stripped museums to bask in the reflected glory of star designers, science museums have been capitalizing on the sexy appeal of beauty products. This has been the case in recent events featuring 'the science of beauty' at the Science Museum in London or 'beauty myths' at the Wellcome Institute[3] featuring scientists, industry insiders, and cosmetics company representatives – which might explain a certain reluctance to probe awkward

1. http://www.newzy.fr/videos/biz/-l-ephemere-n-est-pas-une-mode-ephemere.html

2. http://www.independent.co.uk/arts-entertainment/art/features/the-decline-of-britainrsquos-public-museums-2007613.html. Accessed July 2010.

3. http://www.wellcomecollection.org/whats-on/events/beauty-myths.aspx, http://www.sciencemuseum.org.uk/sitecore/shell/Controls/Rich

4. http://www.wen.org.
uk/wp-content/
uploads/Prettynasty3.
pdf, http://www.
cosmeticsdatabase.
com/, http://www.ewg.
org/newsclip/
Saving-Face-How-
Safe-Are-Cosmetics-
and-Body-Care-
Products, http://www.
safecosmetics.org/.

issues of public health such as the routine use in cosmetic products of hormone disruptors, bio accumulators and other synthetic petrochemicals that are linked to potential toxic effects including cancer.[4]

While even the sciences are not immune to the desire to collaborate with corporate power, fashion scholarship may be just as vulnerable to potentially 'dangerous liaisons'.

'Academic fashion' since the 1990s: A discipline in search of a character

As a field of enquiry until the 1990s (with some notable exceptions such as Hebdige, Eicher and Roach, Kaiser, Polhemus, Steele, Wilson, among others) fashion exhibited very little theoretical or empirical sophistication. Before 2000 there were only a handful of interdisciplinary conferences dedicated to fashion and appearance topics (e.g. *the psychology of fashion* in 1985 (Solomon 1985); *mask, masquerade and carnival* in 1994; *masquerade and gendered identity* in 1996 (Tseëlon 2001). Theoretically fashion scholarship has tended to recycle a number of causal explanations from a limited core of theoreticians (e.g. Veblen's *conspicuous consumption*, Simmel's *trickle down*, Barthes' semiotics, Flügel's psychoanalytic explanations). Empirically fashion research relied on insights or anecdotal evidence, avoiding a systematic meaningful analysis. The early experimental work tended to reify the notion of 'indexical meaning' inherent in the clothes themselves and in certain styles, and to embody all that the critique of positivism in social sciences targeted. However, in the last couple of decades fashion studies has emerged as a broadly defined, constantly evolving and incredibly versatile multidisciplinary field (combining arts, social sciences, textile chemistry and business) in search of an identity and a distinctive character.

The transition from a series of loosely connected research areas on the periphery of established disciplines to an interdisciplinary field in its own right has followed the familiar trajectory of a discipline in the making, whose place is not yet safely secure. When organizations (or societies) enjoy recognition, acceptance and prestige, they tend to display relaxed and generous tolerance of heterogeneity and pluralism, and an appetite for cooperation. But in times of uncertainty and struggle, the level of tolerance goes down, and internal struggles intensify. Remembering this will explain the spirit of 'nation building' described below. I detect three main stages in this fashioning of an identity.

- **Identity formation**
  In the first stage 'fashion studies' was preoccupied with setting boundaries, ring fencing, territorial marking, delineating insiders (exclusive club of those who are invited to participate in special activities, symposia, publications etc.) from outsiders.

- **Agenda setting**
  The second stage involved a production of hegemonic discourse in terms of topics, perspectives and methods. This was accompanied by an increase in platforms – both journals and books – where fashion-related work could be published. While such topics could always occupy the margins of social science, history, art, and/or the up-and-coming cultural studies domain of the more established disciplines (like cultural sociology and psychology), the addition of more dedicated journals like *Visual Culture*, *Fashion Theory* and the *Journal of Material Culture* created a positive environment for the field to flourish. Increasingly, publishers started giving space to fashion studies monograms with some, like Berg for example, specializing in these themes. Another feature in the academic landscape is that in the last two decades the number of fashion themed conferences or panels at conferences has multiplied. Fashion is increasingly the focus of many conferences, symposia, seminars and museum exhibitions.

- **Gatekeeping**
  The third stage in the consolidation of the field is the internal power struggle with certain groups representing certain agendas (e.g. *fashion natives* and *fashion migrants*) trying to establish themselves as 'centre' and position other perspectives as 'marginal' (for example fashion practice vs. fashion theory; costume/social history vs. social theory; production vs. consumption; engagement with special occasion wear vs. everyday wear; focus on designer fashion vs. real people's wardrobes). These groups define the scope of legitimate activity using practices which include production of collections, taxonomies, 'Readers' and textbooks which purport to provide definitive and encyclopaedic knowledge and the authoritative version of the field, as well as deciding who to ignore and who to cite, especially as there are so many 'parallel communities' not very familiar with each other's work (I am sure I am not the only one who has a sense of déjà vu when running into their own ideas worked into another text which is apparently unaware of the existence of prior work). Gatekeeping also involves regulating activities of the kind employed by professional bodies that guard the interests of their members (for example in job references, publication refereeing, interview panels or grant panels).

In fact most of the changes described above occurred *inside the discipline*. In the wider academic context it appears that changes have been slower. Despite improved standing and greater understanding of a cultural agenda, fashion is still somewhat tainted with 'craft image' and a 'not quite *serious* image'. Other than a handful of journals in a number of disciplines which specialize in fashion, the research area is still not considered a proper specialization within the established social sciences as expressed in the structure of associations (e.g. ASA, ISA, ESA, APA), and the content of associations' flagship journals (and other 'high impact' journals), or the publishing lists of mainstream publishers.

What does the 'fashion' label actually contain?

If people from different branches of 'fashion studies' were to compile lists of those they consider to be 'the key players' there would be very little consensus about canonical lists. Every branch (representing different core disciplines, or different linguistic communities) has its own list of star performers and every new 'fashion studies reader' or encyclopaedia is trying to rewrite history as they see it, and to place a different set of celebrities at the core of the narrative. This is obvious not just from the content of the anthologies and the entries of the various encyclopaedias but also from the reality of the market. To get a good idea of what 'fashion' is about outside academe a survey of what is available in a non-specialist bookstore is a handy clue. With five floors and more than 200,000 titles in stock the iconic Foyles is Europe's largest and London's leading bookstore. A visit to the shop reveals fashion to contain a number of themes: a periodization of costume/social history with some work that focuses on a specific period, style or artefact; books which feature a specific exhibition or the work of a particular designer; books about the craft of fashion making; and DIY books (from manuals to reality TV programmes). Many titles are of the coffee table variety. There are also a handful of current books about theory.

Similarly, if one examines the fashion courses that exist in UK higher education a clear trend is visible which revolves around engaging with luxury fashion and the fashion industry (the process of producing collections, the study of designers, branding, collaboration with fashion houses: labels and magazines and manufacturers). Additionally, if one looks at the work displayed in graduate fashion weeks, fashion shows and publicity materials, it is obvious that the industry mindset (whether of the couture or ready-to-wear variety), conventions and practices are followed uncritically; these include the catwalk conventions: the skinny models, the killer heels, the loud music, the mindless walk of mechanical dolls. Except in rare token gestures the standards of designing and displaying adhere to the industry's tendency to design for slim figures, professional models, stylized presentations, or to design for size (a tradition whose origin lies in the military uniform) rather than body shape (as some fashion gurus have been advocating (see Woodall and Constantine 2007)).

Towards defining a 'fashion studies project'

It is only in the last two or three years that fashion studies gained institutional recognition in the form of specialist fashion theory chairs and dedicated degrees (e.g. Stockholm, Leeds, NY Parsons). At this point it seems appropriate to rethink a fashion studies project. In particular I would like to outline how *Critical Studies in Fashion and Beauty* (CSFB) is to fit within that project. On the one hand its role is simply to enhance the gallery of dedicated publications that address issues of dress and appearance specifically. At this juncture any such bolstering is an asset to the field and to its practitioners. Beyond that I would like to clarify the remit of the journal, not so much in terms of content, but in terms of methodology and approach. First, I want to briefly sketch out the vision of the field that the journal will cater for.

The field

The definition of fashion studies I wish to advance here is the study of beauty, fashion and dress as material and visual evidence of social and economic processes, or as an object of contemplation, reflection and critique. More specifically it is the study of the *meaning of body and beauty procedures* in clothes and adornment, production and crafts, practice and symbol, observation and experience, self and identities, fact and fiction, reality and representation.

In principle, such a field contains two levels: visible and invisible. The visible level focuses on details of objects or images, taxonomies and specific examples, and examines them closely and meticulously. It highlights certain periods, locales or styles and uses the rich detail either to paint a previously unknown picture, or as data to support social historical observations. The invisible level is a conceptual layer of meanings, both personal and collective, that reflect the wearer's experience and perspective on *reason giving* and *meaning making*, neither of which are inherent in objects or practices but are contextual in terms of time, place and function. The invisible level is not necessarily anchored in specific details, but can refer to sartorial or appearance elements metaphorically or allegorically, to 'the idea of beauty' or 'the idea of dress' (or other material objects) or to 'generic clothes'. It is also a layer that involves a meta-reflexive approach that examines the assumptions underlying the practices that secure 'fashion' its place, the power relations that sustain or subvert it, the values that inform it and the ideologies that provide it with the certainty of the taken-for-granted veneer.

What the field is not

The task of fashion studies is not merely to record, describe or analyse. It is about engaging by way of innovative research and application of a range of theories in a critical reflection, and challenging and interpreting the received ways of doing fashion, observing fashion, understanding fashion, explaining fashion and talking about fashion.

To engage in research in fashion studies does not necessarily require detailed knowledge of historical styles, technical craft knowledge of designing or making fashion, or an intimate knowledge of the fashion industry. 'Fashion studies' as a field of knowledge is not just about 'fashion icons' and 'designer collections', couture and catwalks, historical styles or the latest trends; it is not just about how to cut, sew, craft a collection or market a label. It is about more than creating synergies with the industry, producing rich descriptive accounts, documenting trends or doing 'fashion tourism'.

What the field is – and what the journal invites

There are many entry points to the kind of scholarship the journal would welcome, particularly any form of critical argument about fashion studies that seeks to provide insight into its meanings as a social activity either through research of artefacts, of wearers or of theoretical reflection. The idea is to genuinely open the journal to a wide spectrum of fields, theoretical frameworks and sets of assumptions and conventions. CSFB is located in the gap between journals at the art, museology and history end of the spectrum (e.g. *Fashion Theory, Costume*) and between the social science, social theory, and cultural studies end of the spectrum (e.g. *Body & Society, Theory Culture & Society*). It aims to provide a space for anyone who would like to contribute a critical argument that will draw on areas and ideas which deal with fashion as industry or as metaphor. It is open for people who are disciplinary experts but also those who are original thinkers and do not subscribe to disciplinary boundaries: to the purists as well as the multi-disciplinary, those who like to build from the ground up and develop specialist knowledge of their craft, as well as those who think in big pictures and paint in broad brush.

Interdisciplinarity

The interdisciplinary face of the journal is to be cultivated by encouraging a range of different perspectives, by ensuring that there is no specific agenda or canonical corpus of readings whose knowledge by contributors is expected and assumed. My notion of interdisciplinarity is the bringing together of areas of enquiry that may not instinctively be grouped together. This idea is part of the fashionable rhetoric of programmes and mission statements of many educational and research institutions and publications. But this discourse appears to be more aspirational than real. Diana Crane (2010) proposes a theory about facilitating interdisciplinary conversations by creating 'trading zones' between fields with little in common, theoretically or empirically. It would require participants to construct a set of terms that permits them to exchange ideas. She also proposes that 'clusters of fields' in different disciplines are linked by 'free-floating paradigms' which would help to diffuse paradigms across disciplinary boundaries. In the same spirit, this journal will also encourage interdisciplinary linkages from unexpected and less predictable partners (education, politics, religion – to name a few).

In terms of content, fashion studies is as much about the fine workmanship of the couture ateliers as it is about the destitution of workers in the sweatshops of fast fashion; it is as much about production of obsolescence in consumer society as about second-hand clothes and traditional crafts, and it is as much about real fashion or beauty practices, conventions and products as it is about the idea of fashion, or the idea of beauty.

Part 2

Conceptual fashion from the museum to reflections on the field

I would like to illustrate the *spirit* of the journal by a paradigmatic example based mostly on an analysis of two recent exhibitions. The origins of the theoretical frameworks that have become influential in many areas of scholarly and artistic endeavours since the 1980s are rooted in the intellectual traditions of post-structuralism, deconstruction and post-colonialism. In particular their challenge to the hegemony of totalizing theories and unifying narratives of nation and subjectivity created a paradigm shift. In fashion this new reflexivity was expressed in two principal ways:

(1) the semantic shift from the indexicality of clothes as reflecting rigid and fixed categories to an appreciation of their contextual nature and the realization that meaning is always negotiated, and
(2) the blurring of boundaries between art and fashion with both artists and fashion designers engaging in reflection and questioning of the assumptions underlying their own craft – fashion design, practice and consumption – through installations and performances. This has been most clearly demonstrated with the emergence of deconstructionist fashion led by Japanese and European designers (e.g. Belgian, Dutch, Cypriot) who rewrote the rules of the game, and managed to combine conceptual fashion with commercial success and to *perform* not just articulate a 'participant observer's' critique.

In this issue I would like to take up one such example of an insightful synergy which highlights a few defining themes that knowingly or unknowingly underlie a lot of the conversations, the observations, the thinking and the theorizing of this rather varied and colourful field of knowledge, and illustrate their presence in recent exhibitions which, in their very different ways, reflect on some core themes.

1. **The role of the visual in reflecting on clothes.**
2. **The role of classification in thinking about clothes.**
3. **The limits of precise sartorial signification.**
4. **The culture of brands.**

Theme 1: The role of the visual in reflecting on clothes

At first glance this theme seems almost common sense: you cannot write anything meaningful about a visual medium without the visual presence of the clothes. This is not self-evident though, and opinions differ. Valerie Steele once critiqued Lipovestsky's *Empire of Fashion* (1994) by pointing out 'There are no pictures in Gilles Lipovetsky's book … the total absence of pictures is symptomatic of a serious problem, since fashion is such a visual phenomenon' and goes on to explain that since Lipovetsky just analyses the cultural significance of the ephemeral in general (though with examples from fashion) it is not relevant to fashion but to political philosophy.

Yuniya Kawamura, on the other hand, has a different take on what fashion studies entail. She sees it as a set of social institutions combining production and consumption. Defining fashion as the process and clothing as the product, she reasons that 'since the process itself is the object of the

5. See http://www.
comme-il-faut.com/
house/bubble-gum.
See also http://www.
comme-il-faut.com/
user_files/06_events/
bait/
newspaper%5B1%5D.
pdf).

study, a fashion-ological perspective of fashion requires no visual materials to explain fashion because it is not about clothing' (Kawamura 2005: 1).

In fact a critical examination of fashion practice highlights that it is as much about *process* as about *content,* and as much about *concept* as about *object*. Therefore it is possible to talk about and theorize sartorial phenomena and ideas without necessarily illustrating one's argument with 'clothes'. When art engages with fashion not as 'aesthetic inspiration' but as a medium of critical reflection the result may be 'clothes-free'. A case in point is an exhibition curated by Orit Freilieh, a fashion designer, an artist and a lecturer at Shenkar School of Fashion Design in Tel Aviv. The exhibition 'Bubble Gum' (September–November 2007) was set up in the stunning conversion site of the old Tel Aviv port which houses the *concept store* complex of the *Comme il Faut* group. *Comme il Faut* is an ethical Israeli high-end fashion label with a feminist agenda. The compound 'Bayit banamal' ('a house in the harbour') is a female pampering centre (*Comme il Faut* label clothes store, health food café on the water, spa, various fashion and accessories shops made by local artists, fair trade products etc.). The exhibition featured a series of meditations by different artists and designers on the relationship between fashion and its subjects; it was defined by the curator as 'meta-fashion' – *about clothes but without clothes.*

The curator explained her choice of the *Comme il Faut* compound as a site for artistic reflection and examination on the ambivalent relationship of the producers and the consumers of fashion. She chose it precisely because of its role as a 'temple for fashion'.

'I was interested in addressing such spaces without actually displaying clothes. It was important for me to represent a range of modes of expression. I chose works that go far in their examination of clothes, that refer to traditions of constructing the clothes and the social semiotic codes that operate on the wearer'.[5]

Some of the works included:

- Hannah Okanin (fashion designer) constructed a dainty garment from hard materials. She presented a photographic installation of a ballerina wearing a layered garment made of PVC pieced together by nuts and bolts. The fusion between metal and PVC creates new body proportions that look like they have been surgically re-arranged.
- Gav Rotem and Yael Taragan (designer and wood artist) produced a 'dress' inspired by a dressmaker's dummy made using a medieval weaving technique; it is designed to be worn over the female body.
- Meirav Peretz (graphic designer and typographer) shows three panels of textiles serving as background for a typographic interpretation of the verses of Dalia Rabikovitz's poem 'mechanical doll'.
- Raviv lifshitz (industrial product designer) displayed shoe and sandal models made of identical size PVC pipes.

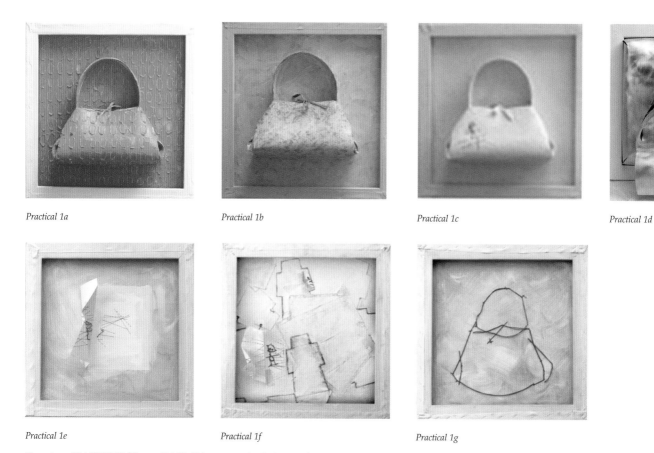

Practical 1a

Practical 1b

Practical 1c

Practical 1d

Practical 1e

Practical 1f

Practical 1g

Figure 1a–g: PRAC(TIC)AL (The word 'tic' in Hebrew means 'bag'). A series of seven images by the artist-designer Dalit Shahar. Photos courtesy of Dalit Shahar.

6. http://www.
dazeddigital.com/
Fashion/article/7670/1/
Maison_Martin_
Margiela_20, Dazed
& confused (2010), 3
June.

- Dalit Shahar (fashion designer and artist) created a series of works, 'PRAC-TIC-AL' (see figure 1), examining the transition of a handbag from an 'object of desire' (in the fashionable field (representing the feminine, the seductive, the sensual)) to an 'object' (in the field of art), from a poetic personal designer artefact to an industrial product, or from a personal object to a generic object. She does this by taking apart a bag she has designed and removing its distinctive qualities one by one: colour, texture, shape, 3D, the quality of a container – transforming it from an 'object' to an 'idea of an object' – or symbol.

In the same way that the artists and designers participating in the 'Bubble Gum' exhibition made statements about the social context of clothes without 'real' clothes, an exhibition of the fashion label Maison Martin Margiela 20 (June to September 2010) displayed 'real' clothes not for wearability but to make statements about the social context of clothes. In reference to this exhibition in London's Somerset house, MoMu Fashion Museum's curator Kaat Debo remarked: 'I think it's important that this exhibition shows people that it's not about costume. When you exhibit conceptual fashion the worst thing that could happen is that people say "Ooh I would never wear that!"'[6] (More on that later.)

Theme 2: The role of classification in thinking about clothes

The history of ideas from the Renaissance to the Enlightenment can be regarded as an offshoot of the encyclopaedic ideal of organizing knowledge (Kelly 1991). Yet while folk taxonomies have existed since the Greeks it is the work of the Swedish Doctor Linnaeus – who in the second half of the eighteenth century introduced the method of identifying and naming species and organizing them into systems of classification – that is credited with laying the groundwork of the modern science of taxonomy. Taxonomy has been enjoying enormous prestige and was rigorously supported by the laws of triumphant rationality. It came to signify rationality, objectivity, and credibility.

Classification systems (from archival record keeping, and cataloguing of museum collections and inventories, to library classification methods or dictionaries) are not in fact neutral methods of organizing information. The *medium*, as Marshall McLuhan suggested, *is the message*, so is the method, as I argued elsewhere (1991). Both are constitutive of the nature, not just the structure or format of the knowledge they store. By virtue of their systematic objective-appearing aura, methods of knowledge organization enjoy a dual vote of confidence: for the *quality of the content,* and for *public trust in the quality of the institution* (trusted custodians of trusted repositories).

There is an interesting corollary to the notion of systematic classification. As Foucault (2000) tells us in *The Order of Things*, in order for the system to sustain itself the 'rules' of every taxonomy require a certain degree of *order and similarity – not originality –* between units. Thus the classificatory logic and the spirit of creativity and imagination are incompatible. Therefore, an element of instability and precariousness is introduced – posed by the continuous challenge of 'difference' that resists the laws of taxonomy.

The principle of resisting the spirit of classification in order to generate fresh perspective can also be applied to challenging the very authorities (of repositories and custodians) that are supposed to provide an objective, neutral and unambiguous sign system. Maciel (2004) proposes an affinity between the unclassifiable – that which resists taxonomies, cannot fit any category or fixed place and cannot be precisely defined – and between the strange and the extraordinary. Indeed as Barthes ([1970] 1973) argues in *Texte de jouissance/The Pleasure of the Text* it is *the original text* that embodies the spirit of 'jouissance', i.e. not regulated by the rules of language, the laws of grammar and the dictionaries. This brings me back to fashion, which is often assumed to have a classificatory quality like that of a dictionary. In fact, the closest one gets to the rulebook precision of the fashion system is in Barthes' *Système de la mode/The fashion system*. When Barthes wrote this he did not attempt to eternalize the trends of summer 1965; rather he used the current narrative of fashion description for illustration purposes in order to derive, by induction, a system of relationships. Indeed there is an argument for comparing fashion as a system of meaning more with Barthes' notion of the 'texte de *jouissance*' than with his notion of the '*Système de la mode*' on account of fashion being so inherently subversive, diverse, and in a state of flow.

Maciel argued that in our 'hyper-textual' age where speed and scope of information 'explicitly de-authorize and disestablish the very idea of classification' (Maciel 2004) a reshaping of knowledge from a more open, dialogical, and even paradoxical perspective is required. This view is a starting point for examining what happens in underground museum corridors to inform how cultural choices are made. Such a 'cultural psychoanalysis' is the focus of a new exhibition (21 August 2010–1 January 2011) in the art museum of Haifa curated by Dr. Gideon Ofrat. The exhibition, 'Lights On: From Storage to Display'[7] gives the viewer a behind-the-scenes view of the collections, and the cultural routes along which modes of classification, traditions of hegemony and trends of critique, influence what is brought from the archives to the display halls. A somewhat similar idea is echoed in the spirit of the exhibition 'A concise dictionary of dress' commissioned by Artangel in collaboration with the V&A.[8] It was set up at Blythe House, the repository store for the reserve collections of the V&A during May–June 2010. The work, which involved collaboration between a fashion curator Judith Clark and psychoanalyst Adam Phillips, challenged notions of classification in words and artefacts while drawing analogies between the process of producing taxonomies or storing a garment.

The exhibition consisted of a series of definitions and a series of instalments placed throughout the five floors of the archive house. Objects from the collection along with specially commissioned works were used. Each instalment was a visual interpretation of a series of definitions of commonplace adjectives associated with fashion. The definitions are original, hence unexpected, as they do not adhere to the stock classificatory rules of interpretation that characterize much of popular culture

7. http://www.hma.org.il/
   Museum/Templates/
   showcase.asp?DBID=1
   &TMID=84&LNGID=1
   &FID=524&PID=403,
   http://www.science-
   museum.org.uk/
   sitecore/shell/Controls/
   Rich

8. http://www.artangel.
   org.uk/projects/2010/
   the_concise_
   dictionary_of_dress

discourse and some academic discourse. In fact the definitions preceded the exhibits and thus constitute an inverse analogy of the psychoanalytic symbolization process. They started out without any concrete object in mind. It is the visual interpretation of the curator that realized the ideas in specific objects. As visitors, however, we were invited to engage in another interpretation, taking into account both the visual and the verbal. We were not given 'proper' captions designating the genealogy of the exhibits, and had to generate our own. We were asked to indulge in what I'd call 'the little prince' experience. In Antoine de Saint-Exupéry's *Le Petit Prince* the author, a pilot, is forced to land in the Sahara – a forced landing that leads him to meet a special little prince with an unfettered imaginative mind. The writer then tells us that grown-ups are pretty hopeless. If you tell them that you saw a beautiful house with red bricks and flowers in the windows and doves on the roof they have difficulty picturing it in their mind. But as soon you tell them just the price – they can easily admire it.

It is this kind of critique of 'grown-up assumptions' that the 'dictionary of dress' invites us to adopt.

'A concise dictionary of dress' is intriguing and it invites engagement on various levels. Just like the idea of the 'dictionary' that is questioned in the exhibition itself, so are the interpretations and meanings one can bring to bear on the structure or the specific messages. For the purpose of this issue I have chosen to illustrate the journal's mission statement by a comparative analysis of exhibitions because they seem to bring out some of the key issues I highlighted in the first part of this editorial. They also illustrate, in a very visual manner, the very critical perspective that does not, in fact, require visualization to articulate its insight. What is interesting about the dictionary definitions of dress is that there is no 'dress' in the definitions. They describe pure emotions, observations, reflections, or insights – in other words nothing which is visual or tangible. And while they are quite versatile, they can be manifested in concrete garments in infinite ways.

The idea of a functional similarity between clothes and words prefigures the exhibition. Phillips explains that they both call attention to the subject of their discourse (dress calls attention to the body, and definitions call attention to the qualifiers they define). Both acquire meaning by their context of use. Both are evocative objects: they can be innocent traces of intense or forbidden emotions. The juxtaposition between 'clothes' and 'definitions' addresses dictionary practices and curatorial practices but also the more general questions of the function of storing, and the possibility of indexing fashion in a dictionary-like manner. The critical challenge of 'the concise dictionary' can be appreciated by combining the various formats the exhibition is packaged in, e.g. the exhibition layout, the exhibits, and the exhibition book. None of these elements are 'traditional'. The exhibition plays off the relationship between the objects and the descriptions. It challenges traditional use by subverting conventions, providing unconventional idiosyncratic unorthodox definitions and bringing to light the covert role of evocative meaning in our casual use of stereotypes. By their 'difference' from some conventions they also highlight the critical challenge of the exhibition, both in content and in structure.

The topography of the exhibition

The layout of the exhibition space reinforces an analogy between clothes and words as elements in dream symbolism, which, because of the nature of fashion as both beautiful and temporary, ties fashion to traumatic notions of fantasy images as well as transience and loss – which are the stuff of dreams, repression and the unconscious.

The archive space with its secretive hiding places is a visual spatial analogy of the unconscious, and the elements of the exhibition come with unpredictable interpretations of the definitions; they are arranged on different floors of the building from the roof to the basement and are hidden in unexpected corners (sometimes from view), in secret places like between rolling racks, in small cracks, a larder, on a rooftop or in a basement, in bespoke cabinets or in the object's original display room. They appear like objects cast in the unconscious memory space, captured as symbolic messages, which in the original nocturnal drama elaborated by Freud are coded in order to bypass the original repression of the desire or trauma they allude to. The journey of the guided tour is like a treasure hunt and is closely guarded to convey a reluctant admission into a forbidden space (which is normally not open to the public). This reinforces the psychoanalytic interpretation of the journey as a 'voyage of discovery' in a new and un-annotated territory of the repressed psychic material. It is designed to 'bring to light', figuratively and metaphorically, those hidden away and forgotten elements.

The set up for this exhibition reminds me of another representation of the unconscious space I have encountered in the exhibition *Traum & Trauma/Dream & Trauma* shown at the Kunsthalle in Vienna in the summer of 2007. *Dream & Trauma* was structured like a dream by setting the various gallery rooms in darkness. This created a space of emptiness and isolation to pursue Freud's sketch of the unconscious as a nocturnal psychic drama (Bronfen 2007) from which remembered images shine.

The exhibits, much like Judith Clark's installations, functioned like dream images, disavowed but allowed into the dream stage in a coded form. The installation that welcomed the visitor to the Kunsthalle museum (*Hunger cradle* by Nari Ward, see figure 2) hung low over the entrance hall in the shape of a big web. In the folds of this huge web were woven many discarded everyday objects, some wrapped like presents, others whole or in fragments.

Both *Concise Dictionary* and *Dream & Trauma* embody Rosalind Krauss's metaphor of 'the optical unconscious' (Krauss 1993), which is repressed from the narrative of modernism. This is a labyrinth which resembles the unconscious in its puzzling structure, mined by a thousand pockets of darkness and its conjunction of passages, unintelligible twists and irrational space.

Figure 2: Nari Ward 'Hunger cradle' 1996. Courtesy of The Dakis Joannou Collection, Athens and Kunsthalle Wien.

In the book that accompanies the 'concise dictionary of dress' (Clark and Phillips 2010) Michael Morris, co-director of Artangel, described Phillips' 'chosen words' and Clark's 'imagined definitions' as 'a cover-up for what might lie beneath: the feelings and desires that need masking; the hidden wounds that must be dressed' (Clark and Phillips 2010). In an article entitled 'Art and Wound: On the aesthetics of dream and trauma' the director and the curator of the Museum of Modern Art in Vienna (which also housed *Dream & Trauma*) point out that dream and trauma are essential for a theory of the unconscious. Their imaginary power is revealed in the tension between absence and presence, and between repression and an excess of emotion. The key to understanding the relevance in the context of the dictionary exhibition is that while trauma is real it need not involve an external event. It represents a state of emotional overload that 'cannot be integrated into the emotional balance-sheet' hence is repressed (Stief and Matt 2007).

Exhibits

By subverting the traditional practices the very construction of both 'definitions' and 'clothes' reflects the personal choices of Clark and Phillips, e.g. using dictionaries and displaying clothes. In fact, it is only through the supplementary talk given by the artists, and the articles that feature in the exhibition book, that one realizes the extent of the personally associative meaning that lies behind the project. In this sense, they constitute an integral part of the experience of the exhibition – they are not add-ons.

The logic of the definitions – in sharp contrast with a normative dictionary – introduces a quirky element into the 'rational dictionary'. Their visual representation (see table 2) which features a familiar title in an unfamiliar typography broken into segments, though not according to any known classificatory system (e.g. syllables), adds surprise and mystery. It subverts the concept of a 'dictionary' in the course of providing one. The content of the definitions breaks another rule of objective rationality: it is pretty original and idiosyncratic. The archive space with its secretive hiding places supports the unconscious or the dream metaphor. The dream, as Elisabeth Bronfen reminds us is 'a subversive place or locality in as much as it insists on ambiguity and overdetermination' (Bronfen 2007: 191). The enigmatic, somewhat ambivalent, personal and unexpected way in which the exhibits have been reconfigured (in their verbal visual combinations) identifies them as cast objects whose coded meaning is buried in the dark recesses of the unconscious.

Like the dream materials that have been repressed from consciousness and return in a disguised and disfigured form, their meaning is not obvious and may rely on typical over-coded symbols and biographical ones. In the dream, one meaning can obscure another: one dream thought can be replicated in different elements, elements may swap places or dream images can be compressed through contradictory traits, or, like screen memory, they can be displaced onto mundane innocuous detail. As a result, dream elements may appear in a seemingly trivial and unconnected, or fragmented format.

Meas				Pret
Ure	or	**Pla**	or	enti
D		in		ous

Table 2: Measured, Plain, Pretentious.

In the journey of discovery of the dictionary exhibition the exhibits function like dream materials in another sense in that the interpretation work, which occurs in the daytime, is given to every visitor: the guide or the exhibitors do not participate in the decoding process. The guide is instructed to be as opaque as possible, and the exhibits are devoid of any biographical details. In a break with museum display traditions the exhibits present themselves as unclassifiable, undated, indeed caption-free, in an attempt to simulate the encounter with the raw stimuli – unmarked by culture. Such an encounter presents the viewer with a pure experience unmediated by labels and classification categories in which the space and the object interact directly with the viewer. This is an experience based on allusions and invocation instead of information. It is this transition to the experiential – not rational – dimension which reinforces the analogy between storage (and retrieving) of knowledge and the psychodynamic process of retrieving and renaming disguised dream symbols carrying traces of repressed traumatic experiences and intense desires. This naming device, as Bronfen reminds us, is equivalent to a gesture of transference.

Book

The structure of the book, with its aesthetic images and lack of traditional indexicality (no page numbers, typography of truncated captions, marginal position of biographic details) reinforces the interpretations that are suggested by the exhibits and the layout. Interestingly, even the book which does contain those classificatory details (which the exhibition avoids) presents them in a rather unorthodox way. The table of contents gives page numbers but the endnotes are not numbered, and the visual images, beautifully photographed in the tradition of art books, guidebooks or coffee table books, have no numbering and no captions. Each exhibit is represented by a number of images that also include the location, and is accompanied by the evocative definitions, not the informative details. Contrary to the visual images that include many close-up photos, the endnotes that give the bibliographical details of the works presented appear like pages torn out of a sketchbook, with some tiny sketches and tiny script. In fact the search for details in the book is no less challenging than the search for them in the storehouse. Even the typographic representation of the captions to be defined is disguised: it rolls across three lines which creates curious breaks in otherwise quite familiar word patterns. For example:

DICTI		CONT		AFT
ONA	or	ENT	or	ER
RY		S		WORD

Table 3: Dictionary/contents/afterwords.

One caption, though, is not truncated, and this is the title of the article by Adam Phillips. It is called **look it up** and seems to apply equally to the dictionary – the habitual act of someone checking a word in the dictionary – and to the exhibits themselves. By looking up and examining the exhibits, instead of looking down for captions and definitions, one is invited to partake in 'the little prince' way of experiencing.

The dictionary exhibition is using the context of the archive but subverting the systematization assumptions that come with it, while introducing the repressed *emotional* element. In fact, foregrounded by this huge, and largely hidden storehouse of treasures, the exhibition problematizes a few key questions about the relationship between knowledge, storage, definitions and pleasure. Starting from an examination of the nature and function of dictionaries, it proceeds by raising fundamental questions about the authoritative voice of 'factual knowledge': safe rather than inspirational, exact rather than idiosyncratic. The exhibition also raises questions about the meaning of the storage of clothes in museums/storehouses and of words in dictionaries, and, by extension, the function of accumulating clothes, material objects, and knowledge objects that exceed our capacity to use them.

In so doing it alludes to the possibility that the pleasure of the collector is different from the pleasure of the user. Storing a dress, as Clark says, refers to both object and imagination (a memory, an aspiration, a fantasy). While this would be true for ordinary people hanging on to meaningful clothes, it has particular relevance to the curator's attitude towards conservation of garments: there for the keeping not for use. Use, which is display, implies degradation of the exhibits and is, in a sense, a distraction. Referring to a dictionary as 'a dressing up box' Phillips implies that storage is the 'fantasy of potential': the knowledge that the information in the dictionary is safe and accurate 'in case we need it', a kind of armour.

The exhibition subverts the storage process by calling into question its predictable routines. In their own way the unusual definitions and the unusual display of costumes, artefacts and the particular spaces they inhabit defy both the classificatory principle of the dictionary, and the logic of the curatorial practice, especially when the exhibits enjoy varying degrees of protection. While some exhibits are protected in cabinets, drawers and racks, others are exposed to the elements or the dampness of the rooftop or the cellar (though they are made of materials appropriately resistant to damp deterioration). In being subversive the exhibition resists closure of meaning by alerting us to the complexity and variety of fashion's voice. It highlights the guiding and restricting role of closed, 'proper' and well-defined classificatory drawers, and well-cared for curatorial drawers – and opens up different ways of looking that disrupt our tendency to reproduce stereotyped looks and concepts, and makes us veer away from the sartorial cliché. In this sense it underlies a principle common to both dictionaries and curation: that *typological knowledge is relational*. Meaning is born out of *temporary groupings in space*: out of *connective possibilities* of various arrangements – not an *inevitable logic*.

In structural terms while the 'dictionary of dress' hints at the unconscious as a repository of meanings that are organized by everyday objects, Maison Martin Margiela's (MMM) retrospective hints at the deconstruction of everyday objects. Neither of the exhibitions adheres to the classificatory principle of costume museums, which tends to chronicle and periodize methodically and systematically. Rather, each exhibition creates its own classificatory logic: an *associative* logic in the case of the 'dictionary of dress', a *thematic* logic in the case of Margiela. What they have in common is the sense of discovery, of uncovering the hidden and the disguised, and the desire to 'bring them to light' by reversing the psychoanalytic interpretation process in the case of Clark and Phillips. In the case of Margiela it is achieved by laying bare the process of tailoring through deconstruction, distortion and subversion of canonical shapes and conventional practices of tailoring, conventional definitions of garment, and of definitions of a sartorial aesthetic.

The Margiela exhibition catalogue starts from a mock dictionary definition of the meaning of 'Maison Martin Margiela' (see figure 3). This is fictitious in that the fashion house name is unlikely to be part of a traditional dictionary and it is fictitious in the contents of the definitions. But the very presentation of the house in this pseudo-dictionary manner is both ironic and critical in one stroke – two adjectives that the house's fashion and the exhibition stand for. Appropriating the format of a dictionary definition the curators Kaat Debo and Barbara Vinger signal a set of objective, normative and widely shared meanings. In fact, the definition blends factual objective information with the critique and commentary that has been levelled at the designer over the years, taking the couture ethos to absurdity. It also contains a paradox: while the content of the house characterization is collegial, unassuming and everything that is not exclusive and not pretentious (the white label, the recycling, the team work and the anonymity as well as the austerity of the garments) those very qualities create the mystique and form the basis for a couture prestige – the defining markers of an exclusive club.

Contrary to the methodical systematization hinted by the use of 'a dictionary definition' as a symbol of a classification system, there is much in MMM's work that transgresses such order: the numbers of the collections (instead of names) are chosen randomly, and the nature of the clothes is not easily categorized. Even the logic of the exhibition is not chronological (as a systematic organization would suggest) but thematic: each theme resembling a metaphor more than a concrete style.

In some sense both exhibitions employ a similar method in their explorations of the relationship between clothes and meanings or wearers. It is what I would call *the uncanny method* whereby

MAISON MARTIN MARGIELA. *Proper noun, plural,* derived from the name of a Belgian stylist. **Fashion company** created in **Paris** in 1988. Registered office situated at number 163 rue Saint Maur, 75011, Paris. Known for its taste for **transgression**, its fashion shows in unexpected places, its 'street casting' mixing all ages. Categorized successively as underground, deconstructive, destroy, grunge, minimalist, provocative, established. ♦1° Garments for women, offering several collections, from ready-to-wear to unique pieces (**Artisanal** collection). The main collection uses a plain **white label*** with no writing, sewn into the garments by hand with four **white stitches***. The other collections, of which there are twelve, are identified by a circled number on the label. ♦2° Male clients have also been taken care of since 1998, with four distinct collections. ♦3° Communicates exclusively in the first person plural 'we', in order to focus attention on teamwork (sixteen nationalities) and to respect the creator's wish for anonymity: *'The only thing we wish to push to the forefront in our fashion'.* ♦4° Known for its taste for **recovery*** and **recycling*** of materials. ♦5° May go as far as to re-release an existing garment (**Replicas***). ♦6° Since its creation, has favoured the use of whites: walls, floors, stands, accessories, hanging wardrobes, in its boutiques, showrooms and offices. ♦7° Its employees wear **white coats*** (from 'haute couture' workshops) as a 'uniform' when serving the public ♦8° *Ext.* Sunglasses, jewellery, perfumes. ♦9° A study subject in fashion schools. ♦10° Name used internationally in books, articles and exhibitions.

Figure 3: Mock dictionary definition of 'Maison Martin Margiela' from the exhibition catalogue. Courtesy of Somerset House & Maison Martin Margiela.

distancing, adopting a deliberately different viewpoint and turning familiar and everyday objects and assumptions into estranged ones is used, thereby disrupting the mode of engaging with the ubiquitous and the taken-for-granted.

Theme 3: The limits of precise sartorial signification

This relates to the inherent limitations of the indexicality of the language of clothes. Part of this limitation lies in the inherent ambiguity of dictionaries which cannot nail down definitive, unambiguous versions or interpretations, and in the impossibility of indexing de-contextualized meanings precisely. Part of the problem lies in the difficulty of translating concepts into concrete objects since the meaning of objects is always contextual and fluid.

There is a tendency to define fashion – based on cognitive or historical rationales – as having precise rules and regulations and with fixed, potentially definitive meanings, like a 'dress' dictionary. As I have demonstrated elsewhere (Tseëlon 1989; forthcoming 2011) this assumption, even if not explicitly articulated, pervades much fashion theorizing and thinking, but it is more folklore than science and does not stand up to scrutiny. In fact the assumption regarding visual transparency and the predictability of fashion language is merely sustained by the tendency of much fashion scholarship, and most popular culture vocabulary, to privilege iconic clothes (like designers' couture frocks) or looks with over-determined meanings[9] (historical and contemporary) over the study of the ordinary wardrobes of ordinary people, which do not lend themselves to easy generalization or straightforward interpretations.

There is plenty of evidence, theoretical and empirical, that the study of fashion as a system is not a search of the kind that would allow us to write the definitive dictionary or encyclopaedia of fashion. Rather it is a more illusory process that involves a discovery of shared principles at the level of ontologies or epistemologies, alongside numerous and changing detailed descriptions of particular cases on the level of methodologies. The notion of a fashion dictionary – a perfect classification –is, therefore, a fantasy of wholeness superimposed over a reality of fragmentation. It is an attempt to fix what Stuart Hall calls 'a sliding signifier'.

Clark and Phillips seem to be deliberately toying with the idea that fashion can be summed up meaningfully in one word or a choice phrase, and, by extension, that it can be sensibly archived into a museum catalogue. The exhibition illustrates how 'a stereotypical bias' (focus on dramatic, spectacular, iconic, cliché) misses a whole layer of meanings. In fact it works like a repressing device of meanings that do not fit – all for the sake of producing a coherent narrative. It is true for personal or national identity stories, for ideologies, for artistic genres, or for scientific paradigms. It is also true for new disciplines. It applies to choosing one's dressing style (whether as a 'fashion groupie' or a 'street-style entrepreneur', for example). It also applies at the level of scholarship to where we direct our research efforts: at the level of the 'dramatic' or the 'everyday'. It is obvious from the discussion of taxonomies above that looks that can be easily pigeonholed are stereotypical and do not carry much beyond predictable information, and that to be original requires one to be unclassifiable. Originality is the escape from stereotypes.

As is obvious from each of the sets of definitions, they are partly subjective, and partly referring to a cultural vocabulary (what Barthes (1983) calls *garment poetics*). As such they are not always synonyms but more like free associations veering in different directions. In the book and the talk that accompanied the exhibition both Phillips and Clark recount some personal, one might say, biographical associations that inform their choices. These associations form another layer of individual meaning, not captured by any cultural configuration.

But if the creative space of the definitions is more diverse, their translation into visual elements is more constrained. And so it tends to capture the essence of many, or to refer to a dominant one. Part of the reason is rooted in the translation from the abstract to the concrete. Part of it is a cultural habit of searching for 'the obvious meaning'. Judith Clark actually reflected that she thought the definitions would 'free her' but found instead that she was almost obsessive about treating them 'as precisely as possible' (Clark and Phillips 2010: 110).

In the following section I highlight one of the distinctive features of Phillips and Clark's approach which one can call 'a refusal of stereotypes' – and a dialogue with ambiguity and ambivalence. For this I have chosen three types of concepts from the exhibition as paradigmatic examples of categories I will define as 'stereotypical' looks (*Conformist, Comfortable, Tight* and *Creased*) and analyse the cultural meanings they evoke and the linguistic and visual manner in which they were realized. I arrange these concepts into three categories, borrowed from an earlier work where I posited three models of female voice that refer to sartorial strategies: *Proper, Mute* and *Provocative* voices (Tseëlon 2001). I also cast a look at how the message of the exhibition (the experiential level of meaning left out of traditional dictionaries and traditional curatorial practices) plays out through the way the exhibition itself is organized.

1. The proper voice

Conformist

The many references to the exhibition in the press and online blogs explained the concept and accompanied it with some visual examples. While each publication chose different pictures, the illustration of conformist was most common.

Adam Phillips' definition of the *conformist* resembles the features characterizing the classificatory principle itself: to be sufficiently similar to other objects so as to be classifiable, and, by implication, unoriginal. But it also implies a valuable way of conforming: by preserving the skills of fine craftsmanship.

Figures 4a: CONFORMIST from The Concise Dictionary of Dress, Judith Clark & Adam Phillips, 2010. Commissioned and produced by Artangel. Photo by Julian Abrams.

Figure 4b: 'Conformist'. Stereotype: 'a person or thing that conforms to standardized image'. Courtesy of Somerset House and Maison Martin Margiela.

Judith Clark's association of the concept is in the form of a dress that blends into the background of a floral motif. Clark asked embroiderer Rosie Taylor-Davies to transpose a William Morris design for wallpaper onto a calico toile for a medieval gown. The choice of a William Morris floral design evokes an English aesthetic and ideal of craftsmanship. The embroidery is on calico, which signifies a draft, 'the idea of a dress', because finished embroidery is normally done on precious silk. Thus the conformity comes across both in the act of 'blending in' and the need to conform to 'a standard of craftsmanship' in scrupulous detail in order to record the methods and store them within a dress.

Phillips' definitions were as follows:

1. A state of essential simplification; safety in numbers.
2. Recipient of an unnoticed demand, complicit; choosing not to choose; compliant, and therefore enraged; unwitting double agent.
3. Blended into a selected background.
4. Committed to difference, and by it; horrified by the idiosyncrasy of desire; uniformly agreeable.
5. Accurate, diligent; wired for surprise; mourning variety.
6. Consensus as spell; idealist.

(Clark & Phillips 2010)

What is particularly instructive is the complexity of motives, and the *non-visual aspects of visual uniformity* that even this, the 'most ultimate stereotypical of looks', can inspire. The notions of conformity that are expressed in different ways, by both Clark and Phillips, speak of a combination of agency and passivity: they refer to a choice of submitting to a standard of workmanship (e.g. preserving a craft and a taste, or 'consensus as spell: idealism'), to a fear of 'standing out from the crowd' ('safety in numbers' 'blending into the background'), to being coerced ('recipient of an unnoticed demand', 'complicit'; 'compliant, and therefore enraged'; 'unwitting double agent') being undecided ('choosing not to choose;'), being intolerant of differences and variety ('committed to difference, and by it'; 'horrified by the idiosyncrasy of desire'; 'mourning variety') and also to deliberately choosing a conciliatory position ('uniformly agreeable').

Interestingly, the Margiela collection features a similar concept in a different way. It is a suit whose label reads a definition for a stereotype: 'a person or thing that conforms to a standardized image' (see figure 4b). In so doing the label uses a trope of elite fashion – the concealed label – but the substance of the label contradicts the message of the 'couture label' in two ways. First it empties the concept of 'label' of its original content. Second, it replaces it with a statement that negates it – implying that to wear 'designer clothes' is not to be any more distinctive than to conform to any other kind of stereotype.

Figures 5a and b: COMFORTABLE from The Concise Dictionary of Dress, Judith Clark & Adam Phillips, 2010. Commissioned and produced by Artangel. Photo by Julian Abrams.

2. The mute voice

Comfortable

This exhibit conveys the protective, pleasurable and relaxed connotations of a loose-fitting garment. It consists of the following definitions:

1. A refuge; a nostalgia; the calm before or after.
2. The affluence of ease.
3. Fear of the future, rehearsed.
4. Pleasure as convenience; measured longing.
5. Space protected to forget that protection is required.
6. Invisibly armoured.

The garment is a simple, 1910 nightgown of chaste but translucent white linen, loose fitting and hanging straight from the shoulders. It is neither constricting nor embellished (save for ribbon-ruched sleeves), and has no fancy stitches or patterns. It conveys a sense of comfort that has not sacrificed aesthetics though an aesthetic of simplicity. However this interpretation is more complex than it first appears; the sense of comfortable protection that the curator had in mind refers not just to the wearing of the garment, but also to the curatorial perspective that protects the garment, not the wearer. This perspective refers to the cabinet where the garment is stored – a glass cabinet in which the mannequin stands in a large drawer in an oversized chest of drawers. Here again the definitions suggest a range of interpretations, some contradictory. They combine a sense of ease and comfort, even pleasure, a yearning for a bygone comfort, and an allusion to the kind of alarming vulnerability that the *comfortable* subtly protects against ('calm before or after', 'fear of the future', 'space protected to forget that protection is required', and 'invisibly armoured').

If the *conformist* evokes notions of autonomy (between having and lacking control), *comfortable* is about emotions (feeling at ease or anxious).

3. The provocative voice

The next two instalments I discuss have a different place in the topography of the exhibition, which reinforces the substantive meaning they offer with a positional one, both geographically (in the landscape of the building) and psychically (in the unconscious repressed material space).

Tight

This is the only exhibit that comes with an air of mystery or secrecy, and the only image that was not available to the press. Indeed, in the pictures of the installation available to the press, even on the Artangel website, the reader can see only the *mise-en-scène* not the actual instalment. The instalment is

Figure 6: TIGHT from The Concise Dictionary of Dress, Judith Clark & Adam Phillips, 2010. Commissioned and produced by Artangel. Photo by Julian Abrams.

a lit-up image of a headless mannequin dressed in a prim and proper, tight, buttoned-up Victorian suit. On the lower part of the suit a Victorian grey-and-white photograph of a naked woman bent over backwards under a gauzy underskirt has been superimposed. The instalment is displayed in a dark narrow constricted larder with viewers having to squeeze in one at a time and observe it through a narrow gap. The set-up for viewing has the aura of coin-in-the-slot 'What the Butler Saw' type machines (alluding to images of a butler peeking through a keyhole at a woman undressing). The machines, common in the late Victorian and Edwardian period at the seaside pleasure piers, provided viewing to only one person at a time and offered peeks at saucy photos from risqué to outright soft-core porn.

Tight consists of the following definitions:

1. The holding in that is a holding out for something.
2. Restriction as exposure.
3. The triumph of continence.
4. Squeezed; mean; tensed; lithe; sleek; close; in readiness.
5. The intimate as threat and embrace; the line between torture and comfort.
6. A gathering, a collecting, a smoothing over.

Here the meanings of the viewing conditions, as well as the corresponding garments, add a contrast between cultural conventions and expectations, and hidden desires. The image appears like a fantasy of the 'proper' Victorian lady, who we know was not the chaste lady a cultural construction would have us believe. The *tight* in the exhibit appears to refer both to the tense Victorian image and to the pressure arising out of keeping it repressed ('restriction', 'continence', 'squeezed', 'gathering', 'tensed', 'torture', 'a smoothing over'). The pretence of the calm of the exterior and the turmoil of the interior is hinted by the contrast between the suit and the photo, and in definitions such as ('the holding in that is a holding out for something', 'restriction as exposure', 'in readiness', 'the line between torture and comfort', 'the intimate as threat and embrace'). After a public talk Phillips and Clark gave in connection with the exhibition, and following the question session, a number of people came to the artists to ask questions in privacy. One silver haired woman wanted to know about the exhibit that 'everyone is talking about' though nobody dares to ask either in the question section of the book, or the talk. The refusal to engage with the erotic symbols or messages in the exhibition re-enacts the drama of the repression of such images that the exhibition mimics. It also explains the rushed and hushed peek at the installation among the visitors I observed during my tour of the exhibition. It was as if nobody wanted to be seen to be showing too much interest in the image, since the singular viewing conditions ruled out the possibility of gazing at the image discreetly. It made one of the definitions 'restriction as exposure' curiously fitting for the audience as well.

Creased

This is the ultimate disguised symbolic object, passed off as devoid of any evocative meaning but which may be considered a visual innuendo that flies under the radar of repression. It appears on the cover of the book, it appeared in the press; it has not been discussed or alluded to as a sensitive image, and the definitions do not seem to evoke it, and yet the imagery is unmistakeable.

Creased is positioned in the coal cellar. The dress is arranged so that only its curly frills are visible against a white pillow, underneath a protective giant Perspex dish hung to catch the drips from the damp ceiling (a certain curatorial anxiety surrounds this dress though we are told that this Comme des Garçons dress is, in fact, quite robust and has been designed from a fabric treated to withstand moisture). This curatorial anxiety is linked to the feared 'fixed folds' phenomena, which is caused by the body's heat, perspiration, and use – and form a common site of deterioration (definitions: 'fold fixed', 'line designed by use').

The definitions are few and simple:

1. The fold fixed.
2. The line designed by use.
3. Spread for conversation, sometimes with laughter.

While *Tight* was meant to be suggestive of eroticism, *Creased* is more ambiguous. There is nothing in the definition that suggests eroticism though the visualization, a combination of dark curly fabric and a white phallic object is evocative of one. What adds to the erotic symbolism is the positioning of that particular exhibit in the cellar, where it is exposed to pollution and dampness. The image clue and the positioning clue recall the topography of symbolic hierarchies of *high* and *low* elaborated by Stallybrass and White (1986). They identify four symbolic domains – psychic forms, the human body, geographical space, and social order – as mechanisms of ordering in European culture. The geographically 'low' are areas of the *abject*: disposal of waste products, pollution, mess and dirt. The lower strata of the body evoke the grotesque body, dominated by images of secretion and elimination of fluids, copulation and orifices. The antithesis of the grotesque body is the classical body: smooth, clean, closed, and symmetrical. Such images feature in other instalments (for example *Essential*). *Creased* is the only instalment that contains an object with gaps and holes.

Finally I would like to compare my sartorial strategies (a product of empirical work and cultural analysis of books and films) with the approach of the 'dictionary of dress' exhibition.

My characterization of the *proper voice* is that

like dressing the part, it carries very little personal information. It is 'dressed for the occasion' and subdues personal expression behind a 'front' of some form of (formal or informal)

Figure 7: CREASED from The Concise Dictionary of Dress,
Judith Clark & Adam Phillips, 2010. Commissioned and
produced by Artangel. Photo by Julian Abrams.

uniform, a business suit, or other conventional and 'safe' solutions. By blending in with the background it avoids calling attention to the wearer, it plays up belonging over individuality, and social awareness over creativity. By following the script of social expectations one's own position is masked.

My definition of the *mute voice* is one that:

signals the desire to be present and absent at the same time; the wish to suppress a desire the wearer dare not display. It wears baggy shapeless clothes that do not define the body contours (and in some societies these include veils). The mute clothes do not call attention to one's bodily presence either because of embarrassment, or 'civil disobedience', which has neither the desire to go along with prescribed codes nor the power or courage of defiance.

The *provocative voice* is distinguished not through conformity but through deviance, which is more revealing of personal information. The provocative voice relates to sexy dressing but also to subversion and outrage. It is designed to shock, to stir, to antagonize, to draw a smile – or simply to provoke a reaction, any reaction. If appearing gauche is the dread of the proper voice, going unnoticed is the dread of the provocative one (Tseëlon 2001).

In terms of process my definitions are a product, not a trigger: they are the end points of a process not its point of origin. In the dictionary exhibition the definitions are the starting point. My definitions are schematic but more convergent, perhaps more in the spirit of informative traditional dictionaries. In terms of semantic space my definitions cover somewhat different space than the corresponding one the exhibition covers. Phillips' definitions, combined with Clark's interpretations, are more open-ended, suggestive and evocative. They question the possibility of a totally informative grammar and invite us to reflect and engage in a dialogue about content but also about the very possibility of mapping meanings. This returns us to the analogy of the dream that is also 'a subversive place in as much as it insists on ambiguity and over-determination' (Bronfen 2007). The juxtaposition of my empirical classification and Clark and Phillips' conceptual one reinforces the value of synergy of approaches.

Theme 4: The culture of brands

Both exhibitions deconstruct, in their own way, the source of meaning and pleasure derived from the cult of designers and other luxury symbolism, particularly focusing on the artifice at the heart of brand idolatry. In the 'concise dictionary of fashion' this is represented through two instalments: *Pretentious* and *Plain*.

Figure 8: PLAIN from The Concise Dictionary of Dress,
Judith Clark & Adam Phillips, 2010. Commissioned and
produced by Artangel. Photo by Julian Abrams.

Plain is set in the hangar-sized, white-tiled textile store room, with its acres of white fabric rolls and a covered group of designer gowns, poised as if waiting to be unveiled for exhibition. They are wrapped in Tyvek, a tough paper-like fabric made from pulped polymer fibre and used by conservators to preserve textile goods. All seven, white ghost dresses are wrapped in the same material, preserving shape and space, with nothing but the creases, wrinkles and billows to suggest the amazing spectacles that lie in wait below. Through this draping, expensive and prestigious Balenciaga dresses are turned into a fantasy of a dress, or an idea of a dress. This has the effect of reducing the experience of interacting with them from the realm of knowledge and experience to the realm of fantasy and imagination, though one of the two definitions of *Plain* hints at the contradictory process that is encouraged by the act of obscuring the status symbol. The first definition reads 'hiding to make room' where the obvious meaning would be 'room to imagine, freed from the constraints of the label'; the second definition implies that the process of fantasizing makes meaning the responsibility of the dreamer, it reads 'nothing special where nothing special intended'.

Pretentious addresses the over-valuation of labels in a different way. It shows two opposite displays like mirror images – both the original and its negative are hidden in rolling racks. One side of the display shows a series of beautiful vintage cocktail dresses bolted to a wooden structure. On the opposite side there is a wax wall with imprints of each of the dresses against the dress it imprints, as if should the walls be joined they would constitute a protective shell for the contours of the dress. The wax casts (recall lost-wax moulds) are normally used for more durable objects like jewellery or sculptures and are destroyed in the process of casting. This unusual use of moulds, and the juxtaposition of the originals with the imprints, underlines the fragility and transience of the mould, and, by implication, the transience of the beauty of the originals. In his essay 'on transience' Freud recalls a nature walk with two friends who did not share his joy at the beauty of nature. While for Freud the 'transience value' of beauty limits the possibility of enjoyment and hence makes it more precious; for his friends there was no joy in beauty, since beauty must fade (Freud 1915–1916). For them, he reflected, the idea that all this beauty was transient and prone to decay was a foretaste of mourning; some sense of this transient beauty accompanies empty dresses by virtue of the fragility of their material, and the absence of the body that once inhabited them. This realization casts a different light on what Judith Clark calls 'iconic dresses'. These types of dresses, which have prestige value, appear without labels in the exhibition, and so their 'pedigree' is not obvious to the viewer at first glance. The masking of labels facilitates the process of contemplation of the beautiful dresses as generic, not highly stereotyped dresses or the creations of iconic designers. But it highlights the fact that death is a leveller, and the iconic dresses, even ones that are so highly prized and beautifully preserved like museum pieces, are ultimately just as vulnerable to decay and disuse as the bodies that used to wear them, which are alluded to in the wax impressions, like 'body prints'. The wax imprints vs. the fragile dresses

Figure 9: PRETENTIOUS from The Concise Dictionary of Dress, Judith Clark & Adam Phillips, 2010. Commissioned and produced by Artangel. Photo by Julian Abrams.

bring to mind Freud's 1925 essay on the 'mystic writing-pad' on the mechanism of memory. The writing pad he refers to is made of a thick wax board covered by a thin sheet of clear plastic attached to its top edge, The user can write on it with any pointed instrument. When the plastic sheet is lifted away from the surface of the waxen board beneath, the written traces disappear; the pad is clean again. But even though the marks disappear from the top plastic sheet, a faint indentation remains on the wax below. In his essay Freud uses the writing pad as a model of the psyche. In the exhibition the dialectic between the *ephemeral* and the *permanent* that Freud refers to in his essay is invoked in two ways. It is in the contrast between the robust wax wall with the imprints as opposed to the fragile period dresses encased in a glass cabinet to protect them from the marks of time. The dialectic also applies to *ephemeral* forms of commentary and documentation (exhibitions, catalogues, reviews, media coverage) and *permanent* forms like archives.

Graham Green's story 'Dr. Fischer and the bomb party' tells of Dr Fischer, who has become rich after inventing perfumed toothpaste. Dr Fischer is known for his notorious dinner parties, which are, as his estranged daughter suggests, an outlet for her father to humiliate the rich sycophants (whom she calls 'the Toads') in his coterie. The rules of engagement require complete submission to the humiliations of Dr Fischer. Apart from the vile food, these include cruel verbal taunts that play on each guest's failings or insecurities. If you follow all the rules you are rewarded with a present (or prize) at the end of the meal. The presents are usually tailored to each guest and are worth a substantial amount of money. Despite the humiliations, the rich and famous queue to be included: to be invited is like a badge signalling exclusive club membership. The content of the event is almost negligible: like red carpet events it is the fact of being there that counts. As well as the visionary anticipation of celebrity culture, and of a brand of reality TV that thrives on humiliation or deeply unpleasant tasks (*The X Factor, Britain's Got Talent, Weakest Link, Survivor*), the story goes right to the heart of the dynamics of fashion in general and fashion labels in particular. It captures the essence of a social ritual that appears to be about aesthetics and identities but actually contains another layer of inclusion and exclusion of the very fashion club itself.

Dr Fischer's invitations are like Margiela's self-conscious manipulation of the cult of glamour with his white label (plain, with four white stitches at the corners), that while looking like an amateur's mending job, for people 'in the know' it is recognized as the authenticated 'label' (one which carries connotations of the brand but at the same time represents an empty gesture at 'labels' themselves see figure 10). Wearing a garment with this distinctive but unassuming label is like displaying a club membership. In fact the blank label is only one part of a series of rhetorical signals that signify the antithesis of celebrity culture. The *incognito strategy* (the anonymity of the designer himself, the blindfolded models, the staff in their white coat uniforms, and the numbered collections) is a deliberate statement against the cult of the designer and the fashion model, trademarks of celebrity culture (see figure 11). Martin Margiela, the elusive Belgian designer who has never been

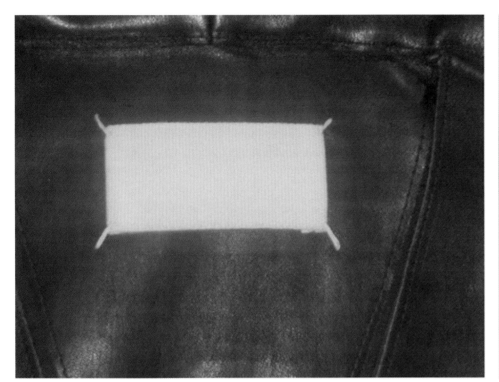

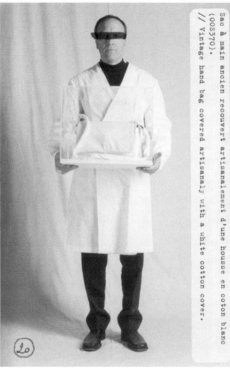

Figure 10: The blank white rectangular label first adapted to incorporate the numbers of the collections (chosen at random between 0–23). Courtesy of Somerset House & Maison Martin Margiela.

Figure 11: 2000–2003. The incognito strategy – models are made anonymous by having their faces masked (or in the look books by a black band over the eyes). © Jacques Habbah. Courtesy of Somerset House & Maison Martin Margiela.

photographed, or fronted his collections, emphasizes the teamwork of his multinational staff. Much like the *plain* instalment from 'the concise dictionary of dress' the group portrait that appears in the exhibition is symbolic: it shows white Styrofoam cut-outs of silhouettes but no personal details, names or faces. The diagram that accompanies the schematic portraits simply lists the occupations and the nationalities (see figures 12a, 12b, 12c). In both exhibitions the use of white connotes the simplicity of the clean line and essential values. In the context of 'fashion', with its ever-changing colour palates and patterns, it lends a timeless quality to the fashion garment and the installation, untainted by the trendiness of fashion cycles. Like the blank canvas on which people project their own associations and meaning, the white reinforces an implicit minimalist understated symbolism of the clothes, creating a new visual language, which, paradoxically, becomes a brand marker.

In the Margiela exhibition the meaning and value of a status symbol are addressed through a critical practice that has become part of the brand's signature. This consists of laying bare the process of tailoring and branding, by mocking the desire for a status symbol while exploiting it, and by exposing the process of make-believe that is involved in, for example, turning a duvet into a coat by sewing sleeves and projecting different patterns onto it (see figure 13); by printing photocopied patterns onto white garments to make them look like different materials, by labelling vintage designs as 'replica' (see figure 14), or by printing a charity logo T-shirt while reminding the wearer that the purchase of a label does not make them a fashionable philanthropist (see figure 15).

Maison Martin Margiela advances an alternative notion of luxury. In sharp contrast with the industry definition of luxury, which relies on the quality of the materials, the prestige of the label, or the craftsmanship of the product, MMM does not use valuable fabrics. In direct juxtaposition with the perfect look of ready-to-wear luxury, Margiela reworks second-hand fabrics and ordinary materials into his creations (see figures 16a, 16b), and pioneered the use of unfinished seams, frays, and clothes in different states of deconstruction (see figures 17a, 17b, 17c) as a visual reference to embellished poverty.

In juxtaposition to couture fashion Margiela's concept of luxury appropriates only the element of workmanship, not the preciousness of the raw materials. The labels of such creations indicate only the number of hours of labour invested in the production of a garment, as the new criterion of luxury (see figures 18a, 18b). Such a designation celebrates the standard of the craft (as in Clark's illustration of the *Conformist*, see above) at the same time as it critiques the value of excess of such labour-intensive investment. By the same token the exhibition, and the collections, are making a stand with regards to idealized standards of perfection, which, together with luxury, make up the fantasy of glamour. The Martin Margiela team is not celebrating the new or the perfect (all the core values of the fashion industry). Instead the collection references the aging process as a creative ingredient (not as a problem to eliminate). Second-hand materials are worked into the designs, dark clothes are painted with silver paints that do not quite cover them, and crack with use, revealing the origin and creating an old patina – even with new clothes (see figure 19).

Figure 12a: A 3D group portrait in Styrofoam. Courtesy of Somerset House & Maison Martin Margiela.

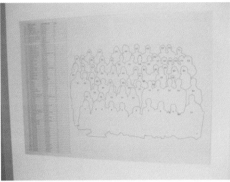

Figure 12b: a schematic table of the group portrait with numbers on the images representing a list of nationalities and role. Courtesy of Somerset House & Maison Martin Margiela.

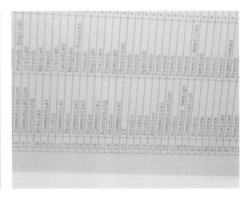

Figure 12c: A detail from schematic table – a list of nationalities and roles. Courtesy of Somerset House & Maison Martin Margiela.

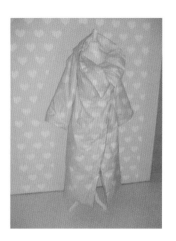

Figure 13: Autumn-Winter 1999–2000. 100% down duvet coat. The pattern is created by projecting different patterned background. Courtesy of Somerset House & Maison Martin Margiela.

Figure 14: Replica of a tuxedo jacket, Spring-Summer 2005. Part of a series of reproductions of archetypal, second hand garments from different style periods. Maison Martin Margiela ensures faithful reconstruction but is not the garment's 'author'. Courtesy of Somerset House & Maison Martin Margiela.

Figure 15: AIDS T-shirt. Since 1994–1995 Autumn-Winter collection each season Maison Martin Margiela produces a T shirt whose proceeds are entirely donated to helping AIDS victims. The text which is printed in black letters over the V-neck. Courtesy of Somerset House & Maison Martin Margiela.

Figure 16a: Autumn-Winter 1989–1990. Waistcoat made from broken dishes and wire. Courtesy of Somerset House & Maison Martin Margiela.

Figure 16b: Spring-Summer 1990. Sleeveless bolero made of street posters stuck together, lined with white cotton. Courtesy of Somerset House & Maison Martin Margiela.

Figure 17a: Autumn-Winter 1993–1994. Skin coloured top with burnt and singed hemline. Courtesy of Somerset House & Maison Martin Margiela.

Figure 17b: Autumn-Winter 2003–2004. Sleeveless dress slashed at the waist to show the lining and patchwork vest made from stitched interfacings normally used for stiffening collars. Courtesy of Somerset House & Maison Martin Margiela.

Figure 17c: Spring-Summer 1991. Dress in lining fabric, with visible darts, combined with a separate cotton shoulder section. Courtesy of Somerset House & Maison Martin Margiela.

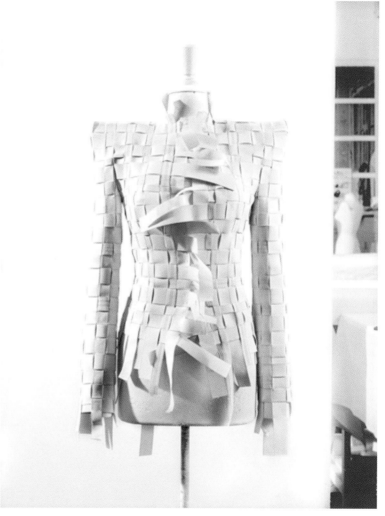

Figure 18a: Spring-Summer 2001 artisanal. Halter top made from second-hand gloves. Production time: 12 hours © Marina Faust. Courtesy of Somerset House & Maison Martin Margiela.

Figure 18b: Spring-Summer 2008 artisanal. A plaiting of elastic bands creates a jacket. Production time: 29 hours. © Marina Faust. Courtesy of Somerset House & Maison Martin Margiela.

Figure 19: Autumn-Winter 1999–2000. Second hand jacket painted over with silver paint. Spring-Summer 2003: Underdress cut to form a sleeveless blouse, partly laminated with silver foil. Courtesy of Somerset House & Maison Martin Margiela. Touch of old: covering garments with paint is part of the Margiela visual language. Wearing causes the paint to crack making the original visible giving way to a hidden past, highlighting the process of aging.

If the dictionary exhibition invokes *The Little Prince* as a method, the Margiela exhibition invokes *The Emperor's New Clothes* as message. Together they illustrate a visual mode of doing a reflexive analysis with fashion as the *object* but not necessarily the *objective* of the analysis, even though (most) authors of the exhibitions are deeply embedded in the theory or practice of fashion.

In subsequent issues of *Critical Studies in Fashion and Beauty* we would like to welcome papers that address the reflexive challenge of fashion from a diversity of perspectives: as an end, as a means to an end, as an associative link, or as an afterthought.

References

Barthes, Roland ([1970] 1973), *Le Juissance de Texte/The Pleasure of the Text* (trans. Richard Howard), New York: Hill & Wang.

Barthes, Roland (1983), *The Fashion System* (trans. Matthew Ward and Richard Howard), New York: Hill & Wang.

Bauman, Zygmunt (1998), *Globalization: The Human Consequences*, New York: Columbia UP.

Bauman, Zygmunt (2000), *Liquid Modernity*, Cambridge: Polity.

Bauman, Zygmunt (2001), *Community: Seeking Safety in an Insecure World*, Cambridge: Polity.

Bauman, Zygmunt (2002), *Society Under Siege*, Cambridge: Polity.

Bauman, Zygmunt (2003), *Liquid Love: On the Frailty of Human Bonds*, Cambridge: Polity.

Bauman, Zygmunt (2005), *Liquid Life*, Cambridge: Polity.

Bauman, Zygmunt (2006), *Liquid Times: Living in an Age of Uncertainty*, Cambridge: Polity.

Bauman, Zygmunt (2007), *Consuming Life*, Cambridge: Polity.

Bronfen, Elisabeth (2007), 'Dream journeys: Shakespeare's nocturnal forest and Freud's other stage setting', in *Traum & Trauma; Dream & Trauma: works from the Dakis Joannou Collection*, Vienna: Kunsthalle.

Clark, Judith and Phillips, Adams (2010), *Concise Dictionary of Dress*, London: Violette.

Crane, Diana (2010), 'Cultural Sociology and Other Disciplines: Interdisciplinarity in the Cultural Sciences', *Sociology Compass*, 4: 3, pp. 169–179.

Davis, Fred (1992), *Fashion, Culture and Identity*, Chicago: University of Chicago Press.

Eicher, Joanne B. and Roach, Mary Ellen (1973), *The Visible Self: Perspectives on Dress*, NJ: Prentice Hall.

Foucault, Michel ([1966] 2000), *Les Mots et les Choses/The Order of Things*, London: Routledge.

Freud, S. ([1915] 1916), *On transience. The Standard Edition of the Complete Psychological Works of Sigmund Freud*, Volume XIV (1914–1916): 'On the History of the Psycho-analytic Movement, Papers on Metapsychology and Other Works' (trans. James Strachey), London: Hogarth Press, pp. 303–307.

Freud, S. (1925), *A note upon the 'mystic writing-pad'. The Standard Edition of the Complete Psychological Works of Sigmund Freud*, Volume XIX (1923–1925): The Ego and the Id and Other Works, pp. 225–232.

Hebdige, Dick (1979), *Subculture: The Meaning of Style*, London: Methuen.

Hedström, Sofia and Ingesson, Cecilia (2008), 'The end of trend', *Bon*, Spring, pp. 62–66.

Hollander, Anne (1999), *Feeding the Eye*, NY: Farrar, Straus and Giroux.

Kaiser, Susan B. (1996), *The Social Psychology of Clothing: Symbolic Appearances in Context*, London: Macmillan.

Kawamura, Yuniya (2005), *Fashion-ology: An Introduction to Fashion Studies*, Oxford: Berg.

Kelley, Donald R (1991), 'History and the encyclopaedia', in Donald Kelley and Richard Popkin (eds), *The Shapes of Knowledge from the Renaissance to the Enlightenment*, Dordrecht: Kluwer Academic Publishers.

Krauss, Rosalind (1993), *The Optical Unconscious*, Cambridge, Mass.: MIT press.

Kritzman, Lawrence D. and Reill, Brian (ed.) (2005), *The Columbia History of Twentieth-Century French Thought* (trans. Malcolm DeBevoise), New York: Columbia University Press.

Lipovetsky, Gilles ([1987] 1994), *L'empire de l'éphémère – La mode et son destin dans les sociétés modernes/ The Empire of Fashion: Dressing Modern Democracy* (trans. Catherine Porter), Princeton: Princeton University Press.

Maciel, Maria Esther (2004), 'The unclassifiable', *Theory, Culture & Society*, 23, pp. 2–3.

Paris Aéroports magazine (2007–2008), 'Conso mobilité mode d'emploi', 26: December–January, pp. 18–19.

Polhemus, Ted and Lynn Procter (1978), *Fashion & Anti-fashion: Anthropology of Clothing and Adornment*, London: Thames & Hudson.

Solomon, Michael (ed.) (1985), *The Psychology of Fashion*, Lexington, MA: Lexington Books.

Stallybrass, Peter and White, Allon (1986), *Politics and Poetics of Transgression*, London: Routledge.

Steele, Valerie (1985), *Fashion and Eroticism: Ideals of Feminine beauty from the Victorian Era to the jazz age*, New York: Oxford University Press.

Stief, Angela and Matt, Gerald (2007), 'Art and Wound: On the aesthetics of dream and trauma', in *Traum & Trauma; Dream & Trauma: Works from the Dakis Joannou Collection*, Vienna: Kunsthalle.

Toffler, Alvin (1970), *Future Shock*, New York: Random House.

Toffler, Alvin (1980), *The Third Wave*, New York: Bantam books.

Tseëlon, Efrat (1989), 'Communication via clothing', Ph.D. dissertation, Oxford: University of Oxford.

Tseëlon, Efrat (1991), 'The method is the message: On the meaning of methods as ideologies', *Theory & Psychology*, 1, pp. 299–316.

Tseëlon, Efrat (2001), 'On women and clothes and carnival fools', in E. Tseëlon (ed.), *Masquerade and Identities: Gender, sexuality & Marginality*, London: Routledge.

Tseëlon, Efrat (forthcoming 2011), 'How successful is communication via clothing? Thoughts and evidence for an unexamined paradigm'.

Tungate, Mark (2005), *Fashion Brands: Branding Style from Armani to Zara*, Philadelphia: Kogan Page.

Wilson, Elizabeth (1985), *Adorned in Dreams: Fashion and Modernity*, London: Virago.

Wilson Trower, Valerie (2004), *Fashion Theory*, 8, pp. 351–354.

Woodall, Trinny and Constantine, Susannah (2007), *The Body Shape Bible*, London: Weidenfeld & Nicolson.

CSFB 1 (1) pp. 55–63 Intellect Limited 2010

Critical Studies in Fashion and Beauty
Volume 1 Number 1

© 2010 Intellect Ltd Article. English language. doi: 10.1386/csfb.1.1.55_1

ZYGMUNT BAUMAN
University of Leeds

Perpetuum mobile

Keywords

fashion
security
freedom
progress
Simmel
utopia

Abstract

In the deregulated, privatized society of consumers, fashion is a perpetuum mobile – a self-feeding, self-sustaining, self-propelling and self-invigorating process. This is due to the interaction of two socially prompted urges: the longing to be a part of a greater whole, and the urge for individualism/uniqueness – in their turn the effects of the dialectics of security and freedom. Fashion casts lifestyles in the mode of a permanent and principally un-finishable revolution. It plays a crucial operating role in rendering constant change to the norms of our being-in-the-world: if you do not wish to sink, keep surfing; obviously, you can no longer seriously hope to make the world a better place to live; but you cannot even make that agreeable place in the social world which you might have managed to cut out for yourself really secure.

Perpetuum mobile: a self-sustained and self-sufficient contraption, containing everything needed to remain in continuous, uninterrupted movement, to be eternally on the move, needing no further outside boost to stay in motion – no stimulus, push or pull, no intervention of an external outside force, no input of new energy …

At least since the time of Galileo and Newton, perpetuum mobile was the dream of sages and mystics, tinkerers and tricksters alike: an object of feverish experimentation and a cause of endless frustration. Time and again its miraculous discovery or invention was announced, only to fail in demonstration, be debunked as an illusion born of dabblers' ignorance, or as a conman's hoax prompted by greed and abetted by spectators' gullibility; all such announcements ended life as footnotes in the long, as yet unfinished, history of unreason. Ultimately, the idea of perpetuum mobile landed on the rubbish heap of popular misconceptions – not so much due to the long string of disappointments, as to the verdict of unfeasibility and sentence of capital punishment passed by modern physics.

There is no quarrelling with the physicists' pronouncements. When it comes to 'physical reality', and so also to the conditions of setting immobile bodies in motion, changing their velocity or the direction of their movement and bringing them to standstill again – physicists have the last word which we cannot but accept in all humility. But at that other level of reality called 'social' – at which bodies, while still subject to the laws of physics notorious for their indifference to purposes and motives, fall under the rule of purposeful change – things happen which (as Shakespeare could have said) physicists would not (and could not!) dream of. There, in that other world, the mythical contraption called 'perpetuum mobile' (a self-triggered, self-propelled and self-sustained change, a movement prominent not because of its inability to continue on its own, but – on the contrary – because of its incapacity of grinding to a halt, even of slowing down) may suddenly become not only a possibility, but also a reality. Fashion is a crowning example of such eventuality.

As Georg Simmel observed 'On fashion […] one can't say that it "is". It is always *becoming*' (Simmel 1992: emphasis added). In opposition to physical processes and yet in close affinity to the concept/ideal type of perpetuum mobile, what is inconceivable in the case of fashion is not the eventuality of keeping on the move (and doing work) endlessly, but – on the contrary – an interruption of the already started string of self-induced change. Indeed, the most astounding aspect of that extraordinary quality is the fact that the process of change does not lose its momentum as its work – its impact on the world in which it operates – is being done. The 'becoming' of fashion is not only inexhaustible and seemingly unstoppable, but it acquires more and more impetus and ability to accelerate as its material, tangible impact, and the number of objects it is affecting, rises.

Were fashion but a run-of-the-mill physical process, it would be a monstrous anomaly, violating the laws of nature. But it is not a phenomenon of physics: it is a *social* phenomenon, and social life as a whole is a startling contraption: one potent enough to suspend the operation of the second law of thermodynamics, cutting out an enclave sheltered from the curse of entropy – that (according to www.princeton. edu) 'thermodynamic quantity representing the amount of energy in a system that is no longer available for doing mechanical work' which 'increases as matter and energy in the universe degrade to an ultimate state of inert uniformity'. In the case of fashion, the 'inert uniformity' is not the 'ultimate state', being instead an ever more distant prospect: as if fashion had been equipped with inbuilt safety valves that open well before the target of 'uniformity' (allegedly one of the essential human motives setting the process of fashion in its perpetual motion) becomes too close for comfort and threatens to undermine or make null and void the potency of fashion's attraction and seduction. Entropy being, so to speak, a 'counter-differentiation' phenomenon, fashion – while drawing its impetus from the human resentment of differences and longing for their levelling – manages to reproduce in constantly increasing volume the selfsame divisions, inequalities, discriminations and deprivations it has promised to mitigate, flatten, or even eliminate altogether.

A sheer impossibility inside the physical universe becomes a norm when ushered into the world of perpetuum mobile. How can it be done? Simmel explains: by bringing together two equally powerful and overwhelming human urges/longings – two companions who are never separable, yet constantly at loggerheads with each other, often pushing or pulling in mutually opposite directions. Borrowing our tropes once more from the vocabulary of physics, we may say that, in the case of fashion, the 'kinetic energy' of movements is gradually, yet completely and without loss, transformed into the kind of potential energy necessary for a counter-movement. The pendulum goes on swinging, and, in principle, can continue swinging indefinitely, by its own momentum.

The two human urges/longings in question are the longing to be a part of a greater whole, and the urge for individualization/uniqueness: in other words, a dream of belonging, and a dream of self-assertion; the desire for social support, and the lust for autonomy; the impulse of imitation, and the drive to separation. We may say, ultimately, the *security* of holding hands, and the *freedom* to let them go. Or, to look at the same emotional coupling/dilemma from the opposite side of the equation, the fear of standing out, and the horror of one's self's dissolution.

Like many (most?) married couples, 'security' and 'freedom' cannot live without each other, and yet find living together a daunting task. Security without freedom is a sentence to slavery, while freedom without security condemns one to nerve-breaking and incurable uncertainty; when one is deprived of the other's support/complementation/outbalancing, both transform from coveted values into terrifying nightmares. Security and freedom need each other and yet cannot endure one another; they simultaneously desire and resent each other – though the proportions of the two contradictory sentiments change with each of the frequent (frequent enough to be deemed routine) departures from the 'golden mean' (temporarily) reached by the momentary compromise settlement.

Attempts at balancing and reconciling these two values prove to be, as a rule, incomplete, stopping short of full satisfaction, and, most importantly, too shaky and frail to exude, credibly, an air of finality. There are always some loose ends still needing to be tied up, and yet threatening to tear up the delicately woven social network with every pull. For that reason, attempts at reconciliation will never reach their explicitly or implicitly pursued purpose, manifest or latent, though all the same they will never be – they cannot be – ever abandoned. This is why the story of the cohabitation of security and freedom is bound to remain full of sound and fury. Its endemic and irresolvable ambivalence makes of it an inexhaustible source of creative energy and obsessive, compulsive change. For the same reason, it is predestined to perpetuum mobile status.

'Fashion,' says Simmel, 'is a peculiar form of life which is to secure a compromise between the tendency to social levelling and the tendency to individual uniqueness' (Simmel 1992). That compromise, let me repeat, cannot be a 'stable state'. It cannot be established once and for all: the clause 'until further (and as a rule abominably short!) notice' is engraved indelibly on its mode of existence. That compromise, just like fashion, is always 'becoming'. It cannot stay put; it needs to be perpetually renegotiated. Triggered by the impulse of one-upmanship,[1] pursuit of the (currently) fashionable leads quickly to the banalization/commonalization of these tokens of distinction – so that a briefest moment of inattention or the slightest slowing of the pace of change, not to mention neglecting it altogether, may, in no time, bring effects opposite to those intended: the loss of individuality. New tokens need to be rapidly obtained: yesterday tokens need to be immediately and ostentatiously expedited onto the dumping site. The precept of 'what is no longer on' needs to be as meticulously observed, and as diligently obeyed, as the precept of 'what is new and (currently) on the way up'. A life status indicated, communicated and recognized by the acquisition and display of the (short-lived and infuriatingly changeable) tokens of fashion is defined, in equal measure, by the tokens on conspicuous display and the tokens conspicuous by their absence.

The perpetuum mobile of fashion is thereby the dedicated, dexterous and seasoned destroyer of all and any standstill. Fashion casts lifestyles in the mode of permanent and principally un-finishable revolution. Given that the phenomenon of fashion is intimately and inseparably linked to two 'eternal' and 'universal', irremovable attributes of being-in-the-world, and so to their equally irreparable incompatibility – its ubiquitous presence is not confined to one or several selected forms of life. At any time in human history and on any territory of human habitation, it plays a crucial operating role in rendering constant change into the norm of being-in-the-world. However, the way in which it operates, and the institutions that sustain it and service it, do change from one form of life to another.

The present day variety of the fashion phenomenon is determined by the colonization and exploitation of that eternal aspect of the human condition by the *consumer markets*.

*

Fashion is one of the principal flying wheels of progress (that is, the kind of change that devalues and denigrates the state of affairs which it leaves behind and replaces). But in stark opposition to the previous uses of that concept, on the rare occasions when the word 'progress' appears (usually on the homepages of commercial websites) it no longer refers to a *forward* drive. Progress is no longer a compulsive chase after a spinning-along, elusive *utopia*, instead the word implies a hard, indomitable, menacing and threatening *reality*: a process that cannot be stopped and whose pressures must be obeyed ('if you can't beat them, join them'); a mortal threat for the slothful, improvident and indolent; a danger that makes a lucky escape an imperative. The imperative of 'joining' or 'moving with' progress is inspired by the urge to run away from the breathing-behind-the-neck spectre of *individually* suffered though *socially* produced disaster. This is not unlike the movement of the Klee/ Benjamin 'Angel of History' – running with one's back turned to the future, pushed on by horror/ repulsion of the putrefying and malodorous leftovers of past escapes …

Progress, to cut a long story short, has moved from the discourse of *shared improvement* to that of *individual survival*. Progress is no longer thought about in the context of an urge to rush ahead, but in connection with a desperate effort to stay in the race, to avoid disqualification or falling out. We do not think of 'progress' when we work for a *rise* in stature, but when we worry about staving off or at least postponing the moment of *fall*. 'Progress' appears in the context of the *avoidance of being excluded*. For instance, you listen attentively to the information that this coming year Brazil is 'the only winter sun destination *this* winter' – mostly to note that you must avoid being seen where people of aspirations similar to yours were bound to be seen *last* winter. Or you read that you must 'lose the ponchos' which were so *en vogue* last year – since time marches on and you are now told that wearing a poncho makes 'you look like a camel'. Or you learn that donning pinstripe jackets and T-shirts – 'must buy, put on, show off' last season – is over simply because 'every nobody' does them now. And so it goes. Time flows on, and the trick is to keep pace with the tide. If you do not wish to sink, keep surfing – and that means changing your wardrobe, your furnishings, your wallpapers, your look, your habits – in short, yourself – as smoothly as you can manage.

I do not need to argue, since this should be obvious, that such emphasis on the disposal of things – abandoning them, getting rid of them – rather than on their appropriation, fits hand-in-glove with the logic of a consumer-oriented economy. People sticking to yesterday clothes, computers, mobiles, or cosmetics would spell disaster for an economy whose main concern (and the condition *sine qua non* of its own survival) is the rapid and accelerating assignment of sold and purchased products to waste; an economy in which swift waste disposal is perpetually the cutting-edge industry.

Increasingly, *escape* has become the name of the most popular (in fact obligatory) game in town. Armies are no longer made of conscripts; instead staying 'with' and 'in' fashion is now achieved by universal conscription, sanctioned with capital (in the sense of social death) punishment for desertion. Semantically, escape is the very opposite of utopia, but psychologically it turns out to be utopia's only available substitute, refashioned to the measure of our deregulated, individualized society of consumers. Obviously, you can no longer seriously hope to make *the world* a better place to live; but you can also no longer even make secure (from progress, from fashion …) that agreeable *place* in the social world which you might have managed to cut out for yourself.

What is left to our individual concerns and individual exertions is the fight against *losing*. The fight against losing is a task which, to be properly performed, will require your full, undivided attention, 24 hours a day and seven days a week; and above all it will require keeping moving – as fast as you can …

Sławomir Mrożek, a Polish writer of world-wide fame with a first-hand experience of many lands, observes: 'In old times, when feeling unhappy, we accused God, then the world's manager; we assumed that He did not run the business properly. So we fired Him and appointed ourselves the new directors'. But, as Mrożek (who loathes clerics and everything clerical) finds out, business did not improve with this change of management. Once the dreaming and hoping for a better life is focused fully on our own egos and reduced to tinkering with our own bodies or souls

> there is no limit to our ambition and temptation to make that ego grow ever bigger, but first of all refuse to accept all limits […] I was told: 'invent yourself, invent your own life and manage it as you wish, in every single moment and from beginning to end'. But am I able to rise to such a task? With no help, trials, fittings, errors and rehashing, and above all without doubts?

The pain caused by unduly limited choice has been replaced, we may say, by no lesser a pain – this time caused by the obligation to choose while having no trust in the choices made and no confidence that further choices will bring the target any closer. Mrożek sees an intimate connection between the world we inhabit and a market-stall filled with fancy dresses and surrounded by crowds seeking their 'selves'. One can change dresses without end, so what a wondrous liberty the seekers enjoy; let's go on searching for our real selves, it's smashing fun – on condition that the real self will be never found. Because if it were, the fun would end …

The odd idea of making uncertainty less daunting and happiness more permanent, steady and secure by the continuous, uninterrupted changing of one's ego, and changing one's ego by changing one's dresses, is the present-day reincarnation of utopia. This is a utopia which services our society of 'hunters' (who replaced the 'gardeners', basic actors of the 'solid' phase of modernity, and the 'gamekeepers' of the pre-modern times): that is, the 'deregulated', 'privatized' and 'individualized' version of the old-style vision of good society – a society hospitable to the humanity of its members and rendering that humanity secure.

Hunting, in a liquid-modern setting, is a full-time job. It consumes a lot of attention and energy and leaves time for little else – and so it averts attention from the infinity of the task and postpones *ad calendas graecas* the moment in which the impossibility of the task ever being fulfilled is faced. As Blaize Pascal noted centuries ago, what people want is 'being diverted from thinking of what they are … by some novel and agreeable passion which keeps them busy, like gambling, hunting, some absorbing show …' People want to escape the need to think of 'our unhappy condition' and so 'we prefer the hunt to the capture'. 'The hare itself would not save us from thinking' about the formidable but intractable faults in our shared condition, 'but hunting it does so'. Pascal's musings have now reached reality courtesy of commercialized fashion.

Once started, tasted and savoured, the hunt (like all other drugs) becomes an addiction, compulsion and obsession. Catching a hare is an anticlimax; it only makes the prospect of another hunt yet more irrepressibly seductive, as the expectations animating the hunting become the most delightful (the only delightful?) experience of the whole affair. Catching the hare presages the end to those exciting, invigorating expectations – and so immediate planning and the prompt undertaking of another hunting escapade is the sole way to relieve frustration.

Is that the end of utopia? In one respect it is – in as far as early-modern utopian thought was inspired by desire for restful security and the end of overpowering, frightening chaos; by the dream of an end to the present unendurable exertions; indeed, the end of time as *history*. Though there is no such point in a hunter's life, no moment where one could say (with conviction passable for certainty) that the job has been done – the open-case shut, the missions accomplished – and look forward to rest and enjoyment of the booty from now to eternity. In a society of hunters, the prospect of an end to hunting is not tempting, but frightening – since it may arrive only as a personal defeat. The horns will go on announcing the start of another adventure, the greyhounds' bark will go on resurrecting the sweet memory of past chases, the others around will go on hunting, there will be no end to universal excitement. It is only me who will be cast aside, immobilized, excluded and no longer wanted, barred from other people's joys: just a passive spectator, watching the party from the other side of the fence, forbidden or unable to join the revellers – enjoying the sights and sounds at best from a distance and by proxy. If a life of continuing and continuous hunting is another utopia, it is – contrary to the utopias of the past – a utopia of *no end*. A bizarre utopia indeed, if measured by orthodox standards: the original utopias promised, temptingly, the end to toil, but the hunters' utopia encapsulates the dream of toil never ending.

Strange, unorthodox utopia it is, but utopia all the same, as it promises the same unattainable prize all utopias brandished, namely the ultimate and radical solution to human problems past, present and future, and the ultimate and radical cure for the sorrows and pains of the human condition. It is unorthodox mainly for having moved the land of solutions and cures from the 'far away' into 'here and now'. Instead of living *towards* the utopia, hunters are offered a living *inside* the utopia. For the 'gardeners', utopia was the end of the road – whereas for the 'hunters' it is the road itself. Gardeners visualized the end of the road as the vindication and the ultimate triumph of utopia. For the hunters, the end of the road would be the lived utopia's final, ignominious *defeat*. Adding insult to injury, it would also be a thoroughly *personal* defeat and proof of personal failure. Other hunters will not stop hunting, and non-participation in the hunt only provokes the ignominy of personal exclusion, and also (presumably) of personal inadequacy.

Utopia brought from the misty 'far away' into the tangible 'here and now', utopia *lived* rather than being *lived towards*, is immune to tests; for all practical intents and purposes it is immortal. But its immortality has been achieved at the price of frailty and vulnerability for all and each one of those enchanted and seduced to live it.

But this is, roughly, what the phenomenon of fashion is about … as if I was speaking of fashion, not of liquid-modern life and its utopia …

Unlike the utopias of yore, the liquid modern utopia, the utopia of hunters, of a life revolved on running after fashion, does not offer meaning to life – whether genuine or fraudulent. It only helps to chase the question of life's meaning away from the mind of living. Having reshaped the course of life into an unending series of self-focused pursuits – each episode lived through as an overture to the next – it offers no occasion for reflection about the direction and the sense of it all. When (if) finally such an occasion comes, at the moment of falling out or being banned from the hunting life, it is usually too late for the reflection to affect the way life (one's own life much as the life of others) is shaped, and so too late to oppose its present shape and effectively dispute its propriety.

For these reasons, the study of fashion is that of the 'grain of sand' in which William Blake struggled/hoped 'to see a world'; a way of grasping and holding infinity 'in the palm of your hand' …

> To see a world in a grain of sand,
> And a heaven in a wild flower,
> Hold infinity in the palm of your hand,
> And eternity in an hour.

(From *Auguries of Innocence*)

The world to be seen in that particular grain of sand called 'fashion' is a world which we, the denizens of the liquid-modern era, all inhabit. And the infinity to be grasped in the course of studying fashion is our *Lebenswelt* – the world conjured up by our way of living and the lives of the conjurers.

References

Bauman, Zygmunt (2009), *Art of Life*, Polity.

Simmel, Georg (1992), Zur Psychologie der Mode; Soziologische Studie – in *Gesamtsausgabe*, vol. 5, Suhrkamp.

Suggested citation

Bauman, Z. (2010), 'Perpetuum mobile', *Critical Studies in Fashion and Beauty* 1: 1, pp. 55–63, doi: 10.1386/csfb.1.1.55_1

Contributor details

Zygmunt Bauman is one of the most significant global social thinkers of our age. His work, spanning nearly five decades, steadfastly refuses to be constrained by arbitrary disciplinary boundaries within the arts, humanities and social sciences.

An extraordinarily productive scholar, his writings continue to be relevant to his host subject of sociology, but also to social and political theory, philosophy, ethics, art theory, media/communications studies, cultural studies, and theology.

His unique contribution – the conceptual framework 'liquid modernity' – has influenced international research within all of these disciplines. By employing the metaphor of 'liquidity', Bauman's later work has captured the fluid and constantly shifting character of our equally individualized and globalized lives and, over the course of a series of related books and articles, has offered one of the most significant interpretations of human societies in the twenty-first century.

Contact: Emeritus Professor of Sociology, School of Sociology and Social Policy, University of Leeds, Leeds, LS2 9JT, UK.

CSFB 1 (1) pp. 65–85 Intellect Limited 2010

Critical Studies in Fashion and Beauty

Volume 1 Number 1

© 2010 Intellect Ltd Article. English language. doi: 10.1386/csfb.1.1.65_1

ANA MARTA GONZÁLEZ
University of Navarra

On fashion and fashion discourses[1]

Keywords

fashion
critical views
social conversation
civilizing process
individualization
self-expression
identity

1. This text is the product
    of a re-elaboration of
    different materials
    previously published in
    Spanish and Italian.

Abstract

While critical views inherited from the past still influence our appraisal of fashion, its pervasiveness in contemporary society calls for an explanation. In this article I attempt to show how the importance of fashion in our society is the result of a combination of a structurally modern space and Romantic cultural ideals. I conclude that, despite its frivolous appearance, fashion is not only a powerful social indicator, but also a particular means of bringing together the diverse and often contradictory demands of our human nature through a peculiar exercise of practical judgment.

The prominence of fashion in our societies demands an explanation and, although this kind of explanation is usually reserved for sociologists, it is also true that changes in society have become one of the dominant issues in philosophical discourse. A glance at contemporary philosophy shows that social issues have become the starting point – and sometimes even the finishing line – for a large section of philosophical debate or, at least, of philosophical debate which is 'relevant' (from a sociological point of view). Whatever the case, this justifies philosophy's novel interest in fashion, an interest that in no way replaces that of the sociologist since the philosopher approaches social life, including fashion, as one of its most striking symbols, with his usual questions – those referring, in the end, to being and changing, to identity and flux, reality and appearance.

From this perspective, the fact that fashion should attract the attention of a philosopher is quite logical. Fashion brings us an ever-changing spectacle (especially accelerated in recent times). It is not simply a social fact or a 'total social fact', as stated by Mauss (1968: 274). It is not merely a coercive fact that imposes its law on the most reluctant individuals; rather, in its apparent superficiality, it implies a deeper dynamic, rooted at the very heart of human life (from which it is extremely difficult to escape precisely because we are social beings). It implies a dynamic of social assimilation and distinction, which, for want of other references, could be postulated as a guiding criterion that determines our very identity.

However, could this really happen? What would social life have to be like? What ideas and values would have to fill (or leave) our minds to allow fashion to set itself up as a criterion for identity? There is every likelihood that fashion cannot take on this responsibility without belying itself – its core is change – and without belying identity, watering it down in fleeting processes, which, in practice, would mean the annulling of all and every project for identity. The fact that, in postmodern times, fashion has been able to present itself as a factor of idenity is a clear sign that, contrary to the common philosophical idea, neither fashion, nor thinking on fashion, imply frivolity.

In fact, it may be true that fashion, despite the contempt in which it has long been held in intellectual milieus, is not so frivolous after all; if we consider that it very clearly reflects our social condition and shows the personal expression of a plurality of human dimensions. Indeed, the way we use fashion – therefore both the way we follow or do not follow it – is evidence of how we situate ourselves in the social world that we inhabit. Without a doubt, it is a powerful social indicator of the position we occupy in the fashion system: as originators or followers of tendencies, as punctual or late followers, as creators or consumers, etc. All this in itself very clearly marks the relative importance we give to a certain kind of common sense and social mobility, but, above all, the use we make of fashion is a way of expressing, in a visible material way, our particular means of bringing together the diverse demands of our human nature, and of doing so with the resources at our disposition, in a specific situation. Thus, the use of fashion means exercising practical judgement; in short, it is an exercise in discretion.

Therefore, the contemporary exaltation of fashion seems – in some postmodern circles at least – to reflect an explicit cult of the most brilliant and seductive aspects of consumer society. But, behind this affected and sometimes perverse exaltation of what is considered, correctly or not, to belong to the area of pure amusement, fashion continues as a social phenomenon that needs a balanced explanation. This will help place it in the general context of human life, in the general context of a life that, as seen by Simmel, takes place at the intersection of a variety of social spheres, and that, for this very reason, cannot be reduced to what prevails in just one of them.

Specifically, while the pervasiveness of fashion in our society calls for a structural explanation, this sort of approach should not obscure the individualized nature of fashion behaviours.

That structural explanation should certainly take into account the social differentiation following the modernization and industrialization process, as well as the acceleration of social time derived thereof; it must also consider the Romantic inheritance that is at the root of the contemporary focus on self-expression and identity.

Nevertheless, it is important to note that while the industrial revolution has certainly influenced the ways in which some fashions are generated and disseminated, romanticism has also increased our consideration of self-expression. Neither of those changes has modified the elusive nature of fashion itself or its ambivalent dynamics of social assimilation and distinction – a dynamic that emerges in unpredictable ways, provided some sort of society exists.

In the following pages I have taken both kinds of reflections into account, in order to understand how the two approaches are linked: the ubiquitous dynamic of fashion in our society and its often discrete presence in our daily lives, where the use of fashion is, in the end, an exercise in judgement or discretion.

With this in mind, I begin by giving a quick summary of two critical views of fashion inherited from the past that still influence the present; I then continue to address fashion as a phenomenon which shapes the social area – an area which modern philosophers, somewhat ambivalently, considered as linked to the civilization process. Fashion is a phenomenon, which, at any rate, can only increase in influence, and may change completely in a world where words are being replaced by images, and where the Romantic ideal becomes more prominent due to the modern insistence that these conventions equate with social order. In line with this thinking, we could say that, although there is a certain structural affinity between fashion and modernity, the importance of fashion in our society is the result of a combination of a structurally modern social space and Romantic cultural ideals.

1. Metaphysicians and politicians: Two critical visions of fashion

The frequent lack of interest in fashion among intellectuals has some eminent precedents. Plato and Rousseau perfectly embody the main two criticisms of fashion: the former metaphysical and the latter political.

In his well-known allegory of the cave, Plato portrayed prisoners as being chained to shadows, and only the free man dared leave the cave and see things are they truly are. On the contrary, those who remain in the cave, enslaved and fascinated by the shadow of things, will never know reality. This text suggests that, as they are enslaved in spirit by the shadows, the prisoners would go so far as to kill anyone who should dare to suggest that true reality lies elsewhere. Nevertheless, in Plato's proposition, there is no doubt that fashion belongs to the shadows. In *Hippias Major,* for example, Plato dwells on the relationship between clothing and beauty using the terminology of fraud [Plato 1982: 294 a–b]. It is clear that fashion, which undergoes constant change, is the antithesis of Plato's immutable ideas, which are the only thing truly real. When describing those involved in the world of fashion, we could use Plato's description of the Sophists, who he referred to as 'experts in producing appearances'. (Plato 1995, Sophist, 236 c)

If Plato can be taken as the main philosopher to scorn fashion for metaphysical reasons, Rousseau may be considered the reference point for those intellectuals who look down on fashion for political reasons. And if Plato's criticism has the virtue of attracting those of a religious nature, the path taken by Rousseau bears a certain similarity to Marxist criticism of fashion. (The case of Thomas More, who, in *Utopia,* describes a fashionless society, belongs, to my mind, to the former group, although, as it is a political treatise, it has been frequently associated with the latter.)

In fact, Rousseau elaborated his political theory in open disagreement with the society of his day, which, unmistakably, had given up the gravity and nobility of classical republican virtue and had surrendered to the enjoyment of private life. Instead of concerning themselves with public life, the nobility – in a process, which, according to Elizabeth Wilson, began towards the end of the Middle Ages (Barnard 1996: 147–8), and according to Fernand Braudel in the sixteenth century (Finkelstein 1998: 6) – were devoted to courtly life, while the bourgeoisie was devoted to business. Looking around him, Rousseau only saw the collapse of republican ideals: the transformation of the republican citizen who had been committed to the good of the republic into either a narcissistic aristocrat or a bourgeois caught up in his own private interests and with copying the whims of the aristocracy. Thus, Jean Jacques concludes that society corrupts; at any rate, it corrupts republican virtue, formulated as a virtue in which one places the common good before private interest. A similar idea is found in Smith when he writes:

> In quiet and peaceable times, when the storm is at a distance, the prince, or great man, wishes only to be amused, and is even apt to fancy that he has scarce any occasion for the service of any body, or that those who amuse him are sufficiently able to serve him. The external graces, the frivolous accomplishments of that impertinent and foolish thing called a man of fashion, are commonly more admired than the solid and masculine virtues of a warrior, a statesman, a philosopher, or a legislator. All the great and awful virtues, all the virtues which can fit, either for the council, the senate, or the field, are, by the insolent and insignificant flatterers, who commonly figure the most in such corrupted societies, held in the utmost contempt and derision.
>
> (Smith 1982: 63)

Rousseau and Smith both refer to social spaces that are governed by the games of seeing and being seen, where human beings vie with one another in an originally corrupt process which must, of necessity, give rise to envy and rivalry. However, this sequence of 'society-vanity-rivalry', which is also very evident in all later social thinking, disturbingly implies that all social dynamics – including fashion – are basically corrupt.[2]

Conversely, the importance of the fashion phenomenon in modern societies suggests that it should be studied in a different light, allowing for a positive approach to the subject. This is even more crucial, as we will soon see, in that the contemporary effervescence of fashion brings essential issues into play which refer to the definition of one's own identity (González 2007). We must not forget that Plato gave no clear answer to this question. By placing reality beyond appearances, he leaves us defenceless in a world dominated by appearances. In this situation, his only option is to escape from such a world, perhaps to travel to 'Utopia'. But that would mean abandoning society to that corrupt logic glimpsed by Rousseau, and echoed by Kant in his description of the 'predisposition to humanity':

> The predispositions to humanity can be brought under the general title of a self-love which is physical and yet involves comparison (for which reason is required); that is, only in comparison with others does one judge oneself happy or unhappy. Out of this self-love originates the inclination to gain worth in the opinion of others, originally, of course, merely equal worth: not allowing anyone superiority over oneself, bound up with the constant anxiety that others might be striving for ascendancy; but from this arises gradually an unjust desire to acquire superiority for oneself over others. Upon this, namely, upon jealously and rivalry, can be grafted the greatest vices of secret or open hostility to all whom we consider alien to us. These vices, however, do not really issue from nature as their root but are rather inclinations, in the face of the anxious endeavour of others to attain a hateful superiority over us, to procure it for ourselves over them for the sake of security, as preventive measure; for nature itself wanted to use the idea of such a competitiveness (which in itself does not exclude reciprocal love) as only an incentive to culture.
>
> (Kant [1793] 1998, Religion, 6: 27)

By differentiating – in the same work – between 'predispositions to humanity' and 'predispositions to personality', Kant emphasizes that this cultural incentive is not necessarily an incentive towards morality (González 2004). Despite this, we can ask if this logic of comparison and rivalry, which, in Kant's own words, is a constituent of culture, really does represent the only social logic, and how the hostility that derives from this logic can be neutralized? It is important to formulate these questions – and even more so to answer them – because, clearly, we live in a world that is fuller of appearance than that of Rousseau or of Kant and this leads to a never-ending comparison; in front of our eyes there is a daily parade of innumerable, often contradictory, models, which have no personality and are simply pure image. This is perhaps one of the points that differentiates our society from those of earlier ones: the rule of image.

2. The shaping of the social space through words or images

In order to define man as social and political animal, Aristotle drew on a feature that distinguishes man from the other animals, and which allows the former to be considered the 'most social' of all animals: the word. Only man has not simply a voice – with which he shows states of pleasure and pain – but also words, with which to speak 'of what is just and unjust, useful and hurtful'.[3] For Aristotle, then, human sociability stands out due to its verbal capacity, which is at the service of the ethical nature of man. In contrast, Rousseau's criticism of the society of his day suggests a very different concept of society, where the centre has shifted from the word to sight, from the ears to the eyes.

Word and action, in Hannah Arendt's view, were the keys to the classical political world. However, as Richard Sennet has observed, sight and appearance triumph in the modern world (Sennet 1997). Thus, however, imitation, which is such a central characteristic of human sociability and, according to Aristotle in his *Poetics*, plays a key role in the process of learning, has many and diverse contents. Imitation of the exploits sung by poets is clearly different from imitation of the more or less brilliant appearance of impersonal, distant models who parade before our eyes as if they were on a stage. Nevertheless, it is in this latter space – the space for 'what is social' – that fashion apparently develops, with the backing – as Smith reminds us – of our willingness to admire and imitate the great.

> It is from our disposition to admire, and consequently to imitate, the rich and the great, that they are enabled to set, or to lead what is called the fashion. Their dress is the fashionable dress; the language of their conversation, the fashionable style; their air and deportment, the fashionable behaviour. Even their vices and follies are fashionable; and the greater part of men are proud to imitate and resemble them in the very qualities which dishonour and degrade them …

(Smith 1982: 64)

Kant uses similar terminology in *Anthropology*:

> It is a natural inclination of man – says Kant – to compare his behaviour to that of a more important person (the child compares itself to grown-ups, and the lowly compares himself to the aristocrat) in order to imitate the other person's ways. A law of such imitation, which aims at not appearing less important than others, especially when no regard is paid to gaining any profit from it, is called fashion. Therefore it belongs under the title of vanity, because in its intention there is no inner value; at the same time, it belongs under the title of folly,

3. 'That is not the fashion which everybody wears, but which those wear who are of a high rank, or character. The graceful, the easy, and commanding manners of the great, joined to the usual richness and magnificence of their dress, give a grace to the very form which they happen to bestow upon it. As long as they continue to use this form, it is connected in our imaginations with the idea of something that is genteel and magnificent, and though in itself it should be indifferent, it seems, on account of this relation, to have something about it that is genteel and magnificent too. As soon as they drop it, it loses all the grace, which it had appeared to possess before, and being now used only by the inferior ranks of people seems to have something of their meanness and awkwardness' (Smith 1982: 194–195).

4. 'It is necessary for us, in our calm judgments and discourse concerning the characters of men, to neglect all these differences, and render our sentiments more public and social …The intercourse of sentiments, therefore, in society and conversation, makes us form some general unalterable standard, by which we may approve or disapprove of characters and manners' (Hume [1777] 1975: 228–230).

because in fashion there is still a compulsion to subject oneself slavishly to the mere example which many in society project to us.

(Kant [1793] 1998, 7: 245)

The scornful tone used by both Smith and Kant when referring to fashion is due to the fact that they believe fashion to be mere vanity, and, simultaneously, they warn that, under the influence of fashion, human beings may behave in ways that are contrary to common sense and morality. But this is precisely proof of the strength of human sociability, encouraged, as both authors mention, by the desire to imitate the great (Aristotle [1991]: 1253a 12). Although a study of contemporary fashion may belie this last point – much fashion has its roots at the street level or in a subculture – the opposite argument is also valid: what has changed is not so much the origin of fashion as the evaluation of who is great or not.

Whatever the case, we must not forget that Kant himself considers this social logic, arbitrated by imitation, as a factor in civilization and refinement – although not of a moral nature – as, in line with Rousseau, he believes that refinement is compatible with the hypocrisy that corrupts the heart (Kant, [1911] 1998, KrV A748/B777). In contrast, Hume has a more positive vision of civilization and its relationship with morality. It is precisely in the moral work of Hume – specifically his theory on the artificial virtues – that we find presentation of the elements of a modern theory of civilization. Here we find the artificial institution of a framework for justice in which commercial activity and the progress of moral sentiments are developed (Baier 1991). This goes hand-in-hand with the 'social conversation' that generates 'common sense'.

Indeed, in a notorious anticipation of the social theory of contemporary social theorists such as Elias (Elias 1997) or Bourdieu (Bourdieu 2002), Hume observes with great clarity that the widening of the circle of conversation required by the transition from family to civil society, involves important modifications of our feelings. He summarizes the nature of these modifications when he speaks of 'making more public our sentiments'.[4] This process takes place when we model those sentiments according to more general criteria that are formed with relative spontaneity; when we feel the need to make ourselves understandable to others in conversation. This social reality – in which Rousseau sees mostly deception – is what, according to Hume, leads to the refinement of our feelings, because it involves a deprivation of the element of passion with which those feelings appear in the first place, and, to a certain extent, make them objective and open to institutional regulation.

The institutional regulation of sentiments has much to do with the importance that Hume concedes to the rules of courtesy, which make up the 'art of pleasing', and, among those rules particularly, the conventional rules referring to social commerce among men and women (Hume [1882] 1964: 192). The logic of this *social commerce* is, ideally, what is reflected in the literary salons so well described by Simmel: a relatively egalitarian logic, based precisely on emphasizing the purely formal elements of sociability.

Indeed, the literary salon created an atmosphere that made treating one another as *equals* possible. This is also what Dena Goodman has in mind as she notes that in the salon one set of differences, based on birth, was devalued and replaced with another, based on comportment, manners, and a shared discourse. To be civil was to act nobly, and thus to be noble. Nobles were people who shared a set of manners and a discourse, both of which were defined by rules of comportment regulating how they were to relate to one another as persons who were admittedly different in a society defined by ranks and orders (Goodman 2001: 132). That sort of society was what the Enlightenment thinkers had in mind as a model for civil society itself.[5]

The echo of Scottish thinking on society is also found in the Kantian characterization of the world as a *Shauplatz* (Kant [1802] 1923, 9:18), as a *Weltbühne* (Kant [1784] 1983, 8: 17), or a *social stage*. However, it is precisely in the way modern society tends to pave the way for the world as a stage that it prepares the ground for the postmodern hegemony of fashion.

Certainly the main difference between modern and postmodern society on the subject of fashion is not so much structural as cultural: whereas modern society gave greater importance to the word – albeit a formal word in consonance with the demands of 'social conversation' – postmodernity grants greater importance to one's image. The hegemony of the word has been replaced by the hegemony of sight. Thus fashion has been strengthened exponentially, perhaps to regulate that which in a social context of 'institutionalized individualism' (Beck 2002) runs the risk of becoming a 'visual cacophony' (Finkelstein 1998: 18). Indeed: as Anne Hollander observes, 'The tyranny of fashion itself has in fact never been stronger than in this period of visual pluralism' (Finkelstein 1998: 18). In any case, the regulation of this pluralism occurs within the context of a social space that, structurally, is still modern, in that what we call postmodernity may be, from a certain view, considered an ambiguous continuation of modernity.

From a cultural perspective also, there is no doubt that modern heritage is relevant in understanding the contemporary destiny of fashion. As we have stated, Rousseau's thesis, which links civilization and corruption, is at the foundation of most modern thinking on society. In this line, vanity and the social vices in general were believed by modern thinkers to be factors for progress and civilization. Mandeville states that the economy advances due to vanity, which promotes rivalry in expenditure; Kant believes that social vices, although blameworthy at an individual level, temper the coarseness of natural leanings, and so, from a historical perspective, may be considered civilizing factors. Thus, despite not having dealt specifically with the phenomenon of fashion, these modern authors proposed a thesis which still frames the postmodern reflections on fashion: for example Lipovetsky, who writes: 'The more ephemeral seduction there is, the more enlightenment advances' (Lipovetsky 1994: 9). Hegel's thesis on the 'Cunning of reason' is itself a secularization of the Christian idea of Providence: what may be fatal individually, may aid the progress of reason at a macro-historical level.

5. 'Commerce, conversation, Enlightenment itself, were all created out of a culture of interaction and exchange among groups and individuals whose differences made such relations meaningful rather than tautological, but which also necessitated rules, structures, and institutions to make them work. The *philosophers* soon looked to salon conversation not only to structure the work of Enlightenment, but as the model for civil society itself' (Goodman 2001: 134).

Certainly, Lipovetsky gives an aestheticist twist to Hegel's thesis. On the one hand, he believes that fashion obeys what is fanciful, ludic, and apparently irrational. But at the same time he holds that fashion has played its role in the modern project for the progressive liberation of the individual:

> The age of efficiency and the age of the ephemeral, rational mastery of nature and the ludic follies of fashion: these are only in appearance antinomic. In fact, the two types of logic are rigorously parallel ... In each case, human sovereignty and autonomy are affirmed, exercising their dominion over the natural world as they do over their aesthetic décor.
>
> (Lipovetsky 1994: 24)

However, in spite of these structural and cultural continuities with modernity, the contemporary effervescence of fashion, at a cultural level, owes a great deal more to Romantic expressivity, which is culturally possible – as Simmel observed – due to the differentiation of the individual promoted by the process of modernization.

Indeed, Simmel differentiates between two kinds of individualism: on the one hand, the individualism of the eighteenth century, which we can associate with emancipation, which was promoted by the Enlightenment and claimed that all human beings have equal rights. On the other, we have the individualism of the nineteenth century, which is the characteristic achievement of Romanticism: every single human being is unique in kind, and true freedom also involves the expression of that uniqueness. Simmel calls the former type of individualism 'numerical individualism' (Simmel 1971: 224), and he believes it to be structurally possible due to the intersection of social circles in which the modern individual ordinarily lives. The second type of individualism, conversely, is called 'qualitative individualism', and it first became possible when the intersection of social spheres left a free space within which the individual, no longer subject to extrinsic norms, could find a space for an original expression of the self. 'Authenticity', instead of courtesy, is then able to thrive as the dominating value in human interaction (Taylor 1992). The self has to appear such as it is without cultural mediation.

3. The affinity between fashion and modernity

'Fashion' represents a peculiar expression of what Kant once described as 'antisocial human sociability' (Kant [1784] 1983, Idea 8: 20–21), that is, the inclination that at times makes us want to associate with our fellow beings and at others to sever connections with them. As is common knowledge, Simmel explains the fashion phenomenon on the basis of that principle. But it is clear that although this two-fold inclination has always been part of human make-up, what each of us considers a 'fellow' varies depending on whether we belong to traditional societies – in which class or family ties are still strong – or to modern societies – which are more autonomous – in which affinities are not, supposedly, pre-defined. It is in this latter case that fashion, with its clear fixation on appearances, may take on a particular relevance as a principle for social assimilation and distinction. This is why, without rejecting its existence in the past, we can nevertheless underline a particular affinity between the development of fashion and the modernization process, which began in western society and is spreading all over the world.

This particular affinity between fashion and modernization can be shown in several ways, some of which follow.

The prestige of novelty

Firstly, we find that the social distinction associated with fashion is linked to the prestige that 'something new' has acquired in modern societies, in surprising contrast to the prestige of 'antique' things in traditional societies. On this basis, we could define fashion as a characteristically modern expression of the social, temporal, and aesthetic dimension of human life. Its modernity resides in the fact that, in contrast with emphasis on what is old and permanent found in classic and traditional contexts, fashion emphasizes what is new and ephemeral. Therefore, even when it returns to manners and styles from the past, it does so in conformity with its characteristic pattern of constant change and it does so in such a way as to avoid settling on any of them. As Kant notes, 'Novelty makes fashion alluring; and to be inventive in all sorts of external forms, even if they often degenerate into something fantastic and even detestable, belongs to the style of courtiers, especially the ladies, whom others follow avidly' (Kant [1798] 1978, 7: 245).

The fashion boom favoured by our modern social structure could thus be taken as a sign of weakening tradition, and of the weakening of social links forged by tradition; in the same way as, according to Gabriel de Tarde[6], modernity has also favoured the substitution of tradition with reason, and of reason with opinion. In any event, we should keep this background idea in mind in order to understand the Romantic-style dialectical reaction with which the cultural area attempts to resist change by appealing to identity. If we do not comprehend this type of reaction, we will never understand the paradox: the irony contained in the postmodern attempt to integrate fashion and identity, change and stability.

Redefinition of social affinities

We find another means of understanding fashion in modernity by remembering that the transition from the old to the new regime, together with the arrival of an industrial society, goes hand in hand with a progressive decline in the traditional significance of attire, which, while not being identical to fashion, is, however, at its 'epicentre'. Thus, while in traditional societies clothing indicated class,

6. 'Mucho antes de tener una opinión general y sentida como tal, los individuos que componen una nación tienen conciencia de poseer una tradición común, y conscientemente se someten a las decisiones de una razón considerada como superior Así, de estas tres ramas del espíritu público, la última en desarrollarse, pero también la más dispuesta a crecer a partir de un cierto momento, es la opinión; y ésta se acrecienta a expensas de las otras dos' (Tarde 1986: 80).

7. There is however, a major difference between Veblen and Simmel. Whereas for Veblen, fashion can be explained in terms of ostentation of status, and therefore, leaves itself open to interpretations where prestige and money are fused together, Simmel offers a more carefully worked out version of the phenomenon, in that he explains fashion in terms of purely formal sociability – as a pure principle of assimilation and distinction in itself indifferent to the content of the expression.

occupation, belonging to a certain region, etc., in modern society – with the exception of those areas where a purely logical function is the rule – clothes alone no longer indicate anything (Finkelstein 1998: 18; Crane 2000: 3), except possibly social position and sexual difference.

However, we find what defines fashion as such within this progressive emptying of significance, which leaves the meaning of attire at the mercy of changing social conventions. Fashion is thus defined by its condition of pure form empty of content and, for this same reason, all its strength and prestige come from social conventions. Accordingly, at a time when industrialization and the progressive democratization of our societies have annulled class differences, fashion, informed entirely by convention, has taken on a double role of assimilation and difference. This guarantees minimal social consistency, because there can be no society unless the dynamics for social assimilation and difference that Simmel, like Veblen before him, considered in terms of class are preserved.[7]

Like many others before him, Simmel emphasizes the role played by *mimicry* in this process. Although the phenomenon of mimicry merits a separate study – attending to the triadic structure of desire (Girard 1978) – here it is enough to admit that, from the outset, we imitate that which, consciously or unconsciously, we would like to be. Granting that this tendency is to be found, partially at least, at the roots of human sociability, we may infer the importance of guiding these ambitions in order to avoid the contamination of the social process, because – in the line indicated by Rousseau – it would be difficult to avoid the emergence and development of fashion itself. Certainly, the phenomenon of mimicry, when referring to fashion, has been expressed in different ways. In other ages, when fashion was a question of class, the bourgeoisie imitated the aristocrats. In the twentieth century, however, the models no longer came from the aristocracy. From the 1950s onwards fashion has clearly changed from being imposed from top to bottom to spreading from the bottom up (Crane 2000: 14) (for example 'cool-hunters', who search for what is 'cool' in the most stylish areas of the main European capitals), and although the need to use celebrity figures as 'loudspeakers' for tendencies has emerged, the mimicry remains.

However, Simmel himself pointed out that the mimicry cannot be complete because both society and fashion demand differentiation. So, for example, although the bourgeoisie did imitate the aristocrats, they always tried to avoid its excesses; and the aristocracy always introduced a new fashion when the earlier one had filtered down to the lower classes. Thus, social difference was preserved. Even now, when a particular fashion has been more or less accepted in the main, the brains behind it – no longer the traditional aristocracy, but creative sectors of the public, urban tribes, etc. – attempt to differentiate themselves again by launching a new fashion. The term 'attempt' does not necessarily mean 'explicit intention', but what is essential in the process is that, by setting a trend, an individual, intentionally or not, tries to be different in the same way that someone else, by imitating them – again intentionally or not – tries to express their social affinities. Meanwhile it is the concept of 'lifestyle', rather than the idea of class, which shapes people's affinities and the dynamics of fashion itself.

The transition from 'class' to 'lifestyle' (Crane 2000: 10), already identified by Daniel Bell in his book *The Cultural Contradictions of Capitalism*, is in itself indicative of a third approach, previously mentioned, which again reveals the modernity of fashion. That is, its harmony with the modern process of *individualization* and, finally, with the Romantic desire to express one's own identity in such a way as to not be absorbed into a genre. In fact, Simmel had already clearly pointed out how, in the anonymity and functionality of great modern cities, fashion had become a channel to express human subjectivity (Finkelstein 1998: 107–108), in paradoxical harmony with the Romantic longing for one's true self and Nietzsche's ethics of distinction.

Qualitative individualism

Undeniably, the individuals Simmel observes at the beginning of the twentieth century are not exactly Romantic types. Living, as they were, in a highly industrialized society they could hardly indulge in Romantic spontaneity. While they still valued their subjectivity, and tried therefore to contest the homogenizing trends of their times, they found it hard to recognize themselves in nature. Leaving the city was no longer an option for them. In fact, the Romantic ideal of *Bildung*, consisting in the reconciliation of nature and freedom in one's own subjectivity, seemed lost forever. In the conditions of a culture, increasingly technical and alienated from its human author, that Romantic longing could only feed a tragic feeling about human destiny.

Simmel was aware of this alienation when he referred to the 'tragedy of culture'– that is, the lack of correspondence and synchronization between objective and subjective culture. In so doing, he was picking up a characteristically Nietzschean theme and it was precisely Nietzsche who first formulated a critique of the Romantic ideal of *Bildung*, suggesting an alternative solution for preserving a sense of one's self despite the conditions of modern life. His proposal no longer required the development of *Bildung*, but rather the acquisition of *style*.

In Nietzsche's view, style – not to be confused with fashion – is a strategy the subject develops to retain control of a situation, avoiding the invasion of the outside world into the realm of one's subjectivity. From this it is clear that having style involves a strong will. It is therefore not a matter for everybody, but for human beings completely in charge of themselves.

According to Simmel, individuals living in early-twentieth-century cities ran the risk of becoming interchangeable pieces in a huge social machine and were thus bound to find Nietzsche's aristocratism attractive. In the development of 'style', they discovered a way to preserve an individual sense of their selves, and control their manifestation. At the beginning of the twentieth century, *style* seemed the last refuge for those who struggled to resist complete functional homogenization.[8]

Clearly, Nietzsche's resort to style, as one mark of the superior human being, may be considered unrealistic and one-sided. In Simmel's view, Nietzsche represents the exaltation of humanity before society; because identity is linked to society, the Nietzschean individual has to resist identification

8. It is important to note that the general relevance of style as a mark of one's own personality is a feature of modern culture. This is not to say that people in the pre-modern era had no style or no interest in style. It is just to say that in pre-modern times having a personal – as opposed to a *class* – style was not deemed so important in terms of one's social identity. Social identity was developed out of other sources. Pre-modern individuals did not have to worry much about their own personal style. In any event, they did not experience it as a matter of self-definition or self-discovery, as a matter of achieving or expressing one's own identity. Their social identity came as a matter of course through the quite fixed position they had in their society by birth. Tradition provided the background against which an individual would develop his/her taste. By contrast, modern individuals came to think of identity as a task to be achieved through personal effort. Romantic thinkers summarized this effort

in a word: *Bildung*. Yet, *Bildung* was an overly ambitious ideal, which became unrealizable as industrial society imposed uniforming trends upon all individuals. At this stage the only way to preserve a sense of one's self was style.

with any social group, with any group of reference. He cannot accept any definitions besides the one he gives himself. Nevertheless, as it turns out, this stylized version of human subjectivity has great difficulty resisting the influence of the consumer society.

Indeed, in the light of subsequent history, we might be led to think that this (supposedly final) refuge could not resist the attack of objective culture. In many cases, it certainly seems as if the advance of capitalist society has fulfilled the dark prognosis of Max Weber, who, through his metaphor of the iron cage (Weber [1930] 1956: 181) sees us going 'from the spirit of capitalism to capitalism without spirit'. In this way, the transition from productive capitalism to consumer capitalism would have finally succeeded in invading the fortress of subjectivity with its productions – to the point of actually shaping people's desires far beyond all natural expectations. Significant in this context is the fact that the pages devoted to 'style' in most newspapers and magazines deal with consumer goods – as if having style were mostly a matter of having certain items. Has style perhaps not surrendered to the dictates of the fashion industry? Has not the subject disappeared behind the objects it consumes? Has not the subject, perhaps, fashioned an identity for him/herself according to the patterns of consumer behaviour? Is not identity something provided by the market, something to be appropriated and discarded like any other property?

Professionalization of fashion

In this final reflection we note the fourth way in which the process of modernization has affected fashion – particularly the production of clothing – by placing it within the general process of the division of labour that, thanks to the breakdown of the guilds, and the introduction of capitalism, led to the diversification of garment production and the professionalization of its manufacture. Thus, when, in 1857, Charles-Frederick Worth opened his couture house in Paris, he introduced the figure of the professional *couturier* and was surrounded by that aura of genius normally reserved for artists, it became clear that fashion would no longer begin in aristocratic circles. The professionalization of fashion brought it into the modern era once and for all.

Although almost 100 years would have to go by before the arrival of prêt-à-porter, and the marketing opportunities offered by the mass media would force the final aristocratic fashion connotations to give way to more 'democratic' fashion (Sommier 2000: 20), the fundamental economic structure has been laid down since then.

4. Fashion and identity

The 1960s marked the beginning of the cultural and social changes that led to the contemporary contentious linking of fashion and identity (Crane 2000: 14). As we have already stated, the seeds for this cultural change had already been sown by Romanticism, to which we owe the emphasis on identity – perhaps as means of steadying the constant movement brought about by modern times – and the emphasis on self-expression, in dialectical contrast with the prevailing conventions of culture.

The 1960s witnessed revolutionary cultural change. Before then, daughters had followed their mother's fashion example; however, in the 1960s it was the mothers who imitated their daughters. Teenagers and young people largely became the focus of fashion – as had already been happening in the US since the 1950s. Haute couture lost ground as the innovator of trends, and in the following decades it was marginal subcultures that, one after another, took over as inventors of styles that were soon found everywhere.

This all seems to indicate that the idea of one single, top-down, hegemonic fashion would disappear and leave instead an unbounded pluralism – just like contemporary art, according to Danto, – that would be impossible to reduce to one single narrative and thus would be in comprehensible harmony with the postmodern exaltation of difference.

But is this difference real? Particularly from the 1980s onwards, we frequently feel that we are watching a manifestation that merely presents '(virtual) variations on a single theme': a manifestation that, far from promoting exceptional uniqueness, encourages – like in the Matrix movie – the elimination of discrepancies to the system. On occasion, the postmodern spectacle is presented as a gallery of identities, which the consumer may freely choose from, as if our very identity were nothing more than appearance and we could make use of it as we please.

Indeed, what is being sold lately in the name of fashion is not simply 'style', but 'identity'. Evidently, the sales departments have seen the demand for identity in a fragmented world and, when introducing a new product – be it a vehicle, a perfume, a vacation or, obviously, clothes – they try to connect it with a more or less stereotyped lifestyle or personality, something, in any event, unitary and superficially attractive. There is no need to be a Freudian or a Marxist to point out that our society, more fetish-oriented than ever, projects its most varied human illusions onto consumer products. In this way, we now sell appearance as identity.

The process that has brought us to this point has been long, drawn-out and not lacking in irony. It has been going on since the first appearance of fashion as a strategy for social assimilation and difference, based on conventional aspects which must be taken seriously – fashion as represented by a Simmel – until its postmodern deconstruction.

Beyond the differences between the diverse postmodern approaches, what they all have in common is the acceptance of the conventional nature of fashion, which Simmel has already underlined. Thus, instead of believing, as Simmel did, that maintaining these conventions is important both for society and for the individual, the different postmodern groups have differing opinions, either in direct confrontation with fashion conventions or by adopting a forcedly ludic attitude towards them.

In general, de-constructionist thinking on fashion begins by accepting the current increasing emptiness of meaning which we associate with clothing and other social manners and then declares that consumer society has carried out this emptying successfully: that we are now 'free' of any other meaning previously associated with objects (and can now use any other arbitrary meaning(s)). According to Baudrillard, the complete emptiness of meaning, which can convert an object into a pure fashion object, occurs when said object has been reduced to mere consumer goods. Once reduced in this way, it is also reduced to the mere condition of a symbol without meaning whose only significant power, therefore, would lie in referring to the remaining symbols of the system.

Continuing with Barthes's analyses, which link connotations of symbols and ideology (Barthes 1967), cultural studies scholars generally interpret the conventional and characteristic aspects of fashion as integral parts of a cultural system for social domination; this system is deemed to be responsible for the perpetuation of class differences and/or gender discrimination. The most evident example of this reading of fashion can be found in the interpretation of nineteenth-century fashion where Flügel identifies the 'Great Male Renunciation' (Flügel, [1930] 1971) as the disappearance of colour and the greater functionality of men's attire. At the same time, women's fashion – rich in ornamentation and poor in mobility – reflected man's conception of himself as an 'active being', in contrast with woman as a 'passive being'. Thus, by accepting the fashion of the period as an expression of their feminine identity, women more or less consciously accepted the position they were destined for within socio-economic structures.

By 'unmasking' the power structures that operate behind such an apparently trivial institution as fashion, the culturalist approach tries to strip fashion conventions of the strength and prestige they had in the modern vision. Thus, it gives the typically postmodern approach a chance; instead of taking the conventional aspects of fashion very seriously, as did the modern approach, it adopts a purely playful attitude towards them, which consecrates the concept of fashion as a mask, and, finally, what Bakhtin would call a 'carnivalesque' conception of life (Bakhtin ([1965] 1968).

So, once the 'perverse' nature of such conventions has been revealed, that is to say, once they have been finally reduced to their purely conventional status, we would be free to play with them, in a never-ending combination. This is particularly reflected in the Lipovetsky approach; in contrast with Baudrillard – for whom fashion, although aesthetic in its effects, is of economic origin – Lipovetsky explicitly emphasizes fashion's aesthetic origin. Moreover, Lipovetsky interprets the global fashion phenomenon in more positive terms than Baudrillard. For the latter, indeed, the fact that fashion has been held up as a self-referential system, which promotes a certain kind of aesthetic liberation, may also reflect the failure of the political system in promoting individual autonomy (Finkelstein 1998: 75–6). In contrast, Lipovetsky believes that fashion, while not free of ambiguity, is a sort of catalyst for the modern process of individualization and it deserves global approval.

In any case, there is no room for anything really new in this self-referential system, nor can we expect it to reflect anything other than itself. Taking an example from Baudrillard, it makes no sense to interpret the miniskirt as a symbol of women's liberation, nor of women's oppression. It can only be interpreted as the opposite of the maxi-skirt. Similarly, consideration of fashion as a self-referential system explains how Baudrillard interprets the aesthetic dimension of fashion in terms of "recurrent circulation of forms" (Baudrillard 1993: 95). And while Lipovetsky does insist more on the idea of 'aesthetic innovation' as the engine for fashion, he does not actually introduce real innovation since the only innovation results from the simple combination of pre-existing elements and is, as Derrida would say, 'bricolage' (Barnard 1996: 167). Precisely from this combination, from this *bricolage*, Derrida draws on the postmodern idea and its peculiar notion of beauty: 'beauty' only comes from combining looks. On this basis, all the hopes of the postmodern individual are pinned on enjoying the seductive images and dreams promised by fashion – immersing himself/herself in the spectacle of virtual realities with changing forms.

In the meantime, what happened to identity? In its attempt to free the individual from the 'corset' of convention, postmodern discourse does not manage to give a positive answer to this question, unless we take the proposal of 'constructing' one's identity by means of the materials offered by the consumer society – including waste materials – as such.

Clearly then, the postmodern discourse – in particular its strange rhetoric of liberation reduced to bricolage – feeds on the situation created by the transition from the primitive capitalist production paradigm to the consumer paradigm of contemporary capitalism. This transition is accompanied by a change in accent in the fashion initiative – from the producer to the consumer – that may largely explain the anarchistic proliferation of styles and trends that have appeared since the 1960s, and which make it almost impossible to speak of a clearly defined fashion. We thus see an apparent mushrooming of offers because the individual is assumed – at least in his use of free time – to have the last word on fashion (Crane 2000: 11). Following this postmodern analysis, then, the individualizing dynamics, which are characteristic of the modernization process, find their ultimate expression in the figure of the aesthetic consumer.

But does this analysis reflect the truth? Is it not perhaps over-simplified?

5. Fashion as an everyday phenomenon

Although macroscopic and conflicting interpretations, such as those of Baudrillard or Lipovetsky, can undoubtedly help us to comprehend the elements involved in the key role of fashion in our contemporary societies, this very macroscopic character is also somewhat excessive. It ignores the everyday phenomenon of fashion, the way in which it appears in the very dynamics of social life, independently of whether it has been cheered on by mass industry or not, independently of whether its agents behave as aesthetic consumers or simply as individuals who want to satisfy a need. As Veblen pointed out, no social class, no matter how poor, ever gives up on conspicuous consumption completely (Veblen 1994: 85).

The everyday phenomenon of fashion is very well illustrated by Laura Bovone when she states that 'most of us have relatively little to do with fashion designers' suggestions, high fashion images, or prêt-à-porter purchases, but for all of us clothing is a duty, for some of us a pleasure, and for many of us a problem. This duty/pleasure/problem may sometimes find a solution in a glossy magazine, but, more often, we make our decisions when we open our full-to-overflowing wardrobes. We live in any case in the world of consumption, but what has been considered for many years as fashion – fashion that every year brings new prescriptions, rules that are temporarily accepted by everybody – is actually affecting our behaviours less. On the flip side, the cultural fashions of the moment – and our personal stock of clothes – have achieved greater importance, imposing slacker standards than before, but leading us away in different directions' (Bovone 2007: 87).

Only by paying attention to these everyday, microscopic decisions can we understand the relationship of fashion with identity and understand how fashion, either because of what we choose or what we involuntarily ignore, is an expression of what we are and, as such, is worthy of attention, precisely in relation to our identity. There are a few more words I would like to add on this issue.

When faced with the modern fixation of the subject in social conventions, or the postmodern 'solution' (or dissolution) of the subject in the flux of fashion, I believe it is of interest to explore the possibilities of an intermediate idea, of Aristotelian origin, repeatedly emphasized by Fernando Inciarte, which I reproduce here in a more conventional manner. The concrete substance (in contrast with the essence) is mutable and surrounded by things (accidents) that change; indeed, it is the substance itself that changes (accidentally) and, for this very reason, we convey, or betray the substance in its accidents. One consequence of this is what Inciarte himself writes elsewhere, 'The circumstances of life are very important, but what is at risk are not the circumstances, but rather the person himself' (Inciarte 2001: 223).

For the topic we are dealing with, we could interpret the idea as follows: identity (the concrete substance, biographical identity) is not conventional nor is it a matter that depends on fashion. However, we decide our identity *in the way* we assume different social conventions, including fashions, which implies an exercise in discernment on the subject of what is permanent and what is not within the changing circumstances of life.

Therefore, by definition, fashion is neither frivolous nor serious. However, a person is frivolous when they play around at an inappropriate moment or do not take something that needs attention seriously. Fashion is not in itself frivolous; in fact, understanding the language of fashion allows us to express our being by means of the demands of social life. As a means of expressing our identity and position in the world, the importance of fashion is based on the importance of the persons themselves, whose identity is strengthened in as far as it is properly expressed (Sommier 2000: 17).

Undoubtedly, we can say that a purely subjective identity, which is not revealed or is shown erroneously on the exterior, does not truly exist because existence implies externality. But this externality is not 'pure appearance', nor is it the more or less erroneous expression of a supposed 'interiority', but is, rather, us, ourselves, as we appear before others and express ourselves to them, mainly by means of behaviour and speech.

Fashion presents images and it may even suggest the illusion of a coherent personality and, in this way, seduce someone with a fragmented life. It may, perhaps, be used as a superficial means of social integration, especially for those who lack a defined identity (this explains groups of teens all dressed in the same way), but fashion, in itself, cannot, strictly speaking, provide identity. Even the teen who dresses in a certain way in order to belong to the group knows that what is truly important, in terms of identity, are the links of friendship with his companions, and the links he has or does not have with his parents (Sommier 2000: 19).

Although some ages and situations in life are more open to the influence of the dialectic logic of fashion, usually this influence is mediated by our awareness of our identity and the position we occupy in our own world. However, this awareness is, in turn, forged and consolidated by the same rhythm as the links that are sometimes real, but never apparent and that connect us to others. Only when these links are strong, only when we grow up in conversation with others, and not merely observing them, can we learn to choose which elements of fashion are suitable to express our identity and which are not. We also learn to choose which may be considered purely conventional, and thus can be played with, and which, in certain circumstances, may even be considered offensive.

References

Aristotle (1991), *Politics*, Cambridge, Cambridge University Press.

Baier, A. (1991), *A progress of sentiments: reflections on Hume's Treatise*, Cambridge, Harvard University Press.

Bakhtin, M. ([1965] 1968), *Rabelais and His World*, trans. H. Iswolsky, Cambridge: The MIT Press.

Barnard, M. (1996), *Fashion as communication*, London, New York: Routledge.

Barthes, R. (1967), *Systéme de la mode*, Paris: Seuil.

Baudrillard, J. (1993), Baudrillard Live. Selected interviews, ed. by Mike Gane, London, New York, Routledge.

Beck, U. (2002), *Individualization: institutionalized individualism and its social consequences*, London, Thousand Oaks, California, Sage.

Bourdieu, P. (2002), *Distinction: a social critique of the judgement of taste*, Cambridge: Harvard University Press.

Bovone, L. (2007), 'Fashion, identity, social actor', in A. M. González and L. Bovone (eds), *Fashion and identity: an interdisciplinary approach*, Barcelona: Social Trends Institute.

Braudel, F. (1979), *Civilisation materiélle, économie et capitalisme, XV–XVIIIe siècle*, Paris: Colin.

Crane, D. (2000), *Fashion and its social agendas. Class, gender, and identity in clothing*, Chicago and London: The University of Chicago Press.

Elias, N. (1997), *Über den Prozess der Zivilisation: soziogenetische und psychogenetische Untersuchungen*, Frankfurt am Main: Suhrkamp.

Finkelstein, J. (1998), *Fashion. An Introduction*, New York: New York University Press.

Flügel, J. C. (1930/1971), *The Psychology of Clothes*, London: The Hogarth Press and The Institute of Psychoanalysis.

Girard, R. (1978), *Mensonge romantique et vérité romanesque*, Paris: Bernard Grasset.

González, A. M. (2004), 'Cultura y felicidad en Kant', *Teorema*, XXIII: 1–3, pp. 215–232.

González, A. M. (2007), 'Fashion, image, identity', in A. M. González and L. Bovone, *Fashion and identity: an interdisciplinary approach*, Barcelona: STI.

Goodman, D. (2001), 'Difference: An Enlightenment Concept', in K. Baker, *What's left of Enlightenment?* Stanford, Stanford University Press.

Hume, D. ([1777] 1975), *Enquiries concerning Human understanding and concerning the principles of morals*, 3rd edition, with text revised and notes by P. H. Nidditich, Oxford: Oxford University Press.

Hume, D. ([1882], 1964), "Of the Rise and Progress of the Arts and Sciences", in *The Philosophical Works. Essays Moral, Political and Literary, vol. 1*, eds Th. Hill Green and Th. Hodge Grose, vol. 3, Scientia Verlag Aalen. Essays XIV (174–197).

Inciarte, F. (2001), 'Entrevista después de una autoentrevista', in *Breve teoría de la España moderna*, Pamplona: Eunsa.

Kant, I. ([1784] 1983), *Idee zu einer allgemeinen Geschichte in weltbürgelicher Absicht/Idea for a Universal History from a Cosmopolitan Point of View* (trans. Ted Humphrey), Indianapolis, Cambridge: Hacket Publishing Company.

Kant, I. ([1793] 1998), *Die Religion innerhalb der Grenzen der blossen Vernunft/Religion within the Boundaries of Mere Reason* (trans. and eds Allen Wood and George di Giovanni, intro. Robert Merrihew Adams), Cambridge University Press.

Kant, I. ([1798] 1978), *Anthropologie in pragmatischer Hinsicht/Anthropology from a Pragmatic Point of view* (trans. Victor Lyle Dowdell, intro. Frederick P. Van de Pitte, ed. Hans R. Rudnick), Carbondale, Edwardsville: Southern Illinois University Press.

Kant, I. ([1802] 1923), 'Physische Geographie', in *Kant's Werke, Band IX*, Berlin und Leipzig: Akk.

Kant, I. ([1911] 1998), *Kritik der reinen Vernunft*, in *Critique of Pure Reason* (trans. and eds Paul Guyer and Allen Wood), Cambridge, Cambridge University Press.

Lipovetsky, G. (1994), *The Empire of fashion. Dressing Modern Democracy*, Princeton, New Jersey, Oxford, Princeton University Press.

Mauss, M. (1968), *Sociologie et Anthropologie*, Paris, Presses Universitaires de France.

Plato (1997), *Complete Works*, ed., with introduction and notes by John Cooper, associate editor, D. S. Hutchinson, Indianapolis, Cambridge, Hacket Publishing Company.

Sennet, R. (1997), *Carne y piedra. El cuerpo en la civilización occidental*, Madrid: Alianza.

Simmel, G. (1971), *On Individuality and Social Forms: Selected Writings*, Chicago, University of Chicago Press.

Simmel, G. (1991), *Schopenhauer and Nietzsche*, Urbana, University of Illinois Press.

Smith, A. (1982), *The Theory of Moral Sentiments*, in D. D. Raphael and A. L. Macfie (eds), Indianapolis: Liberty Fund.

Sommier, E. (2000), *Mode, le monde en mouvement*, Paris: Village Mondial.

Tarde, G. (1986), *La opinión y la multitud*, Madrid: Taurus.

Taylor, Ch. (1992), *The ethics of authenticity*, Harvard University Press.

Veblen, Th. (1994), *The Theory of Leisure Class*, London: Routledge.

Weber, M. ([1930] 1956, *The Protestant Ethic and the Spirit of Capitalism*, trans. T. Parsons, New York, London, Charles Scribner's sons, George Allen & Unwin Ltd.

Suggested citation

González, A. M. (2010), 'On fashion and fashion discourses', *Critical Studies in Fashion and Beauty* 1: 1, pp. 65–85, doi: 10.1386/csfb.1.1.65_1

Contributor details

Ana Marta González is Professor of Moral Philosophy at the University of Navarra (Spain), where she got her Ph.D. in 1997 with a research on the relationship between morality, reason and nature in Thomas Aquinas. Between 2002 and 2003, she was a Fulbright Scholar at Harvard, where she worked with Christine M. Korsgaard on Kant's practical philosophy. She has led several research projects exploring the intersection between moral philosophy and social theory, including, 'Estrategias de distinción social: perspectiva sociohistórica e interpretación filosófica' (2004–2006); 'Razón práctica y ciencias sociales en la ilustración escocesa: antecedentes y repercusiones' (2006–2009); 'Filosofía moral y ciencias sociales' (2009–); and 'Cultura emocional e identidad' (2010–). Her latest publications include, *Practical Rationality. Scope and Structures of Human Agency* (with Alejandro Vigo, Olms, 2010); *Ficción e identidad. Ensayos de cultura postmoderna* (Rialp, 2009); *Kant's contributions to social theory* (Kant Studien 1, 2009); *Razón práctica en la ilustración escocesa* (with Raquel Lázaro, Anuario Filosófico, 2009); *Contemporary perspectives on natural law* (Ashgate, 2008); 'Bioethics between nature and culture' (in *Autonomy and Human Rights in Health Care: An International Perspective*, D. Weisstub and G. Díaz Pintos (eds) 2008); *Gender identities in a globalized world* (with Victor Seidler, Humanities Press, 2008); *Fashion and identity. An interdisciplinary approach* (with Laura Bovone, 2007); *Distinción social y moda* (with Alejandro García, Eunsa, 2007); and 'Global Business in a Plural Society' (*The Journal of Business Ethics*, volume 44, 2003). Since 2004 Professor González has been the Academic Leader of the Culture and Lifestyles branch of the Social Trends Institute.

Contact: Departamento de Filosofía, Universidad de Navarra, Pamplona 31080, Spain.
E-mail: agonzalez@unav.es

CSFB 1 (1) pp. 87–112 Intellect Limited 2010

Critical Studies in Fashion and Beauty
Volume 1 Number 1

© 2010 Intellect Ltd Article. English language. doi: 10.1386/csfb.1.1.87_1

FRANCESCO MORACE
Future Concept Lab, Milan

The dynamics of luxury and basic-ness in post-crisis fashion

Keywords

real fashion trends
luxury fashion
basic fashion
everyday culture
consum-authors
craft
creativity
authenticity

Abstract

Understanding the current moment of the global fashion system and its potential for future development requires that we retrace the dynamics that have characterized this sector in recent years, pre- and post-crisis. This article traces the dynamics to a new sensibility located between simplicity and luxury, which is more than just another 'trend' but 'a new Renaissance'. The new sensibility involves the parallel processes of luxury losing its exclusive aura and diffusing into the everyday, and, at the same time, creativity, authenticity and a spirit of craftsmanship emerging as a form of 'luxurious' basic-ness.

The pre-crisis: Real fashion trends between democratization of luxury and enhancement of basic-ness

Prior to the crisis we have been witnessing a consumer experience that is based on what can be defined as 'a normality that is built on exceptions': those 'normal exceptions' that people construct for themselves during the course of their daily lives in their search for happiness. In aesthetic terms, and from the point of view of consumption experience, this has been characterized by a weakening of both basic-ness and minimalism. At the same time, with luxury acquiring a new centrality and becoming an accessible experience, it has moved away from being an aristocratic prerogative. The happiness that luxury implies is in fact pursued by the vast majority of people who decide to consume in lesser quantity but better quality, searching for an extraordinary satisfaction that can be based on the distinctive and playful, on the excellent commodity, or on an 'artist's' experience (as in the art or design hotels), or on a newly acquired access to 'precious' and top-quality products.

Basic luxury

In their book, *Les battements du monde*, Alain Finkielkraut and Peter Sloterdijk (2003) devote an entire chapter to this phenomenon, which they term 'La démocratisation du luxe'. Thus we see a new reference world taking shape, the world of *basic luxury* that is fostered by the fashion houses, and nurtured by the skill and expertise of the important brands, as well as the creativity of stylists, designers, architects and artists.

This perspective shows us an unexpected convergence between a luxury that becomes democratized and is transformed into quality of life and a basic luxury that is 'enriched' and enhanced by new creative visions: jeans that are beautifully embellished or T-shirts that become pop icons are a clear demonstration of this, as we shall see when we look at the **ultra graphic** trend (see figure 1) (Morace 2007).

Within this context, the occasions of life and consumption constitute potential exceptions, to be stimulated with products and services that become 'happy' by virtue of their surprise about the unexpected element they contain.

The exceptionality of the occasion is created by its emotive relevance, which becomes the echo of a specific happening, experience or consumption act. In this way luxury, on one hand, and basic-ness, on the other, are regenerated and relaunched in a post September 11 cultural context. Constructing *stories* that stimulate, propose and invent – that 'transmit emotive identifications for the occasions of life' starting from the top (the experience of luxury) or from the bottom (the experience of basic-ness) – becomes the new and stimulating exercise for an advanced marketing: a marketing that can only be produced and proposed by passionate managers or entrepreneurs (as in the previous stage of modernity), or in those shops that demonstrate a successful practice in displaying, proposing and supporting 'islands' of advanced experience.

1) Hyper Memorable

The trend that mixes styles from different periods, recognizes object with a capacity for memory and is able to transform apparel into memorable experiences: an ability to narrate **a 'piece' of the past,** either real or imagined.

2) Wonder Simplification

The trend which reflects the changing paradigm with regards to wealth, aesthetics and ethics. Simplifying means possessing the techniques, the taste, the art of existence and the knowledge to recognise the trimmings and trappings of the useless and superfluous aspects. The search for simplicity is lived as a value and as a style that leaves a sense of wonder.

3) Extra Rules

The trend in which the creative challenge of rules is at the research of emblematic traditions. The rule that is invented as a mean to bypass conformism.

4) Ultra Graphic

The trend that works on the unexpected richness of creative surfaces and chromatic effects. The style in which the skin of objects becomes an experimental laboratory.

5) Huge Interlace

The trend in which meeting of styles finds its own combined aesthetic driven by the increasing cross-fertilisation of cultures. People become 'the experts' of their own look fusing worlds that are culturally distant, making personal customisation from hybrid products, creating truly innovative product concepts, experimenting with new 'idioms' – interweaving local traditions and handicrafts with the dynamism of the 21st Century.

6) Super Material

The trend in which the consistency of materials becomes the plot for a story. The style in which aesthetic experimentation from the natural extends to the artificial environments, from nonwoven to recycled materials.

7) Massive Details

The trend in which details conquer the scene through the irony of the icon. A style with vocation for creative wrong-footing. The 'feminine sensitivity' phenomenon has been an important driver in the world of fashion in recent years. It is expressed in the great relevance that small details make as the basis of a daily aesthetic practice. The more classic icons of femininity (flowers, butterflies, high heels, prints of romantic inspiration ...), returned with an ironic twist, becoming 'massive', revealing themselves to be important in the definition of new glamour.

8) Micromega Luxury

The trend in which luxury in its "macro" dimension which is the infraction of the limits set up by society and rationality, meets with "micro" – the sphere of minimal (but by no means minimum) luxuries that have become part of the daily life of many people. The first meaning of the term "luxury" contains the idea of exclusivity, excess, exhibition: not only in having the best, but showing one's wealth. In its creative encounter with the aesthetics of *Partial Paradises* the principle of freedom from every functional aspiration transfers from life experiences to choice of accessories. Personal search and the originality of the "one off" become the key to the planning and commercialisation of objects in fashion, technology or furnishings.

Table 1: The 8 Real Fashion Trends scheme.

Figure 1: Milan (left) Stockholm (right). Courtesy of Future Concept Lab.

The love of everyday things

Within this perspective we see the relevance acquired by the role of the amateur who, recalling the etymological roots of the word, is driven by love and by passion, rather than by technical and specialist knowledge: as Christopher Locke recalls in *Gonzo Marketing*, the contrast with professionalism lies in what the Zen master Shunryu Suzuki defined as *the spirit of the beginner*, 'the ability to look at the world with fresh eyes and an open mind' (Locke 2001).

Against this background a magical meeting between a new conception and perception of luxury, quality and excellence is produced, in which fresh interest is shown in essential, basic experiences which go beyond basic-ness to simplicity and wonderment, such as the **wonder simplification** trend (see figure 2). Thus the great theme of consumption is re-proposed as a style of thinking and a profound and global experience, whose roots lie deep down in a place and a collective experience, which is then channelled into a wholly personal feeling.

Everyday life becomes the 'workshop' of this meeting between accessible luxury and the evolution of basic-ness; Philippe Starck was the first to pick up on this when he launched his project dedicated to essential simplicity, and Conran pursued it for years in his retailing channels, which moved from Habitat to the Conran Shop, ending up in hotels and restaurants that have become – not by chance – emblems of *accessible luxury*. Accessible luxury is no longer imposed upon us from above: it starts from the bottom, while still guaranteeing an excellent experience.

Technically, if we think about the changes taking place in the retail market, it is probable that the money-saving made possible by the large chains (we are thinking here of Wal-Mart, Costco, Home Depot, Lowe's, Kohl's in the US) is being re-invested by consumers in new luxury goods, and even in better taste! Here again, the Japanese are refining their tools, with the growing success of projects that start from the basic – as in Toyota's Yaris, or in Muji's shops and the Wagamama restaurants – and move through to joint ventures such as Yamamoto's partnership with Adidas, which has proved to be such a great commercial success.

In this way a consumer culture is established whose hallmark is the 'historical-poetic biography' of the person, within the context of an advanced modernity. The consumer remains the interpreter of their own modernity, living more firmly in the quality of their own culture, their personal story. In a certain sense they *learn to inhabit themselves*, and in this way become receptive to 'non-essential' everyday experiences, such as the designs of Patricia Urquiola, and to a category of products that we can define as 'excellent commodities' (such as products by Magis and those like the Nissan Micra, which decided to bring in a visionary genius such as David Lynch).

 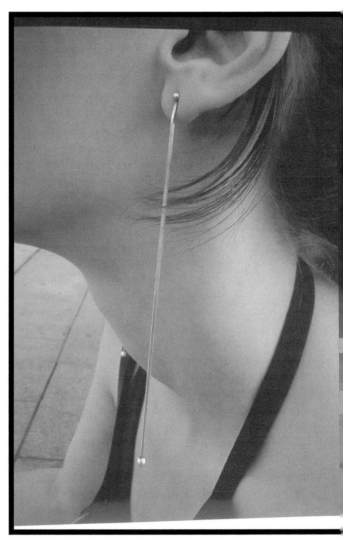

Figure 2: Rio (left), Sofia (right). Courtesy of Future Concept Lab.

The new statute of luxury

As things stand today being up-to-date is no longer enough for a product; it needs to have cultural and emotional substance. Consumption is acquiring new aesthetics and a new culture in which the happiness generated by luxury is even conveyed into the world of basic-ness (Morace 2005). Basic-ness, in turn moves away from the standard, marked by the product's specific quality (such as the materials used, the small details, or the manufacturing process); this can be seen in the two trends **super material** (see figure 3) and **massive details** (see figure 4) and above all by the emotions and the memory that a product can arouse, as we see in the **hyper memorable** (see figure 5) trend. In this development, luxury and its accessories gradually become expressions of a profound experience of quality, through which people can change their own skin and their whole attitude towards the world. Post-industrial modernity recalibrates the standard so as to embrace the creative radicality of experience, by giving centrality to small details, materials and personal memory.

Based on these premises – and reflecting on the changeover from luxury as status, to luxury as a profound and distinctive experience – a number of key concepts need to be presented in order to define the luxury of the present and of the future. A new concept of luxury is required which has the search for happiness as its core, and is offering an interpretation of consumption, of luxury, and of the evolution of both these things over the last few years.

The traditional conception of luxury – thought of as being in a separate, 'superior' and inaccessible world – according to a process of *aristocratic discontinuity from above*, is very close to the French tradition, which guarantees happiness to only a select few.

Instead, the current evolution that is taking place leads the world of luxury to reinterpret and re-process stimuli that come from 'below', from everyday and accessible phenomena. This dynamic offers *everyday continuity from below* in a wholly Mediterranean logic of re-creative creativity. It is on this ground of 'taste' that the new luxury comes into contact with the new basic-ness, understood as essential experience, as we see in the collections of the Greek stylist Sophia Kokosalaki or in those of the Colombian fashion designer Silvia Tcherassi, giving birth to the trend of **micromega luxury** (see figure 6), in which the theme of mega luxury (more flaunted and only for 'genuinely rich people') none the less remains active, too.

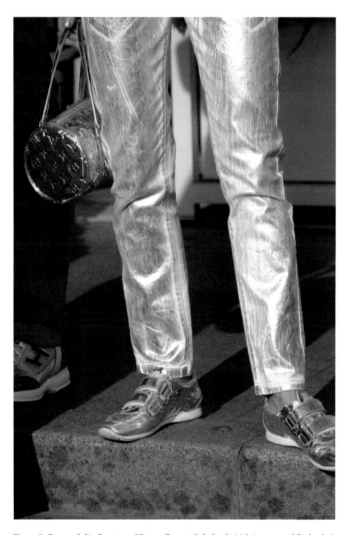 

Figure 3: Cannes (left). Courtesy of Future Concept Lab. Leeds (right): revamped Parka designed by Annabel Burton, Elizabeth Jackson and Kailey Twigge, School of design University of Leeds, Nonwoven project.

Figure 4: Leeds (left). Galliano inspired this 'Flower Bomb' outfit designed by Amy Rodgers, Lauren Crimes and William Coma, School of design University of Leeds, Nonwoven project. London (right): Schuller Opticians.

Figure 5: Madrid (left) and Moscow (right). Courtesy of Future Concept Lab.

Figure 6: Maison Martin Margiela (left): chain covered with black chiffon, creating a necklace, Autumn-Winter 2004–5. Courtesy of Somerest House and Maison Martin Margiela. New York (right). Courtesy of Future Concept Lab.

Intensity and discretion

This means that the codes of privilege are no longer governed by difference alone, but also and above all *by intensity*: if silence comes to symbolize the new qualities, you do not need to take a vacation in a monastery, all you have to do is switch off your mobile, and become unavailable to people. If luminosity becomes a code of elegance, you can buy a high-profile jewel that, like Trilogy, will re-propose this essential and constituent quality of the product itself, but you can also play around with Swarovski crystals. In this way we see a weakening in luxury's variable of externalization from the classical point of view of strategy of appearances, and a strengthening instead of people's relationship and confidence with products that have 'character', together with their more genuine and deeper qualities, in exactly the same way as happened in the early stages of the modern movement. In this horizon, luxury does not perform a role of 'recreation within superfluousness'; on the contrary, it embodies its own ability to differentiate, discern, evaluate and select, i.e. what Guicciardini (1857/1977) has already defined as *discretion* and that is shown to be the opposite of *ostentation*.

The labels and the great fashion houses, like the designers and the great brands of Italian design, can therefore strengthen their own position in the market only if they succeed in interpreting – in a profound and structured way – their own potential for fascination, charisma and credibility linked to personal well-being, without being limited to the classical strategies of brand 'extension'. This sets the backdrop for the need to formulate new rules, as we shall explain in the **extra rules** trend (see figure 7).

Even the narcissistic personalization that typified two decades of personal whims has now given way to a ritual of sharing between similars. In this new ritual symbolic sensitivity, shared excellence and tangible aesthetic experiences successfully fit in with a new civil conscience and an aesthetic of values. This is steadily gaining ground, even in the niches of those few fortunate people who find themselves living this world: Naomi Klein's book *No Logo (2000)* sold very successfully in Armani's megastore in Milan, too. The trend that captures the innovative individual look (born out of fusion of traditional handicrafts with the experimentalism of the twenty-first century) is **huge interlace** (see figure 8).

Figure 7: London (left). Milan (right). Courtesy of Future Concept Lab.

Figure 8: Paris (left) and Stockholm (right). Courtesy of Future Concept Lab.

The following sections (tables 2–4) indicated below define the ways in which luxury has evolved, and help the market to go beyond the concept of basic, proposing instead a new vision of joyous luxury (the *playful luxury* of Dior and Dolce & Gabbana), of the value and prestige of essentiality (in line, for example, with the Lombard matrix of B&B, and with Molteni and Cassina), of distinctive playfulness (as in the Smart car, in Alessi's objects, or in Diesel's communication), or of the comfort of prestige (as found in the home wear of Zegna, Loro Piana, and Malo).

Traditional Luxury	Advanced Luxury
Aristocratic discontinuity from above	Distillation by continuity from below
Privilege by difference	Privilege by intensity
Externalism of luxury	Intimacy/familiarity with the top of the range
Luxury as ostentation	Luxury as discretion
Allows the extension of the label	Suggests the profoundness of the label
Supports narcissistic personalisation	Facilitates ritual participation
Privileges material expression	Works on symbolic sensitivity
Is based on the need to show off	Allows excellence to be shared
Uses the transcendence of fashion	Optimises the immanence of the aesthetic and vital experiences
Places its trust in the ethic of appearances	Interprets the aesthetics of values

Table 2: Traditional vs. advanced luxury.

Luxury and basic in direct comparison

The evolution taking place in the markets, lifestyles, thinking styles and aesthetic trends addresses a medium quality market which, while continuing to be very price-conscious, at the same time shuns all things standard. Europe, and in particular Italy and France – albeit in differing and indeed almost opposing ways – play decisive roles in this paradox, starting either from *the aristocratic taste for beauty* (France) or from the skill in *creatively recreating excellent experiences* (Italy). It is a game that truly oscillates between the perceptions, motives and expressions of *luxury* – and the traits, logics and variants of *basic-ness.*

'Luxury' and 'basic-ness' continue to stimulate and foster controversy by asking questions such as: is luxury in a state of crisis or is it the only consumption variable that continues to show that it is still vital? Is basic disappearing or has it instead proposed a universal way of democratizing quality? We shall try to provide you with an interpretation of this evolution by means of keywords, which continuously meet and overlap with each other.

Luxury	Basic-ness
Joyful	Playful
Essential worth	Everyday non-essential
Comfort of prestige	Excellent commodity
Cult innovation	Innovative basic
Exclusive prestige	Accessible preciousness
Authentic	Eclectic

Table 3: Luxury vs. basic-ness.

The 'new basic'

As can be deduced from the keywords that describe it – playful, non-essential, innovative and eclectic – basic-ness reinforces the preferences that consumers have expressed towards personalization. To conclude our analysis of pre-crisis fashion we present a comparison between the two worlds of *advanced basic* and *traditional basic*. This comparison completes the circle of interpretation of types of luxury, and types of basic-ness. Examination of the keywords contained in the right-hand columns of these tables (2–4) reveals the characteristics of many *real fashion trends*.

Traditional Basic-ness	Advanced Basic-ness
Everyday functionality	Excellent everydayness
Aesthetics free	Perceptive enhancement
Standard type	Character standard
Massification of style	Mass creativity
Economy in scale	Democratisation of quality
Multiplication of the minimum performance	Multiplicity of the performances
Neutral Basic	Basic Pop
Aesthetics of simplicity	Simplification of aesthetics
Centrality of cost and price	Essentiality of processes and values
Everyday routine	Poetics of everydayness

Table 4: Traditional vs. advanced basic-ness.

The post-crisis: The new challenge for the fashion system

The economic and financial crisis we are experiencing is comparable to a sudden storm. This turbulent crisis is transforming established patterns of consumption and communication. *The most consolidated and widely practiced business models lose credibility and are being questioned.*

The cities which symbolize the former 'new era', London, Dubai and Shanghai (which we have been looking at with a mixture of envy and admiration), suffer upon the sudden closure of their businesses, leaving people disappointed and disenchanted by the end of a dream. The countries of the ex-economic miracle – Ireland, Iceland and even Spain – are experiencing the same phenomenon. Everybody thinks about the crisis. *Only a few reflect upon its core*, its reason to exist. Not many view this crisis as an opportunity for a new miracle: a miracle that can offer people a more enlightened vision of the meaning of our existence, a miracle that could form the basis of a new Renaissance. As history teaches us, a new enlightening vision is likely to come in response to a crisis, after the elaboration of a trauma, for example the way people reacted to the black plague which devastated Europe in 1330.

Today we are witnessing a 'change of era'. The rules and paradigms of corporate activities are in the process of change, and this will transform business models and ways of producing, communicating and distributing. The twenty years of Future Concept Lab's activities become a foundation of knowledge to face this challenge, applying 'the trends, the concepts and the scenarios elaborated over time'.

Of all the productive sectors, fashion is certainly one of those that have suffered the most from the crisis, both in terms of sales and advertising investments. This was because for years the world of fashion was the reference model of a phase that has been called 'the era of image and appearance'. At a time when the paradigm has entered into crisis, the world of fashion moved into one of the most dramatic crisis of its long history, a crisis of credibility. But the numbers change if one factors in online sales. In Italy online clothing shopping was forecasted to increase by 32% in 2009, while global orders are predicted an increase by 40%. With regards to the fashion world, the online medium is a winner in communication – not just in retail. In the quarter January–April 2009, Nielsen Media data recorded a decrease of 30% in advertising spending in the fashion industry in comparison with 2008. However, fashion saw an increase when it came to Internet: the fashion-accessories sector in particular showed a growth of 6.1%. This is not the highest of percentage increases, but significant if one considers that the Internet is the only media not in the red (the film industry alone registers a decrease of 90%) and if we consider the successful case studies of a few Internet fashion brands.

In recent years we have observed how speed has changed the entire fashion system through acceleration in production, and from distribution to the act of purchase. The consumer, encouraged by the wide choice available and the cheapness of the product, begins to consider quality, processes and the social responsibility of production less important. Slowly the value of fashion has also decreased, design with a capital 'D' is a world of reference for very few and the brands have re-dimensioned (victims of a culture that promotes fragmentary and provisional identities). Today, however, a consumer emerges from the grassroots in search of experiences that go beyond the surface, careful and ready to welcome new meanings from the fashion system. For starters, the interest of the consumer in the genesis of the fashion-product has increased. Products with a virtuous history are appreciated, through a new model of consumption that brings into light alternative thoughts. The demand for ethical products that respect the environment and have a greater responsibility towards society has grown. Fashion that makes original use of materials and available resources, and puts into circulation critical projects in which the originality of style, comfort and sensoriality are not in contradiction with sustainability, is popular, as are clothing garments and accessories that distance themselves from the rules of short-lived fashion and present a 'natural' life cycle.

With the *Stolen Jewellery* collection, designers Mike & Maaike from San Francisco explore the relationship between true and perceived values, creating a short circuit between the tangible and immaterial world. They search on Google to find photos of some of the most famous and precious pieces of jewellery in the world, use software to elaborate the images and then create necklaces, replacing the precious stones with coloured pixels printed on leather. The project makes the viewer reflect on the complexity of the construction and reduces the cost of the jewellery, without damaging the visual intensity, the original history, or the accessibility of each piece (e.g. the 'Golden Jubilee' pin belonging to the King of Thailand, or the Imelda Marcos ruby and diamond necklace created by Van Cleef & Arpels).

Similarly, Afterheels shoes, designed to allow 'freewalking' (to walk as if barefoot), are thought to give immediate relief to those who use high heels and so constitute a comfortable alternative at the end of an evening. Like a second skin, these ballerina style shoes, ultra compact and light enough to be carried in one's handbag, act as a barrier against water and protect feet from sharp objects such as stones or small fragments of glass. Their low cost (£5), the wide range of colours, and the alternative sales channels all contribute to the success of the project: they cannot only be purchased online, but also from vending machines positioned in some UK clubs. As well as being comfortable, their life cycle is also virtuous: the upper part and the sole of the shoes are made from biodegradable and recyclable materials.

With the project Yooxygen, the Yoox virtual boutique has started down a path towards environmental sustainability. It encompasses a new area dedicated completely to eco-friendly products, starting from fashion, design, and jewellery, and including books and music. This window dedicated to ecology also becomes a showroom for designers like Katharine Hamnett and Stella McCartney, who have developed exclusive, limited edition collections for Yoox. One such collection is *Venetian Bags* by Ilaria Venturini Fendi, whose design philosophy is 'creating without destroying'. It features original clutch bags made from thin aluminium sheets once used for Venetian blinds. Another collection is the project *Aperitivo*

Bio, a fun limited edition aperitif set made up of unique objects designed by Pandora design, in Mater-Bi, a polymer created from maize and 100 per cent biodegradable.

The art of Ayurvastra is a branch of traditional Indian medicine that is literally translated as 'Ayur = life + Vastra = clothes'. A.D.O Clothing is a line of garments that is based on the principles of Ayurvastra. The brand has developed shirts and trousers designed to improve wellness to the consumer. Anjelika Krishna, the founder and designer of the brand, explains: 'Each yarn is soaked in natural ingredients, such as pomegranate seeds or eucalyptus. By wearing these garments, the infusion of herbs is absorbed by the skin, helping you to feel rested and rejuvenated'. The collection, produced entirely in a factory in India that has a holistic approach towards its workers, uses natural fabrics, above all organic cotton, without synthetic colours, pesticides or chemical substances.

The above examples are important in order to understand some key points for the future:
- Moving away from the rules of short-lived fashion towards systems and products that have a 'natural' lifestyle
- Embracing projects that go beyond the surface, and offer new meanings to the fashion system
- Searching for stories of origin about fashion-products in order to better share thoughts and values

The return of 'true qualities'

In the panorama of style, fashion and expressions of taste, there is evidence for a *return to substance* understood as the search for *consistency in projects* and *excellence in products*. The great thought at this moment focuses on the theme of *true* qualities. The world of fashion is re-establishing its new rules on parameters of authenticity, competence, virtuosity, ability and genius, creativity and excellence. The products of the textile and fashion industry have become, in certain ways, *unique pieces*, following the logic of the *Serie Fuori Serie* (Series and Out Series) well presented in the exhibition hosted by the Triennale Design Museum in Milan (an exhibition examining Italian design).

In the world of style there is a desire to return and to 'touch beauty with one's hands'. The ability to produce aesthetics is expressive of the textile, clothing and accessories sectors, which are all facing a new challenge – maybe the most difficult of all – that of overcoming the logic of image and focusing instead on their tailoring origins and on a taste for detail. This extensive renewal corresponds to recovering the artistic touch that comes from the grassroots, from the talent of the 'maker' of fashion, who shows himself/herself able to give value to the character of the chosen material, and to mould new shapes and chromatic presence, allowing for *the definitive death of the trend book*.

The SS 2009 collection by Prada marked an important passage for the Milanese fashion house. Following a number of seasons marked by the use of prints and excessive decoration, garments were presented stripped down and coarse, apparently not finished, in the pursuit of a primitivism that signals a radical return to grass roots. And even if the clothing line proposed unusual materials (like the cotton fabric with a metallic thread) and aesthetic experimentation (prints which reproduce reptile skin, but 'pixelated'), the most interesting innovations were seen within the accessories and the jewellery line, which interpreted the same yearning towards roots, but with a much more visible and deeper craft ability. These new Prada jewels are a mix between ready-made and craft: in fact earrings and necklaces are created using shells, linked to one another with gold thread or even applied to fabric. The most elementary and primordial of decorations becomes a 'craft object', cared for in every detail, but still with 'authentic flavour'. Each piece is nothing short of unique and sees the work of nature woven in with that of knowing craftsmanship. This desire for authenticity is also clear in the collections for the coming winter, for Prada as well as MiuMiu, in which embroidery becomes the true protagonist, achieving a level of craft ability that is very close to high fashion.

In recent years we have witnessed the surprising growth, on a global level, of everything linked to 'do-it-yourself' creativity in daily life, discovering 'the craftsman' as theorized by the American sociologist Richard Sennett in the book of the same title published in 2008. Even the recent exhibition 'Diritto Rovescio' held at the Triennale di Milano, illustrated, with precision and poetry, the current scenario of 'threads woven between art, design and creativity for the masses', using weave and embroidery as the common dominators. The English clothing brand 'Folk' is certainly one of the most interesting interpreters of this aesthetic and value-based phenomenon. Created in 2001 (thanks to the initiative of Cathal McAteer), from the very first collection of male clothing the objective was to create something that could be liked by friends. The rustic style, with the typical handmade feel, at a first glance seems simple, but closer inspection reveals the care taken over every detail, often with strange operations, which, for example, play on the closeness between knitwear stitches and pixels. The materials are chosen with care and arrive from all over the world, like the Japanese cotton used for the double-face shirts or the cotton from the US used for the cardigans. The shoes line, *Shöfolk,* is completely handmade in Portugal, with coarse hides in natural colours: this aspect is decidedly craft and authentic. In the London outlets of Folk (voted by *Monocle* as the third most interesting clothing store in the world) one can find the homewear lines, but also other brands that are in sync with Folk's aesthetics and values.

Emerging creativity gives rise to new aesthetic languages that, with a free spirit and an apparently naive outlook, are able to catch one unprepared and to supply experiences at the limit of the surreal. The Korean designer Min-Ji Cho is sure to represent a generation that is able to give life to new grammars, mixing areas, materials, and inspiration. Following his studies in Seoul, Min-Ji gained his masters in jewellery at the Royal College of Arts in London, where he also successfully acted as a researcher. His signature style is the use of the usual materials for the realization of jewels (such as gold, silver, pearls) but always accompanied by common rubber gloves: the contrast really catches one's senses unawares, with a hint of poetry of great impact. The colourful gloves are first meticulously worked, cut with craft precision and assembled in order to create decorative elements that allow one to forget their humble, almost vulgar, nature. Necklaces, bracelets and brooches are also crafted in this way with unusual combinations of chains and rubber strips, pearls and small, multicoloured domes guaranteeing a unique experience, both to behold, and to touch. Min-Ji's future plans include a series oriented towards the decoration of the body, and also one for the home.

Finally, earlier this year the Italian Trade Commission and the Genuine Italian Vegetable-Tanned Leather Consortium introduced the Tuscan leather handicraft tradition in a special exhibition 'Hand Made in Italy', in New York, Seoul and Tokyo. The exhibition featured exquisite handcrafted items made by Italian brands and artisans including video performances and multimedia displays designed by Oliviero Toscani.

From these examples we can underline some other elements for fashion of the future:
- Re-establishing a fundamental equilibrium between image and substance, within the system starting from real 'know how'
- Recovering the concept of 'made to perfection' beyond the intrinsic value of the *product* to the creative *process*
- Restoring dignity to single materials through creative talent and deep motivation

New communication strategies in the fashion system

The economic and financial crisis is actually rooted in the idea that a (basically invented) story is enough – if well communicated – to justify and legitimize a promising business. This typically postmodern idea has produced devastating results, not only for the financial world but also for the manufacturing world and above all for marketing. The idea that the *true quality* of the product is *less important than its communicative ability* (leading us to make a choice between a number of similar stories all offering products, services and experiences that invest more on image than *true quality*) is no longer sustainable. People and consumers have unmasked the game and the toy has broken.

Today the world of style and fashion registers the need to look elsewhere, to develop new strategies, to rethink its business model. This fundamental need is based on the success of a 'make-believe' story that has lasted too long. The sector is now finding itself in a quandary, but it made its bed and now must lie in it. The weight of the communication (and the imaginary) has played an essential role in this dynamic and it is from this that one should probably restart, and experiment with new paths and new languages, wrong-foot one's counterparts above and below, and shuffle things as if in a game of cards.

Over the last thirty years all the sectors have considered the fashion system as a pioneer of advanced communication, with the ability to sell and to captivate consumers. In fact, in the phase that we are living through, it should instead humbly learn from other sectors: technology and body care, the car and above all food. This 'looking beyond' cannot be reduced to the classical mimetic that the fashion system is used to trigger, offering glimpses and stylistic provocations. Instead fashion should aim for a comprehensive regeneration of processes and communication strategies.

In this difficult task fashion must look carefully to the world of music, cinema, art, and to those creative phenomena that, until now, have been limited to the emphasis of the power of fashion. The following examples convey the spirit of this new creative direction. The first example is from the 2009 film/mockumentary *Brüno* produced, co-written and interpreted by Sacha Baron Cohen. The film is based on the character of the same name created by Baron Cohen for *Da Ali G Show*. As with *Borat*, this film mixes fiction with real life situations. The film tells the irreverent story of Brüno, a gay Austrian reporter, who, in his own way, makes fun of the fashion world and entertainment industry. Baron Cohen, in the role of Brüno, went to Milan Fashion Week in September 2008 bursting into the show by designer Agatha Ruiz de la Prada and trying to seduce Republican Ron Paul, a determined opponent of gay marriage. Promotion for the film has become part of the Brüno phenomenon and perhaps more significant than the film itself. With regards to the printed press, Baron Cohen/Brüno appeared alongside the model Alessandra Ambrosio in an ironic photo shoot for the magazine *Marie Claire*; he also appeared nude on the cover of *GQ*. For the European launch of the film, Brüno visited all the major capitals where he put on hilarious shows. In London he marched with fake British royal guards dressed in hot pants and the famous fur headgear; in Madrid the comedian was a guest on Spanish TV, where he stripped and exposed his underwear (printed with the face of Zapatero); he also crossed the city in a skin-tight bull outfit.

Another example is from the new project by the Italian clothing brand 'Hogan' – known for its distinctive design agenda, which takes inspiration from Andy Warhol's The Factory. The company – under the art direction of Formapura – has created a contemporary and temporary factory, a place to talk about fashion and life using the instruments closest to the new generations – from photography to online short films – and giving free rein to personality and creativity. It is here that the photographer Jessica Craig-Martin created a special Hogan advert campaign: the protagonists were seven young talents with different artistic backgrounds (actors, DJs, artists of various kinds) who, in addition to posing for the campaign, told of their experiences in art and life (visible on the site www.hoganworld.com.)

In the same spirit of the factory, another project by Hogan, *Artribe*, exemplifies this forward-thinking trend. *Artribe* is a street-art inspired venture that has collaborated creatively with the New York City-based 'muralists', Tats Cru (renowned on the international stage as authors of graffiti). Spraying 600 cans of paint on 200 square meters of canvas, the artists created massive graffiti paintings that were on display during Men's Fashion Week in June at Pac Milan. Micro-versions of the works became 20 pairs of Olympia sneakers and five trend bags, all unique pieces exhibited around the world in the brand's storefronts and also in Hong Kong in October at a dedicated event. In December they were auctioned on the site www.hoganworld.com and the proceeds went to charity.

Another example is a new type of traditional communication medium: *Paperdoll Magazine* is a British publication whose first issue came out in June 2009. The magazine is aimed at a young female target market, passionate about fashion, art and music, and explores new narrative and expressive directions. No more glossy photographs typical of photo sets but images conceived with a simple teenage graphic, or 'cut out' from other fashion magazines; no more advice from experts and gurus, instead excerpts from blogs by regular girls are used; no longer focused solely on the aesthetic, instead focusing on linking fashion and music, catwalks and daily life, the world of fame and the galaxy of 'simple fans'.

In *Paperdoll Magazine* fashion leaves the catwalks and the jet set in order to become part of the life of everyone in a playful way. But it is also innovative with regards to languages of communication. The originality of the project lies in the inspiration taken from the game of paper dolls, not only used in the name of the magazine, but also in the structure and execution of the articles and contents. The fashion and trends columns in fact use cut outs for the appearance of Barbie-size patterns (especially but not only for the teen brands). The graphic design is colourful, saucy and sometimes irreverent, inviting the reader to investigate, and above all to play and have fun with the object in itself. The whole magazine is downloadable and printable from the site, demonstrating a new way of doing fashion print.

Finally, Iqons, a social networking site for the emerging world of fashion, is a meeting place for young and aspiring designers, photographers, stylists and accessories designers who can register and show their creations, in a way similar to the music networking site MySpace (www.iqons.com).

In conclusion we can indicate some final activities that are compatible with the future fashion perception:

- Utilizing other creative areas as the stimuli for 'lateral thinking' in communication
- Proposing a new vision of the sector through 'wrong footing' messages, which moves communication into areas unexplored by fashion
- Regenerating strategies and business models, adopting a critical and experimental approach, for everyday and glamorous products

Future Concept Lab has identified **talent, simplification, exploration** and **sharing** as four highly influential themes in contemporary consumer culture. *Social innovation* and *design thinking* are indeed the challenges of the years to come, both in institutional and business terms. This is the context in which *people will become the authors of creative enterprises.* The more identity is based on a network of social relations, the more people are the protagonists at the centre of a scenario in which technology, brands, products and the media overlap. The aesthetic of 'made to perfection' shows itself to be a guarantee for disenchanted consumers, who always appreciate the craft dimension more than the flattening caused by mass production. New forms of personalization for a slow equilibrium between 'made to measure' activity and well-being seem to capture the spirit of the age. 'I am the protagonist', 'I am the product', 'I am the media', are not simply slogans but a new religion, and one that the marketing world needs to embrace in order to face future challenges.

References

Guicciardini, Francesco (1977), Ricordi [Maxims and Reflections]. Milano: Rizzoli (originally published 1857).

Finkielkraut, Alain and Sloterdijk, Peter (2003), *Les battements du monde*, Paris: Fayard.

Klein, Naomi (2000), *No Logo*, Toronto: Random House.

Locke, Christopher (2001), *Gonzo Marketing*, New York: BasicBooks.

Morace, Francesco, (2005), *Società Felici*, Milano: Libri Scheiwiller.

Morace, Francesco (ed.) (2007), *Future Concept Lab: Real Fashion Trends. The manual of the cool hunter*, Milano: Libri Scheiwiller.

Morace, Francesco (ed.) (2008), *Consum-Authors: The generations as creative enterprises*, Milano: Libri Scheiwiller.

Sennett, Richard (2008), *The craftsman*, New Haven, CT: Yale University Press.

Suggested citation

Morace, F. (2010), 'The dynamics of luxury and basic-ness in post-crisis fashion', *Critical Studies in Fashion and Beauty* 1: 1, pp. 87–112, doi: 10.1386/csfb.1.1.87_1

Contributor details

Francesco Morace is a sociologist, writer and journalist who has been working in market research since the 1980s. He is the president of the innovative market research company Future Concept Lab which has been since 1989 a pioneer in its field both in Italy and abroad. It was the first company to set up a network of cult researchers in cities worldwide to follow and observe trends connected to daily life, clothing, food products, life styles and mind styles.

Future Concept Lab (FCL) of Milan integrates *global values* based on a genius loci (spirit of the place) approach, and *local behaviours* collected using the street & body signals method – into a combined system of the *MindStyles*. The **MindStyles Program** is the result of a consistent monitoring of the cultural influences affecting the collective imagination, based on an analysis of mass media contents and the influence of "opinion leaders" on values, styles and taste in the cultural industries: anything from music to literature, art, fashion and design. It articulates both *short term trends* (based on the monitoring of signals by worldwide "cult researchers"), and *long term values*. The values emerge from the dynamics of globalization and represent the framework for social change.

CSFB 1 (1) pp. 113–132 Intellect Limited 2010

Critical Studies in Fashion and Beauty
Volume 1 Number 1
© 2010 Intellect Ltd Article. English language. doi: 10.1386/csfb.1.1.113_1

FUTURE CONCEPT LAB

The real fashion trends in a global context

This summary presentation is based on an annual series of seminars at the Future Concept Lab.

INTRODUCTION. THE URGENT NEED FOR NEW ENLIGHTENMENT

We urgently need a new age of enlightenment to ensure that knowledge and experience come back to hold a crucial role in our daily experience and to protect ourselves from the risk posed by obstructionism and ignorance.

La tête bien faite, by Edgar Morin

007.145

Future

INTRODUCTION. THE URGENT NEED FOR NEW ENLIGHTENMENT

In this, the work by Edgar Morin will serve us well. He advocated a distinction between rationality, or reason – through being open to experimentation – and rationalisation – which is often reduced to a little less than a paranoid system in which we are expected to answer all questions. This view implies a completely inward looking approach to our daily life experience.

Family monument, by Gillian Wearing

 008.145

INTRODUCTION. THE URGENT NEED FOR NEW ENLIGHTENMENT

Rather than taking nourishment from the «logic» of advertising images, the New Enlightenment is nourished by those things, which we have already experimented in full. This is embodied by a constant need to experiment, to broaden the nature of human enquiry. It is an awareness of the need to restore a proper value to experience and has, in itself, a hint of experimental experience and tangible innovation. It requires a radical reform in the way we «sell» our experiences and re-evaluation of insight.

011.145

INTRODUCTION. THE URGENT NEED FOR NEW ENLIGHTENMENT

While for many years producers had great difficulty reconciling beauty and functionality, for example, New Enlightenment demands that we define and audit not only tangible production process, but also those which affect our senses. If we are to reinvigorate our lives, we will need to first understand and then define new functions. In this way we will arrive to a new way to «illuminate» our reality through a clear responsibility for planning.

012.145

INTRODUCTION. THE URGENT NEED FOR NEW ENLIGHTENMENT

The merging of the more radical languages of the 60s and the 70s with modern holistic values, has allowed the current horizon of Experimental Enlightenment to define our future ever more clearly...transforming the vision of 18th aristocratic intellectuals into a shared collective vision for this millennium.

Traité d'athéologie, by Michel Onfray

 013.145

INTRODUCTION. THE URGENT NEED FOR NEW ENLIGHTENMENT

By overcoming the idea that history
is a record of human improvement, we can start
being the author of our destiny, of our real aims
which is marked by our individual uniqueness.

The *Time* magazine cover dedicated to the person of the year

014.145

INTRODUCTION. SOME TENETS OF NEW ENLIGHTENMENT

**The establishment of where intuition
– from which knowledge originates –
and reason meet, through the verification
of empirical experimentation.**

**The emotive and cognitive relevance
to Enlightenment as the basis for
new educational and training models.**

018.145

Futuxe.

INTRODUCTION. SOME TENETS OF NEW ENLIGHTENMENT

The importance of technique, scientific knowledge and skills, which merge in a new type of creativity that is inspired by new functions.

021.145

INTRODUCTION. SOME TENETS OF NEW ENLIGHTENMENT

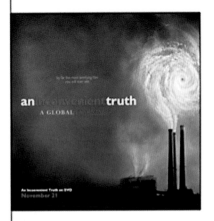

An Inconvenient Truth,
by Al Gore

**The importance of universal themes
to protect the environment
while upholding our civil rights.**

INTRODUCTION. SOME TENETS OF NEW ENLIGHTENMENT

The Architecture of Happiness,
by Alain de Botton

The importance of the individual's quality of life, of well-being and health, within a holistic discussion of happiness.

HYPER MEMORABLE

MEMORY WEAR	1997 ⇒ 1999	NOSTALGIC SEASON	2000 ⇒ 2002

Memory Wear indicates the growth in the phenomena of vintage, no longer lived as «fashion» of the moment, but as personal memory, to interpret in an absolutely subjective way. In these years the work conducted by the fashion industry on the concept of revival – through recovery and quotes relative to the history of fashion – have contributed to the awakening of a general taste for clothes in relation to the personal memory.

With the name **Nostalgic Season** a first important passage is indicated, towards research that is deeper and individual and also the recovery of the past, inspired by the fashion of recent decades and the historical traditions of their countries. People express values like attachment to roots with a retrospective glance. Difficult to define as conservatism, because to relive or evoke a place or the atmosphere of the past serves to satisfy profound feelings and emotions.

HISTORICAL ARTICLES

THEATRICAL UNITS

	2003 ⇒ 2006		2007 ⇒ 2009

In these years the interesting passage has been represented by the taste for the liter, historical, recognisable quotation. Classic items mixed with the basic, transform into «tributes» to epochs and characters of the past. For people **Historical Articles** become the punctuation of daily life and individual style.

With the rules of the game understood, enjoyment becomes fundamental. The theatrical metaphor is therefore more adapt in recounting the desire for interpretation that characterizes the evolution of this long passage of memory. With **Theatrical Units** we witness the game of masks brought to the day to day life of style, that in this way becomes a possible game on different levels.

035.145 ◖◗

Future.

WONDER SIMPLIFICATION

CITY KIT | 1997 ⟹ 1999

The geography of the end of the century seems to have been defined by the principal metropolis, that dictate the new rules of cohabitation within which it becomes necessary to navigate. It is in this moment that the search for basic clothing emerges, a «Survival Kit» constituted by common elements that find a place not only because of their transversal nature in fashion, but above all for their interchangeability. The **City Kit** becomes the emblem of a style of life, shared by a growing number of people.

BALANCED ESSENTIALS

2000 ⟹ 2002

The search for the essential and a deeper quality of life define this phenomenon, that is expressed through the choice of clothes that have a strong classical content. The subjects involved in the **Balanced Essentials** sensibility conciliate the search for formal purity with a more careful evaluation of the quality of products, maintaining a critical equilibrium in their consumption choices and above all keeping an interest in products with a history and soul.

ESSENTIAL BASIC | 2003 ⟹ 2006

These are the years in which the satisfaction of the basic on one side and peoples capacity for choice and combinations reach the maximum levels. With the **Essential Basic** phenomenon a new grammar of style is defined in which essential clothes of ones own wardrobe become the pieces with which to compose ones own daily narration, in a constant search for simplification.

IMMATERIAL LINES

2007 ⟹ 2009

Today an important desire for designers and people in general is to work on the aesthetics of simplification, on the essence of form. The concept of **Immaterial Lines** is not founded on the banalization of the project, on the contrary it aims for the maximum valorization of lines as a constructive element with much creative potential.

050.145

EXTRA RULES

NOBLE SPORTS	1997 ⇨ 1999

The influence of sports clothes profoundly marked the style of the period. The trend that emerged in these years is that of **Noble Sports.** The sports activities mainly linked to the canons of elegance and status inspire the collections of fashion houses and designers, entering and becoming part of daily life. Sports such as golf, equitation, skiing and tennis become sources of inspiration even for occasions outside sport.

ARCHI-SHAPE	2000 ⇨ 2002

This passage is marked by a greater and more profound search for the archetypes of elegance, widening the vision of sport towards fashion and its «rules». Formal or informal classics, icons of good taste, characterise the **Archi-Shape** phenomenon, that opens fruitive and design paths to the passion for a wealth of rules, that are chosen but no longer imposed.

HYPER REGULAR	2003 ⇨ 2006

One of the more interesting and advanced archetypes of the present day can be defined as **Hyper Regular** and is expressed through the search for forms, colours and experiences that underline the great richness of normality. An aspiration (beyond that of an inspiration) towards the recognition of the habitual, essentialism that has nothing to do with minimalism, but that deepens the pureness of the project, giving back an aesthetic that nourishes on functions and representations of modernity.

FORMAL SHAPES	2007 ⇨ 2009

A phenomenon that we can define as **Formal Shapes** represents the actual evolution of taste for rules. The recovery of iconic elements of elegance emerge: from the tie to cufflinks, from the sartorial chalk-stripe to the most classic polo shirt. In this way we assist the recovery of ever more rigourous proportions, put into play through the delicate balance and fine adjustments to a body that appears to be of a grand modernity.

065.145

ULTRA GRAPHIC

UNIVERSAL POP	1997 ⇒ 1999

The **Universal Pop** phenomenon, that has defused in these years, refers to adrenaline culture that is enriched with values of experimental proposition. For the young generations pop art and cartoons become the instrument for «protest» against the tired and confused system of values. The use of strong colours, the mix of styles from musical inspiration, the surreal accessories and decorations well represent the desire to express one's own personal creativity as an emblem of an extraordinary and at times positive vision.

JAP 2-D	2000 ⇒ 2002

With the phenomenon that we have defined as **Jap 2-D**, a reference is not only made to a sensibility of geographical density, but above all to the weight of the Japanese two dimensional graphic culture that has seen the evolution of this trend. The return of prints, of graphic design, the need for decoration of mostly primary colours, are clearly traceable to Japanese culture, that has had the capability to awaken desires towards typologies that have almost vanished from the world of style.

NONSENSE DECORATION

	2003 ⇒ 2006

The evolution of this sensibility, **Nonsense Decoration**, is above all expressed through the transposition of the world of *disco* on occasions more shared and daily. The T-shirt becomes the privileged platform, the perfect instrument of communication to transmit the messages of this generation. Messages of sense or nonsense express a renewed desire for decoration, for sometime hidden to clothing.

BLACK & LIGHT	2007 ⇒ 2009

Black & Light constitutes the more advanced frontier of this path, in which graphics and play of contrasts, recover black as a background element. White, as well as bright colours, become the touch of light that illuminates the project as a whole. Light reveals itself to be a surprising, capturing, catalyst of attention, giving value to graphic design that remains important in the definition of this style.

HUGE INTERLACE

NAVIGATORS	1997 ⇒ 1999	HYPER LAYERING	2000 ⇒ 2002

The **Navigators** phenomenon opens this trend path. The theme of travel be it real or virtual and exploration in these years assumes growing importance for youth culture. Also, the diffusion of internet, break down the remaining barriers, so contributing in the spreading of a common language above all within the younger generations. Surrounding this scenario clear codes of apparel began to delineate including that of neo tribal decoration and elements that belong to the web culture.

In these years the evolution of sensibility, has placed the importance on the mix of language. With **Hyper Layering** we have seen how people start to layer objects, inspirations, worlds of reference in a totally new way free of prejudice. Again the internet results in being a fitting metaphor, not simply for its language, but also for the horizon of information and navigation. This approach also arrives to fashion, giving people new creative opportunities and great expressive freedom.

COMBO CHIC	2003 ⇒ 2006	DISGUISE GAME	2007 ⇒ 2009

As often happens, when we talk of change of paradigms that give life to new aesthetics, the stylistic combinations and the evolutions become infinite. In this way the competencies of people increase, until they transform into «self stylists». With **Combo Chic** we witness the sophistication of this new way of understanding personalisation that gives life to interesting stimuli in all fields.

As in a Catherine wheel of possible games, what emerges today is the need to experiment new combinations. Like when children play with a mother's clothes, dressing up without having in mind a precise person (as instead happens in the Theatrical Units sensibility), the only intent is that of having fun. The phenomenon **Disguise Game** is similar and expresses the same freedom for interpretation, but a greater mastery of the stylistic rules, maybe to break with.

095.145

Future

SUPER MATERIAL

HEALTH MATERIAL | 1997 ⇒ 1999

In the delicate phase of the passing of the millennium, the theme of protection concerning health assumes central importance in the lives of people. In parallel materic experimentation proposes fibres and fabrics that are always more advanced and performing. **Health Material** affirms itself as a important phenomenon on the level of the search for well being and protection, but above all as an aesthetic expression: technical materials, futuristic coatings, become an absolute must.

EXPERIMENTAL DRIVE | 2000 ⇒ 2002

With the passing of time, material experimentation, has been cleansed of anxiety causing aspects, remaining an interesting frontier both on a project and fruitive point of view.
With the **Experimental Drive** phenomenon, we can witness the diffusion of great creative freedom in experimenting on the body unusual materials and new combinations, that place the aspects of sensorial perception at the centre.

SYNTHETIC AESTHETICS | 2003 ⇒ 2006

With the theme that we have defined as **Synthetic Aesthetics**, the materic starts to work on the aspects of surface and aesthetic languages. Materials such as rubber and metal, that were not originally linked to clothing, are reinterpreted following new rules of style. The synthetic, artificial aspect is emphasised through colours that support the originality and the perceptive wrong footing.

SHINY BOLDNESS | 2007 ⇒ 2009

This final evolution, that we have called **Shiny Boldness**, does not overwrite the previous aspects of material experimentation: it simply implies a use of the matter privileging the aspects of opulence and wealth that only precious materials can guarantee. This pushes for a major use of gold in all its possible variants and design sectors. A sensibility that is also expressed through the return of shiny surfaces, chrome plate, mirror, precious and «sumptuous».

110.145 ◖◗

MASSIVE DETAILS

EDGE OF WOMAN	1997 ⇒ 1999

In the **Edge of Woman** concept, femininity plays in aggressive terms and sensuality becomes the key element to express people's identity. This sensitivity does not involve only the youngest generations but also mature women, who express a certain degree of preference for a soft provoking style. The use of strong colour in maquillage and hairdressing become the first choice for many women.

SEXIRONICICON	2000 ⇒ 2002

The phenomenon of iconic femininity is one the most important drivers in recent years' fashion and aesthetics. The world of accessories, the return of high heels, tiny bags and foulard are some privileged testimonies. The **SexIronicIcon** trend refers to specific icons of the 50's and 60's female imagery. The ironic dimension becomes crucial to the experience of new femininity.

DECISIVE DETAILS	2003 ⇒ 2006

The phenomenon grows with the use of accessories and aesthetic details as a privileged means of expression. With the **Decisive Details,** details become the protagonists and enrich different styles (from the most classic to basic ones). Often characterised by a surreal approach, very predominant details can be found in bags, shoes, decorations of different kinds on both classic and modern items.

EVERYDAY STAR	2007 ⇒ 2009

Careless of time and place, the act of choosing one's wardrobe becomes a way to play a role through which people emulate the star system's aesthetics and behaviours. **Everyday Stars** wear «*red carpet*» clothes, but also use those accessories, such as dark or shiny sunglasses, worn by celebrities who try to protect their image from public scrutiny. Hairdressing and make-up that accurately replicate celebrities' styles, are part of a trend that is in great expansion throughout different age groups.

▢ ▢ ■ ■ ■ 125.145 ◖◗

MICROMEGA LUXURY

HAUTE STYLE — 1997 ⇒ 1999

What we have called the **Haute Style** phenomenon finds its expression through highly sophisticated sensorial structures, the preciousness of the garments and the accuracy of the accessories.
In the last few years, many advertising campaigns have been contributing to creating a link between the world of *haute couture* and people's dreams, stimulating their interest for high street fashion and exclusive clothes, made with particularly refined production techniques.

EXPERIMENTAL PRESTIGE — 2000 ⇒ 2002

The consolidated interest in high street fashion and the concept of exclusivity fit in the context of street styles, highlighting people's desire for the ownership of little «daily» items of prestige. Materials and icons that belong to the artisan tradition are the protagonists of the **Experimental Prestige**, characterized by the merging between ordinary people's creative experimentation and products' new forms and functions.

BASIC LUXURY — 2000 ⇒ 2002

The evolution of **Haute Style** overlaps with a process of sophistication of the «basic» which has brought what we call the **Basic Luxury** phenomenon, the result of the convergence between these two originally very distant worlds.
In this context, accessories undertake a predominant role. It is enough to consider how the pashmina has become a worldwide cult phenomenon. Prestigious and well known brands also contribute to valorize accessories, like hats, belts or glasses, which themselves become forms of decorative patterns, following *Gucci* and *Louis Vuitton* trend.

DELUXE MASHUPS — 2007 ⇒ 2009

The term **Deluxe Mashups** finds its origins in the world of music, precisely that of *mashup*.
In aesthetic terms, this phenomenon is expressed through an almost shameless ostentation, that is particularly predominant in emerging markets where people attribute a high status to clothes and accessories as a way to reduce the gap between worlds. Within consolidated markets, instead, ostentation becomes part of an ironic dynamic in which influences coming from far away countries mix in new creative combinations.

140.145

TRENDS TIMELINE

		1997 ⇨ 1999	2000 ⇨ 2002	2003 ⇨ 2006	2007 ⇨ 2009
1	HYPER MEMORABLE	MEMORY WEAR	NOSTALGIC SEASON	HISTORIC ARTICLES	THEATRICAL UNITS
2	WONDER SIMPLIFICATION	CITY KIT	BALANCED ESSENTIALS	ESSENTIAL BASIC	IMMATERIAL LINES
3	EXTRA RULES	NOBLE SPORTS	ARCHI-SHAPE	HYPER REGULAR	FORMAL SHAPES
4	ULTRA GRAPHIC	UNIVERSAL POP	NONSENSE DECORATION	JAP 2-D	BLACK & LIGHT
5	HUGE INTERLACE	NAVIGATORS	HYPER LAYERING	COMBO CHIC	DISGUISE GAME
6	SUPER MATERIAL	HEALTH MATERIAL	EXPERIMENTAL DRIVE	SYNTHETIC AESTHETICS	SHINY BOLDNESS
7	MASSIVE DETAILS	EDGE OF WOMAN	SEXIRONICICON	DECISIVE DETAILS	EVERYDAY STAR
8	MICROMEGA LUXURY	HAUTE STYLE	BASIC LUXURY	EXPERIMENTAL PRESTIGE	DELUXE MASHUPS

145.145

CSFB 1 (1) pp. 133–143 Intellect Limited 2010

Critical Studies in Fashion and Beauty
Volume 1 Number 1
© 2010 Intellect Ltd Reviews. English language. doi: 10.1386/csfb.1.1.133_4

FROM THE NOTICEBOARD

100,000 Years of Beauty, **Elizabeth Azoulay (ed.) (2009)**
Paris: Gallimard, 15000 pp., ISBN: 978-2070128440, Paperback, $300

Courtesy of L'Oréal

For their 100th anniversary, L'Oréal commissioned a large-scale research project on beauty, which has been published in a set of five books.

Volume by volume overview
Foundations/prehistory (Middle Palaeolithic, 100,000 BC to Neolithic, 5,000 BC)

The earliest humans sought out colours, wore ornaments and made artistic representations of their own bodies. For *Homo sapiens,* the pursuit of beauty was important both on earth and in the afterlife. All that we know of prehistoric beauty comes from surviving artefacts – intricately carved necklaces, voluptuous Venus figurines (more mother-figure than seductress), the ochre powder found in the earliest prehistoric tombs – and cave paintings.

Neanderthal man was generally thought to be an ugly, stupid brute, despite evidence to the contrary (decorative garments and other forms of artistic expression, such as pigments and pierced shells which appear to have been worn as jewellery, dating back 100,000 years). *Homo sapiens,* who appeared in Europe around 38,000 years ago, were not thought to have much interest either, though surviving ornaments show that they were fascinated by beauty and, like Neanderthals, decorated their bodies with ash, ochre, tattoos and jewellery. Even in this age, when survival was paramount, beauty still mattered.

Antiquity/civilizations *(from old-kingdom Egypt, 2,700 BC, to Meso-America's Aztecs, 1519)*

Volume II traces beauty through the remarkable civilizations of Egypt, Ancient Greece, Rome, China, India, and the Olmecs, Aztecs and Mayans of Meso-America (now Mexico). Here, the evidence of physical beauty, and how it conveyed both taste and identity, is more abundant, as is evidence that all these societies moulded the body to conform to their preferred ideal, whether by binding the feet (China, from around 1,000 AD), or by deforming the shape of the skull (Meso-Americans, around much the same time). All these civilizations had complex beauty rituals involving cosmetics – powders of gypsum, perfumed with extracts of frankincense and myrrh, compounds that worked as foundations to make aged skin seem healthy; creams and perfumes. Many were expensive; even then luxury was an indulgent aspect of beauty.

Hairstyles, especially in China, were dazzlingly intricate; the ancient Greeks were keen on long hair, but women were expected to have the minimum of body hair – *plus ca change*. Egyptian ladies favoured wigs, which held erotic significance and were worn for intimate encounters and were never without kohl, which was more than a mere cosmetic; it protected the wearer from diseases such as conjunctivitis.

The philosophy of beauty becomes complex, too, for the Greeks, who celebrated athletic male beauty to a great degree: order and harmony were the founding principles of beauty, and outer appearance was the key to inner reality. The Romans were particularly fond of perfumes, and the men of sunbathing (women were expected to retain a pale face). India celebrated the sensual body, and felt that no body can be truly beautiful without sufficient ornamentation (the same went for the gods, hence the garlands and decoration on deities in temples). India placed particular emphasis on feet, while Chinese civilization of the Tang and Song dynasties kept strict tabs on beauty because their overriding desire for order and regulation meant hairstyles, clothes and ornamentation were regulated by law.

Classical age/confrontations *(from the eighth century to the nineteenth century)*

The medieval and early modern periods saw faster changes in fashion, both in dress and in beauty. From Dar Al-Islam to mediaeval Europe, from Renaissance Italy to the golden age of Spain, and from the Sun King in France to Japan, China and sub-Saharan Africa – as global trading links developed, fashions and practices were brought from one culture to another along with silks and spices. How people actually looked, and how their ideals of beauty were perceived, is much easier for us to grasp thanks to the explosion of artistic talent during this period.

One common thread through all this was the identification – from Raphael and El Greco to Reubens – of female beauty as the dominant mode of beauty. While science entered into the beauty equation (with Leonardo's *Vitruvian Man* anatomy drawings), religion frowned on too much deliberate beautification. In Renaissance art, Venus – and other fleshier, more sensual representations of womanhood – began to vie with the Virgin as the chief subject for artists' devotion, and beauty walked a tightrope between the sacred and the profane. For the Mughal Empire, on the other hand, beauty, sex and divinity were tightly entwined. For them, earthly beauty was a mirror of heavenly beauty.

Modernity/Globalization 1841–1990

With the advent of the Industrial Revolution the pace of change increased, as did developments in notions of beauty. The advent of photography proved shocking to many because they'd grown used to more flattering portraits– did they really look like that? As mirrors became more widespread, people became more concerned about their appearance. Scientific and industrial discoveries led to the creation of myriad new products: from face creams to nail varnish. The old moral suspicion of cosmetics as corrupting disappeared, and the advent of mass marketing brought these new products within reach of the many, rather than the elite few.

Nations with darker skin tones sought increasingly sophisticated ways to make them lighter; then, once tanning became fashionable, the light-skinned pursued a more bronzed idea, whatever the consequences. Cinema and, later, television sent images of the new, idealized beauty around the globe. Women's liberation, and the struggle for social equality, led to very different ways of seeing beauty. The science of allure has been increasingly studied to try to work out what we like to see best. A homogenized ideal of beauty? Or is that bland, and should true beauty deviate from the norm, just enough to make it interesting? It is not something on which people are ever going to agree, though plenty of famous, beautiful faces, both male and female, have worldwide appeal.

Projections: Future beauty

Beauty is the focus for cutting-edge medical and bio-technical research. Where will it lead? What are the fundamental aesthetic truths about the human body, and what do they mean for the future of beauty? As in this paragraph, it's a case of questions, rather than answers. Science could have the opportunity to replace nature. Will we see downloadable kits that enable purchasers to make their own cosmetics at home? Or a transsexual president? Beauty-pageants for centenarians? Will beauty be male, female or androgynous? As each individual has the opportunity to pursue their own interpretation of beauty, and, through modern technology and social networking, share it with the world, will we see, for example, tattoos on the bones as a secret code of personal beauty?

Depending on your viewpoint, you may find all this thrilling or, just as easily, disturbing. It is certainly mind-boggling, and the most challenging of all the volumes in this extraordinary work. Old age and eventual death remains the greatest challenge to bodily beauty – a challenge that all the inventiveness of humankind has yet to surmount.

Charlotte Waite's Fairy Project: Rethinking the fashion show
West Yorkshire, UK, 31 July–7 August 2010

Efrat Tseëlon, University of Leeds

1. http://www.elleuk.com/
    catwalk/collections/
    chanel/spring-
    summer-2010.

At Chanel's spring/summer 2010 show in Paris the runway was transformed into a pastoral scene, with wooden boards, and a flower-decorated barn complete with enormous haystack. The surprising spectacle, complete with a pop-up stage on which Lily Allen performed a song, did not signal a change of concept any more than Marc Jacob's collection for so called 'plus sizes' (size 14) suggests that the 'size zero' debate is over. The rustic barn provided a rural romanticism for country-inspired garments (aprons, laced sun-frocks, poppy prints, straw bags etc.), but even though the models trotted on grassy paths with bits of straw in their clothes or hair they sported the characteristic 'runway walk' tropes. Their clogs were high heeled, the waists painfully thin, the music, the gestures – all were runway standard (except for the occasional smile).

If there were a prize for the season's most brilliantly executed presentation, this would have won, said British *Elle*.[1] In fact, if there had been a prize it should have gone to Charlotte Waite who single-handedly produced a mini spectacle for her final-year high school fashion show in April 2009. Charlotte Waite, from Wakefield in West Yorkshire, masterminded a show that was not just a decorative gimmick but also a thoughtful story. More importantly, it questioned some of the basic assumptions of the conventional runway show, and the role of the fashion model.

The genealogy of the fashion model is tied to the tradition originated in the Court of Louis XIV where French miniature mannequins dressed in the latest trends were passed on throughout European Courts as a way of conveying the latest vagaries of dress. This was before the advent of mechanical reproduction. Modernity brought a shift away from this brand of bespoke tailoring to mass market production through the developments of Taylorism and Fordism at the beginning of the 20th century.

The 'scientific management' of production developed by Frederick Winslow Taylor - refers to the efficient organization of workers within the productive process. In contrast with eras prior to the industrial revolution in which skilled craftsmen could take pride in a complete "job well done" – Taylorism focussed on measureable and quantifiable benefits achieved through compartmentalizing work into simple, precise, repetitive and skill-reducing tasks. Taylorism was the inspiration for the industrial mechanized paradigm of Fordism – originating in *Ford Motors*. Fordism, whose emblem was the assembly line of the Ford factories immortalized so well in Charlie Chaplin's *Modern*

2. Caroline Evans discusses the Taylorism-Fordism roots of the catwalk in an article entitled 'Jean Patou's American Mannequins: Early Fashion Shows and Modernism', *Modernism/modernity*, 15: 2, April 2008, pp. 243–263. The article was also presented at a Business History Conference, Bocconi University, Milan, 11–13 June 2009.

Times – was characterized by large industrial processes producing standardized commodities for mass markets.

The fashion show which evolved in the 1920s appeared as a visual manifestation of processes of mechanized production[2]. Ironically, even contemporary catwalk with its associated body, facial and movement characteristics evokes a regime of operation associated with the principles of labour management designed to increase productivity. But the fashion model concept as a vehicle for transmission of visual information – a walking advertisement for fabric creations embodied in a *real person* with an *object-like* frozen expression, mechanical rigid routines and 'made to measure' proportions – evokes additional types of *body-simulating objects*.

The first object is the *mask*, which most strikingly combines the schism between appearance and reality. Though masks are inanimate while separate from the body, when the mask is donned by a human actor it takes on animate qualities and 'comes to life' through the gestures of the wearer.

> We respond to the mask in a mixture of fascination and avoidance. We regard the mime artist as reaching perfection when his pale made-up face appears like a mask and his gesture mimics a clockwork doll, and we admire dolls for their capacity to look like a real baby … Like the uncanny, it is familiar and unfamiliar simultaneously. The mask stands in an intermediary position between different worlds. Embodying the fragile dividing line between concealment and revelation, truth and artifice, natural and supernatural, life and death.
>
> (Tseëlon 2001: 20)

The second object is the *marionette* – the deceptively lifelike human or animal-shaped doll that owes its liveliness to the puppeteer.

The third object is the *Victorian automaton*, a mechanical doll which – when set into motion – follows the sequence of instructions that are its design features. What is common to these objects is the dual quality of animate and inanimate features. They appear human, vivid and capable of voluntary movement when worn, or pulled by a thread, or activated, but lack agency. The discourse of the fashion model is based on cultivating a similar mix of human and doll-like qualities, complete with the prevailing norms of body management which currently appear excessively and controversially thin. This paradigm is reproduced unthinkingly in fashion shows of seasoned couture designers as well as by aspiring fashion students everywhere.

Even lavish, imaginative or subversive couture productions displayed in the various 'fashion weeks' subscribe to the structural framework of the mechanical doll captured so well in the poem by Dalia Rabikovitz *Clockwork Doll*.

Clockwork Doll

That night I was mechanical doll
and I turned right and I turned left, and in all directions,
and I fell face down and smashed to pieces
and they tried to piece me together again with a skilful hand.

Then I returned to be a proper doll
and my manner was studied and compliant
but by then I was a different kind of doll -
like an injured twig hanging by a tendril

And then I went to dance at a ball,
but they left me in the company of cats and dogs
though all my steps were measured and rhythmical.

And I had golden hair and I had blue eyes
and I had a dress the colour of flowers in the garden
and I had a straw hat trimmed with a cherry

(Rabikovitz 1959)

Charlotte Waite had a different vision for her dress design, which was partially inspired by the story of the Cottingley Fairies (produced by young cousins Frances and Elsie who claimed to have photographed fairies near the Yorkshire village of Cottingley in 1917). Sir Arthur Conan Doyle used these photographs to illustrate an article on fairies he had been commissioned to write for the Christmas 1920 edition of *The Strand Magazine*. The story of the cousins, which was believed to be true at the time but was later admitted to be 'a fairy story', inspired a film *Fairytale: A True Story*. This was the context Charlotte drew on to produce a dress designed to represent something that might have been worn by the fairies the children are looking for. Inspiration for embellishment was drawn from natural sources: frayed edges and a green dip-dyed hemline that could almost have been stained by dew-filled grass, trailing embroidered flowers and printed dragonflies hiding in layers of diaphanous muslin.

To showcase her creation in her graduation fashion show Waite departed from habitual catwalk conventions. She produced a story, a Victorian childhood scene situated in Nostell Priory – an eighteenth century National Trust Georgian mansion nestling in the midst of beautiful grounds with lakeside walks in the heart of the West Yorkshire countryside. Her 'fairies' motif recreates the Cottingley story through a screening of a series of black and white photographic slides as a backdrop to the dress display. The slides feature two girls in period costumes looking for fairies as they play in the grounds. In parallel with this, a girl appears on the stage wearing the fairy dress walking barefoot in slow dreamy movements. She then disappears to the tune of the song *Perfect Day* which is from the title sequence of a *Peter Rabbit* 1990s children series, and the girls' cheerful voices appear like a response to the 'real fairy' who has just appeared on the stage. Yet, while the children are looking for fairies in the photographs, it is not *the fairies* that are the true theme of Waite's project, *but the joy of the children as they play*. In evoking happy childhood memories the project casts a nostalgic look at childhood as something to be cherished, especially in a time when there are such pressures on children to grow up so quickly (of which the catwalk is a contributor).

Thus on every level, visually, aesthetically, musically, rhythmically and conceptually, the presentation of the fairy dress marks a departure from conventional conceptions of a 'fashion show' and offers an alternative paradigm that draws more on cultural narratives than on the production line. In fact so radical was Waite's departure from the norm, that her secondary school textile teacher expressed a concern that it would be 'too boring' and 'too slow' for the audience. In the event, the audience was treated to a fresh approach indeed. In Barthes' reading of *The face of Garbo* ([1957] 1989) he sees the snowy thickness of Garbo's mask-like make up, like the white mask of the mime artist, as having the effect of transforming her face into an 'idea', while the individualized face of Audrey Hepburn is an 'event'. If the current catwalk portrays the role of the model as an 'idea' and the cult of the celebrity model as 'an event', Waite's approach offers an 'event' which does not derive its meaning from the celebrity status of the models; meaning is derived from the distinctive story the fashion show tells, and the model is neither an object (clothes horse) nor a fetishized star, but a part of the plot.

The story of Waite's mini fashion show (complete with the slide presentation) has been displayed in an exhibition at the Nostell Priory, for 300 years home to a textile merchant family, one of whose members, Sir George Winn was rewarded, in 1660 with a baronetcy by King Charles II for services to the crown.

Figure 1: photographs taken by Elsie Wright and Frances Griffith in 1917, showing 1a (left) Elsie with a winged gnome, and 1b (right) Frances with the alleged fairies. Photos courtesy of The Science & Society Picture Library.

Figure 2: Charlotte Waite's storyboard where she recreated, in a series of black and white images, the atmosphere Frances and Elsie created in their Cottingley fairies photos. Her images were the backdrop for her fashion show presentation of her 'fairy dress'.

Figure 3: The fairy dress: 3a the dress, 3b embroidered flower detail, and 3c beaded dragonfly detail.

References

Barthes, Roland ([1957] 1989), 'The face of Garbo', in R. Barthes, *Mythologies* (trans. Annette Lavers), London: Palladin.

Rabikovitz, Dalia (1959), *The love of an orange* (Hebrew: Ahavat Tapuach Ha-Zahav), Tel Aviv: Machbarot Lesifrut.

Tseëlon, Efrat (2001), 'Reflections on mask and carnival', in E. Tseëlon (ed.), *Masquerade and identities: gender, sexuality & marginality*, London: Routledge pp. 18–37.

EDITORIAL

DIANA CRANE

University of Pennsylvania

Auction prices of fashion collectibles: What do they mean?

1   Both fashionable clothing and fashion collectibles need to be distinguished from 'clothes art', pieces of clothing that are deliberately created so as not to be worn (Wollen et al. 1998). They are intended for exhibition in art galleries.

2   Previously, fashion collectibles were included in the Victoria and Albert Museum in London as early as 1852 and in The Costume Institute, which was created in 1944 in the Metropolitan Museum in New York.

When studying fashion, it is important to distinguish between fashionable clothing, which is currently on the market and therefore 'in fashion', and fashion collectibles, which were formerly but are no longer in fashion.[1] In this article, I interrogate the importance of fashion creations as material culture by using the auction prices of fashion items as an indication of the cultural value of fashion artefacts.

The value of fashion artefacts as a form of cultural heritage began to be recognized in the 1970s with the creation of fashion museums in France, Japan and the United States.[2] Today there are fashion museums all over the world, including in other countries in Europe and in Asia. Beginning in 1983 with an exhibition of the couture designs of Yves Saint-Laurent at the Metropolitan Museum in New York, art museums have occasionally organized retrospectives of the work of fashion designers, alive or deceased (Steele 2008).

Aesthetic criteria for evaluating fashionable collectibles and fashionable clothing in general are underdeveloped, as indicated in a recent review of scholarly works on fashion (Gonzalez 2010). Most scholarly discussions of fashion theorize the characteristics and effects of fashion that is *in fashion*, rather than the aesthetic criteria of fashion collectibles. In fact, most such discussions ignore the possibility and implications of fashion collectibles. Analysing fashion collectibles is different from recounting fashion history. The latter tends to be a description of a succession of creators and styles.

The similarities and differences between fashion and art have been the subject of a sizable literature (for the latest contribution, see Geczy and Karaminis 2012). Tseëlon (2012) argues that while fashion is generally classified as a craft rather than as an art, the differences between couture and the Old Masters have been exaggerated.

An indication that fashion collectibles have become a form of cultural heritage is the fact that designer clothes are sold in auction markets. For example, fashion entered the French auction market in 1987 (Bénaïm 1992: 22). In France, the major buyers appear to be fashion museums, private collectors, couture houses (which buy back their own creations) and occasionally the French government on behalf of a fashion museum.

Auction prices of designer clothes are an important indicator of the relative value of fashion collectibles in comparison with other types of collectibles, particularly contemporary artworks. How do the prices attained by major fashion designers compare with the prices attained by major contemporary artists during the post-war period? What do these prices signify about the importance of fashion in contemporary society in comparison with art collectibles?

Prices of fashion collectibles in the auction market suggest that fashion collectibles are perceived by art collectors, art dealers, museums and auction houses as having relatively little economic value in comparison with contemporary artworks. It is not unusual for auction prices of artworks by leading post-war artists to attain over one million dollars (approximately 770,000 euros) (Azimi 2008). For example, paintings by post-war American and British artists, Andy Warhol and Francis Bacon, have been auctioned for over $70 million in the past decade (Bellet and de Roux 2007; Sabbah 2008). By contrast, fashion collectibles created by leading post-war fashion designers are seldom sold for over 10,000 euros.

Two auctions in 2011 support this conclusion: (1) an auction in Paris in June 2011 of 485 items designed by major twentieth-century designers, mainly in the last 60 years (Artcurial 2011) and (2) an auction in London in December 2011 of 82 items, many of them designed by major twentieth-century designers (Christie's 2011a). In the Paris auction, the average price obtained by these items was 391 euros. Only 6 per cent of the items sold for over 1000 euros. Four items sold for more than 5000 euros. Only one item sold for over 10,000 euros.

The London auction was more successful, but again very few items obtained high prices (Christie's 2011b). The average price of the items was 4053 euros. Approximately 48 per cent of the items sold for over 1000 euros, but only the highest price in the Paris auction, 13,631 euros, was paid for a dress designed by Yves Saint Laurent – one of the most important French, post-war designers

– at the beginning of his career when he was employed by Dior. The highest price in the London auction (73,961 euros) was attained by a dress designed by Dior in 1948. By contrast, paintings by Abstract Expressionists created in the 1940s were virtually worthless then but are now worth millions (Crane 1987).

A major factor, which influences the price of fashion collectibles, is celebrity validation. Dresses worn by former movie stars may be auctioned for prices as high as important artworks. In 1999, a dress made to order by an unknown designer for Marilyn Monroe was auctioned for 1.78 million euros (*Le Monde2* 2007). In July 2011, the white dress, which Marilyn Monroe wore in a famous scene in the film, *The Seven Year Itch*, was auctioned for 3.54 million euros in the United States (*Le Monde* 2011).

Other examples of celebrity validation include: (1) a dress designed by the French couturier, Givenchy, and worn by Audrey Hepburn in the film, *Breakfast at Tiffany's*, was auctioned for approximately 681,000 euros in 2006 (Reier 2007); (2) a dress worn by Princess Diana shortly before her marriage to Prince Charles was auctioned in London for £192,000 in 2010 (*International Herald Tribune* 2010); (3) a dress owned by Elizabeth Taylor was auctioned in New York for $362,500 in 2011 ('Buying frenzy greets Liz Taylor auction' 2011).

Why is celebrity validation so important in auction sales of fashion collectibles? One hypothesis is that celebrity validation is important when many buyers are not familiar with the aesthetic criteria for evaluating collectibles. As a result, items with high aesthetic value may be ignored in favour of items with similar or lesser aesthetic value, which have been associated with celebrities. Comparable behaviour sometimes occurs in antique markets. For example, newly wealthy Chinese, buying antique Chinese vases at auction, prefer items that have formerly been owned by famous collectors (Melikian 2011).

To date, the highest auction prices for fashion collectibles without celebrity validation have been attained by pieces designed by well-known, pre-war French couturiers. The highest price for a pre-war fashion collectible (175,000 euros) was obtained in 2009 for a jacket designed by Elsa Schiaparelli ('Drouot Richelieu: Vendredi 3 juillet 2009 SVV Millon Cornette de Saint Cyr' 2009).

The Schiaparelli sale indicates that a second explanation for high auction prices of fashion collectibles is an association with the fine arts. Working in the 1930s when the surrealist movement was at its height, Schiaparelli collaborated with surrealist artists and attempted to apply the principles of surrealism to fashion design (Martin 1987). The jacket that obtained the record price was decorated with embroidery designed by Jean Cocteau, a leading surrealist artist, and carried his signature embroidered in pink thread.

The second highest price (34,689 euros) in the London auction was obtained by a dress designed by Yves Saint Laurent in 1966. The auction price of the Yves Saint Laurent dress benefited from the way in which the dress alluded to the arts, specifically Saint Laurent's use of a familiar motif from the work of the Dutch abstract artist, Piet Mondrian. Saint Laurent did not collaborate with artists, but he incorporated themes from the works of major artists, such as Matisse and Picasso, in his couture designs. Nevertheless, the auction prices of his designs are nowhere near the auction prices of post-war creators of comparable stature in the fine arts.

Significantly, designs created by Paco Rabanne, who is considered to be one of the most innovative designers of the post-war period (Kamitsis 1996), have been much less successful in the auction market. Rabanne's creations are avant-garde in the context of fashion design, but they do not incorporate themes or motifs from the fine arts. In a recent auction (Artcurial 2012a) of fashion collectibles created by Paco Rabanne, only two out of 73 dresses attained a price over 5000 euros (Artcurial 2012b). They sold for 6880 euros and 10,000 euros, respectively. According to Christie's director of costumes and textiles, an exceptionally expensive fashion collectible 'ties the object into popular culture and historical movements' (Menkes 2011).

These statistics raise the question why the prices of contemporary art are so high, while the prices of fashion collectibles are so low. In the post-war period, the art world has built an increasingly elaborate set of institutions for selling art. The number of art collectors has soared. In major art centres, such as New York, Paris, London and Berlin, the numbers of art galleries have steadily increased. The art world is now global; an increasing number of galleries have offices in several countries and successful or would-be successful artists exhibit in galleries on three continents. International art fairs, such as ArtBasel and ArtBasel Miami Beach, bring together artists, collectors and dealers for short periods where many major sales take place.

By contrast, the infrastructure for selling fashion collectibles is relatively underdeveloped. Few art galleries handle fashion collectibles. Auctions of fashion collectibles are relatively rare. It is difficult to estimate the numbers of private collectors, but collectors whose collections consist of clothing that was not acquired for their own use are unlikely to be numerous. Christie's, which names owners of objects auctioned in its sales, mentioned only five collectors for 82 objects in their December 2011 fashion auction. Museums are the main market for fashion collectibles but their funds are limited.

Another less obvious but important factor that influences the prices for fashion collectibles is gender. Fashion is a medium that primarily serves to enhance the attributes of women. This may explain the apparent dearth of private collectors who tend to be male. For example, most art collectors are male or heterosexual couples in which the male member actually pays for the collectibles and presumably makes the final decisions concerning what will or will not be purchased (Esterow 2008).[3] It is also significant that, in the contemporary art world, paintings by women sell for much less than those by men, both in art galleries and in the auction market. In a list, compiled by the author in 2008, of 52 post-war artists whose work had been auctioned for over one million dollars, only four were women.

3   In a list of the world's top 200 collectors published by Artnews, less than 10 per cent were single women.

Will fashion collectibles increase in value in the future? Should they be considered a promising investment that will be profitable for collectors in the long run? The answer will probably depend in part on the extent to which the aura of femininity, which surrounds them, can be transformed from a liability into an asset. The value of fashion collectibles will also depend on recognition of the aesthetic qualities of fashion collectibles, apart from their associations with the fine arts. This would entail a transformation in the status of collectibles that have a useful purpose to one in which crafts were on an equal footing with the arts.

References

Artcurial (2011), 'Results for sale 1967, haute-couture – Alaïa', http://www.artcurial.com. Accessed 10 July 2011.

_____ (2012a), 'Paco Rabanne: Fashion materials', Vente no. 2075 (catalogue), Paris: Artcurial.

_____ (2012b), 'Results for sale 2075, Paco Rabanne "Fashion Materials"', http://www.artcurial.com. Accessed 4 February 2012.

Azimi, R. (2008), 'L'insatiable appétit des collectionneurs des pays émergents', _Le Monde argent!_, January 20-21, p. 2.

Bellet, H. and de Roux, E. (2007), 'Les nouveaux collectioneurs', _Le Monde_, 17 July, p. 2.

Bénaïm, Laurence (1992), 'Des griffes sous le marteau', _Le Monde_, 7 April, p. 22.

Christie's (2011a), 'Sale 3139 fashion', South Kensington, London, 1 December, www.christies.com. Accessed 6 February 2012.

_____ (2011b), 'Results for sale 3139, fashion', www.christies.com. Accessed 6 February 2012.

Crane, Diana (1987), _The Transformation of the Avant-Garde: The New York Art World, 1940–1985_, Chicago: University of Chicago Press.

Esterow, M. (2008), 'The ARTnews 200 top collectors: The ship sails on', _ARTnews_, Summer, pp. 121–35.

La Gazette de l'Hotel Druout (2004), 'Enchères haute couture', _La Gazette de l'Hotel Druout_, 28, 16 July, p. 14.

Geczy, Adam and Karaminis, Vicki (eds) (2012), _Fashion and Art_, Oxford: Berg.

Gonzalez, Ana Marta (2010), 'On fashion and fashion discourses', _Critical Studies in Fashion and Beauty_, 1:1, pp. 65–85.

International Herald Tribune (2007), 'Collecting fueled by personal passions', _International Herald Tribune_, 19–20 May, pp. 18–19.

_____ (2010), 'People', *International Herald Tribune*, 10 June, p. 14.

Kamitsis, Lydia (1996), *Paco Rabanne: Le sens de la recherche/A Feeling for Research*, Paris: Editions Michel Lafon, pp. 7, 50.

Martin, Richard (1987), *Fashion and Surrealism*, New York: Rizzoli.

Melikian, Souren (2011), 'Scooping up the trophies', *International Herald Tribune*, 16–17 July, p. 16.

Menkes, Suzy (2011), 'Vintage fashion on the auction block', www.nytimes.com/2011/11/29/fashion. Accessed 6 February 2012.

Le Monde (2011), '4.6 million de dollars pour la robe de Marilyn dans "Sept ans de réflexion"', *Le Monde*, 21 June, p. 23.

Le Monde2 (2007), 'Marilyn and "Mister President"', *Le Monde2*, May, p. 61.

Reier, S. (2007), 'Collecting fuelled by personal passions', *International Herald Tribune*, 19–20 May, pp. 18–19.

Rich, Holly (2007), 'The quirky couture market: A discussion of mechanisms', Sotheby's Institute of Art, London, http://www.juliensauctions.com/collectors-guide/couture.html. Accessed 17 May 2007.

Sabbah, C. (2008), 'Une pause salutaire?', *Le Monde*, 20–21 January, p. 2.

Steele, Valerie (2008), 'Museum quality: The rise of the fashion exhibition', *Fashion Theory*, 12, pp. 7–30.

Tseëlon, Efrat (2012), 'Authenticity', in A. Geczy and V. Karaminis (eds), *Fashion and Art*, Oxford: Berg, pp. 111–22.

Wollen, Peter et al. (1998), *Addressing the Century: 100 Years of Art and Fashion*, London: Hayward Gallery Publishing.

(2009), 'Druout Richelieu, Vendredi 3 juillet 2009: SVV Million Cornette de Saint Cyr', http://www.druout.com. Accessed 4 February 2012.

(2011), 'Buying frenzy greets Liz Taylor dresses auction', www.gg2.net, 12 December. Accessed 6 February 2012.

Contributor details

Diana Crane is a specialist in the sociology of culture, arts, media and globalization. She is the author of several books, including *Fashion and Its Social Agendas: Class, Gender, and Identity in Clothing* (Chicago, 2000). She is professor emerita of sociology at the University of Pennsylvania.

E-mail: craneher@sas.upenn.edu

CSFB 1 (2) pp. 151–159 Intellect Limited 2010

Critical Studies in Fashion and Beauty
Volume 1 Number 2
© 2010 Intellect Ltd Editorial. English language. doi: 10.1386/csfb.1.2.151_2

Part 2
EDITORIAL

EFRAT TSEËLON
University of Leeds

Is identity a useful critical tool?

Identity between being and becoming

The contributions to this issue address various angles on the issue of identity. Identity and fashion are so regularly addressed side by side that it does appear as the most 'natural' and 'normal' of unions. It is for this reason that my introduction problematizes the nature of identity and the way we apply it, and questions the case for such a seamless alliance between fashion and identity.

Identity is a story we tell ourselves about ourselves or about our group. It is a story with real and imagined dimensions. Within the extensive literature on identity there seems to be a key idea that is pervading, almost irrespective of research tradition. It is the idea that the concept of identity negotiates the relation between self and the Other, identity is always created though setting boundaries which demarcate an 'inside' from an 'outside', a 'self' from an 'other'. There is also broad agreement that identity is generated in social interaction, mediated by cultural instruments, and is contextually situated. 'Social identity theory' developed by Henri Tajfel is a paradigmatic example of theorizing the mechanisms and motivations of group membership. It proposes a cognitively mediated account of the process of identity formation and consists of three stages. The first is 'categorization' and classification of group members and non-members, the second is 'social comparison' for the purpose of determining the relative status of one's own group and distancing oneself from non-group members and from groups which do not share the same beliefs and ideas of their own group. The third stage is using group membership as a source of positive self-esteem.

When considering attempts to naturalize processes of identity formation, whether sociologically or psychologically, it is well to remind ourselves that historically identity is a new concept. Its origins lie in the Enlightenment tendency to categorize, classify and create typologies, and in the emergence of nation states in modernity. The nation-state was premised on the tendency of dominant cultures to appropriate the national narrative by claiming a coherence and uniformity that, on closer inspection, often proved to be more imagined than real. The discourse of the imaginary is a quintessential feature of theorizing identity. Perhaps we can liken identity to a story, not in the sense of 'fiction' but in the sense of 'the documentary' which Grierson said is 'the creative treatment of actuality'. The fantasy of coherent and homogenous sociality, superimposed upon a reality of contradictions and fragmentation that make up the real sociality, is exemplified in the notion of 'national character', which has been of crucial importance not only for so-called 'organic' or 'Romantic' philosophers from Hegel to Heidegger, but also for military strategists. In its conventional usage, it masks an underlying mix of desire and power while legitimizing certain power structures and naturalizing certain types of conflict. Eric Hobsbawm observed that 'imagined communities' were used more indiscriminately when they became hard to find in real life, Jock Younge similarly noted that 'just as community collapses, identity is invented', and Bauman analysed the emergence of the notion of identity at the point where processes of globalization and privatization erode real community as a safe and cosy shelter. Identity becomes a source of security and confidence, 'a surrogate of community'. Since neither is available in our privatized and individualized, fast globalized world, each of these qualities can be safely imagined.

In psychology, a similar fantasy structure is revealed in the unity of the subject represented by an ideal of a well integrated self and is expressed in constructions such as 'self concept', 'character' and 'personality'.

In the social sciences the concept of 'identity' has been critiqued for its failure to address contested and reflexive aspects. As a result it has increasingly evolved from a *national* narrative to a *multicultural* one in order to accommodate emergent, contingent and ambivalent aspects. Thus conceptions of 'identity' have moved from *structural* to *processual.* Identity has come to be seen more as a process of negotiated positions where members define their belonging out of the cultural materials available to them – rather than as a process of reification of permanent properties. In fact already in 1908 Simmel discussed identity as 'never a finished project' but as a 'work in progress'. No longer able to draw on structural forces like kinship and religion, or on traditions which have lost their determining potential to make-up people's total identities, and with locally anchored or loosely connected unstable tribal communities taking over from stable categories such as class, gender, race or nation, 'identity' has come to rely on cultural narratives, images, symbols, and lifestyle alternatives.

In social psychology Rom Harré and his colleagues illustrated this shift by using a social constructivist paradigm to articulate a narrative approach to reading and understanding the dynamics of human relationships. Their 'positioning theory' defines the concept 'identity' not by a particular set of attributes but by a particular position. And in order to avoid essentialist reductionism they replaced *role* with *position* as the central organizing concept for analysing how people do 'being a person'. Positioning theory recast the relations between people and their conversations and used 'relationships' or 'stories' as important analytic variables. This privileged the dynamic aspects of encounters, in contrast to the way in which the concept of role served to highlight static, formal and ritualistic aspects in developing a social psychology of selfhood.

Cultural theory adopted a similar view articulated, for example, by Stuart Hall in *Representation: Cultural Representations and Signifying Practices* argued that identity can no longer be theorized in terms of a stable core that unfolds unchangingly through all the vicissitudes of life. Instead, identity must be thought of as shifting, as a process of becoming rather than being, a discursive practice rather than a given. Hall stresses 'identity construction' as relating to the politics of exclusion and speaks about identification not in terms of recognizing some common origin and consequent solidarity with others, but rather as a construction – a process that reproduces difference.

Postcolonial theory took the notion of 'producing difference' as a core principle. Its multiculturalist model, which seeks to address the legacy of colonialism and conquest is founded on the shared experiences of injustice of members of certain social groups. Their experience fuels the project of rethinking the national narrative, and give voice to groups that are excluded from it. Its 'identity politics' has shifted the focus from 'difference' to 'hybridity' politics, which, accept an irrevocable mixture as a starting-point, rather than as a problem. However, writing in the forum openDemocracy the journalist Neal Ascherson reminds us that even *hybrid identities* face the danger of essentialism because they are constructed around a narrative, albeit a multifactorial one.

Categorical thinking

In the context of the trajectory of the concept of identity it is worth noting the resilience of a *categorical thinking*. This approach to knowledge, which informs the essentialist concept of identity, has not disappeared but remained under the surface. I will mention three examples. The first example is the phenomenal influence of Samuel Huntington's *The clash of civilizations* where he extended the traditional concept of 'national identity' to civilizations. Huntington argues that while nation states are less capable of defining a national identity, this same sense of identity now resides at a 'civilizational' level. According to him inherent differences between these identities (irreducible to mere national interests or misperception) are the fault lines along which conflict and security will increasingly be defined. This thesis has relevance beyond the realm of political conflicts: it represents the resilience of concepts that draw sharp, simple and stereotypical lines around group membership. As such they seem to represent popular culture better than the more nuanced academic theorizing (as the popularity of best-sellers such as *You just don't understand: Women and Men in Conversation* or *Men are from Mars Women are from Venus* attest to in relation to the binary categories of gender – long surpassed by post-feminist thinkers). The second example is David and Bar-Tal's (2009) state-of-the-art thinking in social psychology. Their article *A Sociopsychological Conception of Collective Identity: The Case of National Identity as an Example* theorizes the structure of identity as twofold. The micro-level pertains to individuals' recognition of and categorization as belonging to a group, with the accompanying cognitive, emotional, and behavioural consequences. The macro-level pertains to the notion of collective identity that is made of 'a sense of belonging' to a collective. This is further divided into two aspects containing the 'features' and 'content' characterizing the collective identity.

The third example comes from popular culture. Rachel Shields from *The Independent* asks 'A cup of tea and a game of cricket? What is it to be English today?' Her article that explores the elusiveness and fluidity of the meaning and content of 'English identity' - also toys with definitions based on customs, rituals, habits, history, humour, foods and tastes. Tellingly it attracted numerous readers' comments opening a window into the essentialist undercurrents of the public mood. Among others we find such sentiments as the following:

One cannot change the identity of a particular culture. You can't suddenly say that a European culture is Islamic because some Muslims decided to live there, you can't say that the Italians are a black African race of people because some black Africans live in Rome, etc.

Being English is being descended from the Angles, Saxon, Jutes, Danish and Norwegian ancestors who came together to create that essence of Englishness our remarkable language. My ancestry is documented back to the 11c. and can say I am so proud to be English not British.

The English do not discuss what it means to be English. They just know.

The real problem of identity concerns the recent immigrant populations which in many cases have been encouraged by the mindless application of over-zealous political correctness to continue living with imported customs and languages of their various countries of origin. It is now increasingly recognized that the *multi-cultural experiment has* by and large *turned out to be a disaster.*

I have lived in other countries where I have felt like a stranger for a while, but that quickly subsides, and I have given little further thought to identity, minority status, or being alien.

(Shields 2010, emphasis added)[1]

1. Shields, Rachel (2010), 'A cup of tea and a game of cricket? What is it to be English today?', *The Independent*, 21 November, http://www.independent.co.uk/news/uk/home-news/a-cup-of-tea-and-game-of-cricket-what-is-it-to-be-english-today-2139728.html. Accessed 10 December 2010.

One reader even articulates the nature of the paradox of *defining* a *fluid* category:

> There is really only one thing about being English that makes me proud and that is that we aren't a very proud nation. *Who really needs to be proud of the particular place they happened to be born in, as though by that very incident it makes the place better.* No, I am first and foremost proud of being a citizen of the world. Englishness comes bottom of my list and that's the only worthwhile thing about it – it is a position that many of us modest English folk share. The day we redevelop a sense of national pride is the day I stop being English.

When applied to the realm of fashion as social phenomena and as an object of study, similar tendencies are apparent. On the one hand in the last two decades we have witnessed a shift which is equivalent to moving from 'national identity politics' to 'politics of difference'. In the field of academic fashion, and in the other social sciences, there appears to have been fundamental progress from *categorical* to *conversational* thinking. In other words, there is a move away from modernity thinking, in terms of fixed groups, group membership and existential qualities, to a postmodernity thinking, in terms of meaning that is negotiated, contextual and resists fixing and permanence. It applies both to the theorizing of 'groups' (from fixed to ad hoc), the theorizing of 'dressing practices' (from fashion normative rules dictated in a top-down manner to grass-roots fashion innovation that can allude to, but is not bound by, rigid rules) as much as it applies to the 'meaning of dress' (from stereotypic meanings to subjective meanings). In my own work I call this process the shift from the *stereotype approach* to the *wardrobe approach,* or from researching the *external* dimensions of clothes (e.g. features of fabric and tailoring, historical styles, fashion trends) to the *internal* dimensions (expressed in the lived or reflexive experience of wearing particular clothes in particular contexts for particular reasons or ends), and expand the project of reading collective meanings into modes of dressing to focusing on the subjective meaning of the wearers. This is achieved by moving from a semiotic to ethnographic epistemology. In short, it is a transition from stable, rigid, collective-ideological concepts and conduct that characterize what Bauman defines as 'solid modernity' to the fluid, changing contingent and globalized-individualized universe of 'liquid modernity'.

This transition is two fold: (1) from 'layered' to 'flat' world, as Baudrillard has intimated in his notion of simulacra and Friedman elaborated in *The world is flat*, and (2) from overarching 'universal' categories to a nuanced 'local' picture. But on another level fashion as a field of knowledge and action seems to have kept categorical thinking, despite changes to its rhetoric and many of its research practices and contents.

A few examples from popular culture and scholarly work will illustrate the claim I am making. One example comes from the press' regular habit (bolstered by the trend of fashion manuals written by self-appointed gurus and celebrities) of providing 'fashion advice' and nominating the 'best' and

2. Oxford Mail (2010), "'You tweet' "badly-dressed" students send message to Council leader as they stage "posh" protest', 3 December. Accessed 10 December 2010.

'worst' dressers. This advice is about both appropriateness (what to wear for particular occasions) and fit (what the tall or plump or square faced ought to wear).

The 'fashion advice' genre is based on the assumptions of categorical membership, together with a set of meanings and normative behaviours that are expected as part of membership of these categories. To adopt the postmodern idiom and claim that instead of belonging to 'one major group' we now belong to 'many groups' increases our choice but does not challenge the notion of group membership as a conceptual tool. Another example is one of the fundamental categories that runs through much theory and practice of the field of fashion: the distinction between *formality* and *informality* – perhaps the last remaining bastion of *stereotypical thinking*. But its voice is not diminished. It is expressed, however implicitly, in fashion scholarship's tendency to define as fashion the more 'glamorous' world of regal historical clothing, couture and designer fashion than the less glamorous world of *wardrobe research* of 'ordinary' people. It is represented in the collective desire to 'dress up' for special occasions as well as the collective fantasy of the 'queen for a day' motif, whether in weddings, makeovers or photo-shoot portfolios. Finally, it is expressed in the assumptions underlying popular culture representations in news, not just in fashion columns. The following example captures this point. In a recent event Oxford school children staged a protest during school time against the projected rise in university fees. The council leader was not impressed and branded them on his twitter-feed an 'ugly, badly-dressed student rabble' and suggested that he can 'guess the lifestyle and location' of parents of such children. As a response, the children turned up to the County Hall the next day in formal gear (suits, boiler hats and paper masks of the councillor) to protest against his comments carrying banners, one of which was addressed to that councillor and read: 'Is this good enough for you?' (Oxford Mail 2010).[2]

The point about this last example is that it captures, in a nutshell, both a behaviour which stereotypes a certain type of people, and certain types of conduct as a function of their dress (or as illustrated by their dress), and at the same time it shows that those members of society who do not adhere to this code in their daily life are still familiar with it. Yet it was 'the official' who invoked the importance of categorical difference.

Given the fundamental changes that the concept of 'identity' has undergone – from representing a stable and homogenizing entity of modernity to the transient and contingent process in some parts of the academic landscape of postmodernity – we might question its usefulness as an explanatory category.

There are a few fundamental problems with the concept as a critical category:

1. 'The ship of Theseus'

Over time identity has accommodated so many changes that rather like the Theseus' paradox (or even more aptly the (John) Locke's socks paradox, which refers to socks with holes being patched until there are more patches than sock) the question remains as to whether an object that has had all its component parts replaced remains fundamentally the same object. A concept, like identity, which was initially invoked to represent an entity that comes out of group membership with given qualities, has been transformed to accommodate an ever-changing number of entities and memberships, contextualized and localized. If that is so, we may wonder, what is left of the notion of 'identity' except for an essentialist legacy?

2. Essentialist connotations

Further, the concept of identity reifies categorical and essential thinking even as it concedes that we have many identities and that identities are in a process of change. The very term may enhance (imaginary) monolithic notions. As the exhibition 'A concise dictionary of dress' so beautifully illustrated, the very act of cataloguing, archiving, and defining is at the same time 'fixing'. It is similar to the way we think of the act of capturing a movement (by filming or painting it) which freeze-frames and solidifies a single moment in what is, in reality, a process of continuous change. In order to maintain a critical discourse it may be better to replace the notion of identity (with its essentialist legacy) with concepts that refer to ongoing processes instead of entities. While in metaphysics, the term 'essentialism' originally implies the belief that an object has a certain quality by virtue of which it is what it is; in contemporary critical discourse the term is used more loosely to imply, most commonly, an unwarranted generalization about identity.

Even the metaphor that is required to engage in matters of identity needs to be rethought.

3. Poorly defined concept

Identity is one of those polysemic concepts evidencing a conceptual confusion between identity as process, as entity, as experience, as structure, as discourse and as content. In a similar way as instinct theory, which reduced the complexity of motivation of human behaviour to a catalogue of instincts, lost its explanatory power, so identity theory is risking becoming so many things to so many people and thus losing its purpose and distinctiveness.

4. Reifying 'difference'

However much we think we have left categorical, stereotypical and binary thinking behind, there are many signs both in popular and in scholarly culture that the polarizing notion of self and Other is here to stay. On the one hand a critical use of the concept needs to problematize its assumptions and challenge its claims about the relations between 'identity/difference', and question in whose interest it is to maintain those divisions, and their impact in motivating and shaping the contours of thinking and 'doing', both in the global fashion market and in the sartorial behaviour of people around the world. In the field of fashion one notices the absence of a critical interrogation of the concept of 'difference' expressed in popular culture: in advice columns about the best (and worst) way to dress for certain occasions, in style guides and manuals for certain body types, sizes and occasions; in accepting uncritically the polarity between the standard figure of fashion and the super-size figure of 'most women'; even by promoting the idea of 'style wars' between political wives or female politicians that enact symbolically the political agenda of national conflicts.

From identity to phatic community

I recently came across Annette Jorgensen's research of emotion markers in teenage language in several countries. Invoking Malinowski's notion of *phatic function* she observed that teenage talk is first and foremost a phatic activity due to its social nature. Phatic talk, like the speech act, is one which is meta-linguistic: more than a particular content or 'story' it conveys emotion and connectedness: maintaining contact, communion and solidarity, creating a strong bonding effect, expressing affection. Despite being a verbal medium of communication, affective talk, especially talk that conveys emotion through evocative discourse markers, is a good analogy to non-verbal behaviour that uses a visual medium. Both convey denotative information directly and connotative information indirectly.

There is further analogy between the nature of 'identity communities' that can be theorized around dress, and phatic communities that are produced by teenage talk. Both are partial (referring to some aspects not the totality of the person), temporary, 'becoming' and specific. I want to propose to replace the concept of identity, which evokes stability and an essentializing quality, with the concept of *phatic community*, which suggests a community of affect, connectedness, and transience. A phatic community is not the same as a 'language community' or a 'discursive community', not even a 'style community'; instead it shares features with *global online communities* of interest *of strangers* and with *local location-based communities* of *familiars*. The metaphor of such phatic collectivity I have in mind is that of the traditional *town square* or the *contemporary retail space,* which are increasingly taking on this function (the shopping mall or the concept store). Such commercial spaces turn into spaces of connectedness and conviviality. The advantage of using a 'location' rather than an imaginary construction as a focus of connectedness is that it captures the dual contemporary social trend towards both globalization and localization. Maffesoli refers to this trend as 'tribalism', while Seth Godin's more recent best-seller, *Tribes: We need you to lead us*, refers to the need to belong which is expressed in setting up or joining 'interest communities'. Online media, from blogging to social networking, facilitates this development, which Godin identifies as the new form of marketing.

The dual global/local trend has in turn influenced retail strategies towards the development of large spaces where non-consumption activities can take place, where 'experience', not necessarily the utility of consumption, is enhanced. The Milan-based research trend agency Future Concept Lab characterized this emerging trend in the following manner:

> The retail industry has rapidly become a fascinating and compelling field of knowledge that does not only involve people at a commercial level but also at a *relational and at an emotional* one. What it appears is that what people would like to 'experience' in the point of sale is much less defined and predictable that what is was just few years ago. An engagement which is delicate/subtle and spontaneous, but also flexible and based on shared values and reciprocity. Shops are no longer to be designed as points of sale only. They have increasingly become places where people expect to find some sort of connection or *dis*-connection with different worlds, in a way that is intimately intertwined with the 'momentous experience' people enjoy whilst they shop (mood, personal feelings, time availability etc). For this reason, the point of sale has shifted from being the last to becoming the first area of commerce to be strategically designed in order to convey the identity of a brand. Retail is therefore the platform on which producers and consumers meet and, like in traditional market, 'talk to each other'.
>
> (Retail seminar. The Real Trends, 22 November 2007)

CSFB 1 (2) pp. 161–171 Intellect Limited 2010

Critical Studies in Fashion and Beauty
Volume 1 Number 2

© 2010 Intellect Ltd Article. English language. doi: 10.1386/csfb.1.2.161_1

JOANNE FINKELSTEIN
University of Greenwich

Fashioned identity and the unreliable image

Abstract

High street fashion is an important industry in economic as well as aesthetic and cultural terms. Fashions not only provide a social language based on easily recognized, high-circulating items but they also generate massive wealth. These visual icons and images globalize human experience to a significant extent while, at the same time, remaining problematic to read. For example, how well-recognized and globally accepted are the meanings around images of a full red-lipsticked mouth, an unbuttoned pristine business shirt, or spiked multi-coloured hair? The history of the visual suggests that every image has multiple readings; there is no essence to the image, no limits to its commentary, no reassuring boundaries restricting its suggestions. The image is ubiquitous, problematic and enduringly pleasurable, even as its meanings are tantalizingly concealed. A fascinating example is explored in this article of the ethno-methodological folly of the late 1960s, when a hormone pill-popping young man convinced a myopic medical team to undertake the desired surgical reassignment of his gender. The con was affected on the basis of a skilful and smooth gender-bending performance that rested on the persuasiveness of the unreliable image.

Keywords

image
identity
appearances
deception

Valentino: the Last Emperor (Tyrnauer 2008) and *September Issue* (Cutler 2009) are two recently released documentary films that take the audience behind the scenes into the glamorous world of haute couture. Each focus on charismatic figures – Valentino Garavani of the Valentino fashion house and Anna Wintour, Editor-in-Chief of American *Vogue* magazine. Each individual occupies Olympian status in the fashion world: Anna Wintour has propelled *Vogue* to a circulation of more than a million copies per edition and garnered advertising revenue of tens of millions of dollars for Condé Nast. The September issue of the magazine is renown for its size – more than 800 pages in this 2008 edition – and for its far-reaching influence in shaping the fashion aesthetics for the next season, if not the next era. Valentino, in contrast, is less the entrepreneur and more the artist-creator who has shaped classical fashions for three decades and become synonymous with the establishment. The roll call of celebrities who appear in his documentary include Anna Wintour, Diane von Fürstenberg, Giorgio Armani, Karl Lagerfeld and Donatella Versace. Valentino understands his own importance: in the film he is asked what follows after him, how can he be replaced, and his reply is a biblical reference to extinction – 'After me, the flood' (Tyrnauer 2008). The presence of these two films on the global circuit, each with a similar focus to explore the mystique of fashion glamour, reinforces the view that fashion continues to be a central topic, and the images it promulgates remain a conspicuous problem.

The world of fashion resembles the entertainment industry in many ways. It has its legendary stars – from Charles Worth, Coco Chanel, Christian Dior, Louis Vuitton to Vivienne Westwood, Paul Smith and Issey Miyake – just as Hollywood has its great actors and directors. Behind this celebrated facade there are intricate links to industries that reach across the globe. The fashion industries, like other manufacturing industries, have an elaborate chain of suppliers that draw together local fabric makers from, say, the highlands of Scotland to the southern regions of India. Chanel's braided trim that outlines the famous jacket is still made by hand by the aged Madame Pouzieux on an elaborate loom that defies modernization.[1] There is, in short, a submerged underworld of manufacture, engineering and innovation that underlies the high street fashions, making these industries significant in economic as well as aesthetic and cultural terms, although not always in expected ways. The clothes of the haute couture runway, for instance, translate into huge perfume sales – the most lucrative aspect of all designer merchandise. Fashion continues to be a sociological phenomenon; it is an interesting community that talks to itself, an industry that generates massive wealth, and a spectacle that millions of people observe. The questions for me about this industry are not about what fashion does, but how it does it at all.

Some images are so insinuated into public consciousness that they seem factual and not symbolic: the strange gait of ultra-thin models who strut the runway; the stiletto-heel shoe; the theatrical cosmetic make-up that transforms the fashionista's face; the signature logo of intertwined initials

1. House of Chanel, www.bbc.co. uk/bbcfour/ documentaries/ storyville/chanel-episodes.shtml

and stylish script used variously by Dior, Vuitton, Westwood, Coca-Cola and McDonald's. These icons and images are social texts; they speak. Yet behind this easy elision is a long historical training through various styles in art, from Renaissance experiments in perspective to the postmodern surface. The privileged image is a communication system but, at the same time, its potency makes it problematic. In the first quarter of the twentieth century, the surrealists played with new forms of drawing and image-making; they used automatic drawing as a direct expression of the human unconscious. In his *Manifesto* (1924) Andre Breton argued that such methods could visually expose the mind. Even if the visual appeared as a squiggle, as if from Pitman's stenography, still the surrealists argued, it was a communicative sign, a social text. For them, the visual was loquacious, and even when it could not be readily interpreted; it nonetheless held an inner truth – whatever that may be. The surrealists, Dadaists, impressionists, expressionists and so on, introduced the possibilities of multiple readings of the image that emerge from the edge, at an angle, from below or above, with irony, humour, absurdity and anger.

Following the efflorescence of art, the visual has been recognized as a narrative form that simultaneously conveys various meanings, distortions, exaggerations and deformities. There is no essence to the image, no limitation to its commentary, no reassuring boundaries restricting its suggestions. The image is ubiquitous, problematic and enduringly pleasurable. Oscar Wilde stated 'it is only shallow people who do not judge by appearances. The true mystery of the world is the visible, not the invisible' (Wilde [1890] 1973: 32). This quip alerts us to how we read the obvious. The visible, of course, means more than everyday cultural categories of local history and culture made flesh, say, with gender, race and age. The visible that Wilde problematizes is how readily we read the invisible from the visible, how we see character and moral inscriptions in the cut of cloth and shape of the face. Richard Sennett (1976) describes how the stylized and fashioned body is used to influence the opinions of others. He described how the Victorians were highly conscious of the number of buttons on a coat sleeve, the quality of leather used in gloves, and the colour of the cotton shirt collar, as they demonstrated the social class and rank of those casually encountered in the public domain.

The fashionable look

Fashion, entertainment and high street consumption impact on our everyday lives by emphasizing the importance of physical appearance. Certain body styles become signifiers of character and define femininity, masculinity and beauty for each new audience and generation. Key features of the body are transformed into iconic symbols of identity. Such categorization was once the prerogative of the legal-medical professions. The Italian criminologist, Cesare Lombroso (1835–1909), famously used the size of human ears to indicate criminal potential. Now the entertainment industries have that power. In the animated version of Lara Croft, Tomb Raider, the size of Lara's breasts noticeably

2. See Four Humours: http://en.wikiversity. org/wiki/Personality/ Types.

increases when she is acting as the masculine avenger serving the call of justice. As her actions become more brutally aggressive, her enlarged breasts reassure the audience that this fighting machine is still a woman.

Appearance and presentation have welded interpretations of character onto the visible body. 'People don't always look like they look,' writes Graham Swift in the novel *The Light of Day* (2003: 57). This is the lamentable conclusion reached by the private detective who has been seduced and ruined by a mysterious beautiful woman. He learns too late that appearances can be deceptive, and that the woman he fell in love with was not all she appeared to be. This narrative line has been a successful device in western literature; Shakespeare used it repeatedly in the comedies – *Midsummer Night's Dream, Romeo and Juliet, Much Ado about Nothing* – as did Robert Louis Stevenson in *Dr Jekyll and Mr Hyde*, Oscar Wilde in *The Portrait of Dorian Gray*, and Patricia Highsmith in the Tom Ripley novels. The idea that human character is evident in appearance has persisted through western culture, despite its sometimes ludicrous and dangerous implications. From Aristotle to Paul Ekman, attempts have been made to systematize physical appearances as ciphers to character and human will, and with every attempt there have been persuasive rebuttals. Nonetheless the association of physiognomy with temperament (as illustrated in the well-known images of the melancholic, phlegmatic and choleric individual[2] continues to carry acceptable meanings.

The history of portraiture adds to the evocative association of appearance with human character. At first, a portrait might appear to be a translation between life and reproduction. Before the technology of the camera, the skilled hand of the painter or sculptor showed the subject as realistically as possible, bequeathing to the viewer an insight into another's life and times. The verisimilitude of the early portrait is assumed to be reliable. Thus, the fifteenth-century portrait of an *Old Man with a Young Boy* by Domenico Ghirlandaio (*c*.1490 Louvre, Paris) shows a vivid skin defect discolouring the old man's forehead and flowing into disfiguring lumps on his nose. The young boy, in contrast, has pale soft skin. The portrait appears to capture a tender family moment: the grandfather embracing his heir. The blemishes of age and disease are not disguised. Thus the classical portrait offers the viewer a trustworthy reflection. At the same time, it is more than a realistic representation of the subject; it is also a commentary on age and youth, beauty and affection.

In the case of Albrecht Durer' s *Self Portrait with Gloves* (1498 Prado, Madrid) and the *Self Portrait* (1500 Pinakothek, Munich) the realism has another purpose. Commentators on Durer's *Self-Portrait* describe the composition of the picture – the steady full-frontal gaze, the squared shoulders, luxuriant mass of hair and the transecting beard – as a figuring of the artist's triangular trademark signature A. The self-portrait is thus an advertisement: Durer painted himself in this way in order to promote his profession. Five hundred years later, we can see the portrait was not intended to be

3. See Magritte: http://
onesurrealistaday.
com/post/146305933/
the-pretre-marie-the-
married-priest-by-rene.

hung on the walls of the family home, but to be displayed and admired by potential clients, as a commercial promotion of Durer's talents. Other portraitists such as Rembrandt use painting differently, not as a means of advertisement but to make comments, say, on mortality, honour and human frailty. Rembrandt produced more than eighty self-portraits over a period of forty-odd years and noted in them his own physiognomic changes, not only as a reflection of life's ravages but as a record of the enduring nature of his character. While the body changed, becoming aged and mottled, the inner personality remained as powerful and purposive as ever. The painted changes to his physical shell were defiantly not a reflection of any diminution of the personality that illuminated the life.

The capacity of the portrait to comment, and the viewer's capacity to read more from the image, means it is not and perhaps never was a reliable reflection of reality. Guiseppe Arcimboldo (1527–1593), the innovative painter who used images of animals, fish and vegetation to compose portraits, used the face to make satiric and witty comments on character and social status. He preceded the surrealists in his use of illusionary compositions that nonetheless effectively revealed well-understood personality or character traits. Similarly, René Magritte was fascinated by paradoxical depictions. His image of two identical apples each wearing a face mask (covering up the eyes as if the fruits were human heads) illustrates the point. This was originally produced in the 1940s for the cover of a fashion magazine. At first, the image seems frivolous, just another visual joke but, then, like his other teasing image, *Ceci n'est pas une pipe*, it provokes doubt – what is being concealed by the mask? What is revealed? Do appearances lie? Does the mask suggest distinctions that are being hidden, or similarities that need to be disguised?[3]

We live in an era of dense visuality where images are readily and quickly reproduced and distributed globally. The ubiquitous camera shows us what is important, and we have learned to accept its viewpoint, and to rely on the visual to explain the connections between what we see and understand to be true. As the visual image has proliferated, its value has increased. The brand images of consumer goods and the logos of international companies now function as endorsements of the quality of the product itself. The Nike 'whoosh', McDonald's golden arches, the Dior initials, and Ferrari red are shortcut claims of quality, identity and status. What we see is what we get: thus the visual is elevated and comes to dominate daily life; we believe what we see, and vision appears to be the most discriminating and trustworthy of the senses (Jay 1993: 50).

However, at the same time that the scopic regime has gained in value, it has also been vigorously challenged, principally by the creation of visual products that have no referents in the real world. The Magritte painting of the two masked apples is a case in point. The surrealist, cubist and Dada artists were highly successful at separating the image from the world by creating objects and visions that exceeded reality. Similarly, Hollywood movies and the advertising industries have also created hyper-realities, but unlike the avant-garde artists, they are not concerned with warning the viewer (*caveat emptor*) of the perfidy of the image. What we see is what we see, unmodified by explicit rules of how to look. As a consequence, we could be living in an illusory world as the surrealists suggest; we could be inhabiting a hyperbolic spiral where sensory perceptions constantly infuse one another in a whirl of idiosyncratic private meanings that, in turn, make every social exchange highly ambiguous. If this were the case, would it mean that the visual may be the most ubiquitous but also the least reliable of our languages?

Doubt and dissemblance

In 1694, John Locke posed questions about the reliability of the supposedly self-evident by asking if he was the same person today as yesterday and what, if any, guarantees could convince us of an answer. If our thoughts and actions are constantly interrupted by different states of mind – tiredness, drunkenness, euphoria, stress, forgetfulness – then would it not be possible to say that even though I may appear to be the same person, I am not? I might, as Locke suggested, have several identities and be different by day or night. Such an idea resonates in various popular forms; *Dr Jekyll and Mr Hyde* for instance plays out the possibility of harbouring opposed desires within the same body. Like Jekyll we do regularly speak of ourselves as having multiple facets, some more dominant than others. Am I the same person when I am in love, or drunk, or feel under threat? Stanley Milgrim's celebrated psychological experiments reveal the ease with which individuals can be directed to act 'out-of-character' and these experiments have been widely cited to illustrate how people become alien to themselves. The same idea reverberates through popular reality television programmes such as *Big Brother, Extreme Makeover,* and *Survivor,* in which individuals test themselves in uncommon situations and find they are capable of acting in uncharacteristic ways. Patricia Highsmith explores this in her popular Tom Ripley novels, as does Bret Easton Ellis in *American Psycho* where the Wall Street financier, Patrick Bateman, transforms himself after office hours into a serial killer.

How do we manage to live coherently in a visually dense culture when the image itself is chimerical? How do we act in circumstances where we know that appearances can be deceptive? We are, after all, good actors, trained through impression management to convince others of what we want. Look at me in a smart Savile Row pinstriped suit and think of me as a trustworthy professional; look at me in my Tod's stilettos and think of me as sexually desirable; look at me in my new sports car and think of me as debonair and fun-loving. Each day involves a series of visual performances where I can, as I wish, mask an identity or produce an identity with the use of a mask.

Dror Wahrman (2004: 194–5) reports on the 1740 memoirs of Martin Scriblerus as an instance where appearances were amusingly misleading. In the first half of the eighteenth-century, the Scriblerus Club, which included Jonathan Swift and Alexander Pope, produced a satirical document recounting the misfortunes of the hero, Martin Scriblerus, who was in love with one half of a pair of

Siamese twins conjoined at the sexual organs. As the romance developed and love became marriage, Martin finds himself subsequently accused of rape and incest by the angry other half of the twin. What point did the Scriblerus Club wish to make with this hypothetical? Is Martin's new wife one person or two? Is he married to one person with two bodies (in part) or two different people encased in one unusual body?

Hollywood films have long used this idea to great effect; disguised, confused and misleading appearances are the narrative devices driving *Mr and Mrs Smith* (Dir. Doug Liman 2005*), True Lies* (Dir. James Cameron 1994*), Mrs Doubtfire* (Dir. Chris Columbus 1993), and *Some Like It Hot* (Dir. Billy Wilder 1959). In these films the respectable are not as they appear, instead they are spies, embezzlers, soldiers of fortune, con artists or worse. The message is that appearances are better thought of as hieroglyphics that need to be deciphered. What we see is not a mirror reflection of reality but a surface that is itself unreliable. In such films, characters transform themselves with a change of clothes, a fake moustache, a new set of friends. The world according to *My Fair Lady* (Dir. George Cukor 1964) means we can dress for success and be royalty for a night.

Yet seeing the obvious is not always easy, as Shakespeare suggested in *A Midsummer Night's Dream, The Merchant of Venice* and *Much Ado About Nothing*. The transfer between what is presented and what we perceive (between what is intended and what we understand) is not unambiguous. Our engagement with the visual, with what is presented to us, is more like a rapid and continual series of intersections, collisions and switching points. Ideas and images energetically circulate and we juggle to understand what is being said. Stories like *The Picture of Dorian Grey, Tarzan-Lord Greystoke,* and *Affinity* demonstrate the value of dissemblance. These narratives support the view that dissemblance and concealment create attractive opportunities to live in two or more worlds at the same time.

The image

Magritte's painting of the masked apples is playful and ludicrous; it summarizes the surrealist injunction that the 'world is out of joint', that it does not make sense. We know enough about spin, conspiracy and advertising to concur with the surrealist view. The entertainment industries thrive on the same ideas; appearances matter but not always in predictable ways. Popular television programmes have developed a successful formula for playing with appearances: *The Jerry Springer Show, Judge Judy, The Apprentice,* and *Big Brother* all make use of unreliable appearances as a form of entertainment. They emphasize the importance of the obvious and instruct the viewer in the multiple readings of what appears to be self-evident but, at the same time, they show, often through *Schadenfreude*, that normal social behaviour is highly calculative and often hard to predict. The message that the visible is not obvious and that the surface appearance is misleading is constantly proffered but simultaneously undercut and resisted.

Kant observed, 'the more civilized men become, the more they become actors' (Hundert 1997: 81). Developing such a double consciousness is the first step toward civility, to understanding that daily life requires the management of play-acting, dissemblance and invention. As social beings we have learned the value of a good performance, of being able to switch between the background and foreground, between authoring the situation and being a fantasy of the other's invention. At the same time, this cultural emphasis on appearances has elevated the performative nature of everyday exchange into a narrative through which an identity and personality are realized. Sculpting appearance with fashionable clothing or cosmetic surgery is now a normalized practice. Yet forty years ago, from the annals of American social psychology, there is a remarkable case of mistaken identity that further illuminates the ambiguity that surrounds the fashioning of appearances.

Agnes

In November 1958, a young woman was referred to Dr Robert Stoller at the Department of Psychiatry of the University of California, Los Angeles who was working on intersexed individuals, some of whom had severe anatomical irregularities. Agnes arrived at the clinic seeking surgical modification having been directed by her own physician to seek specialist assistance.

Agnes was nineteen years of age at the time. She maintained she had been raised as a boy even though she knew she was a girl. Agnes is described as having attractive feminine proportions, 38-25-38. She had a smooth facial complexion and was softly spoken. She wore tight sweaters that flattered her narrow shoulders and waist, and emphasized her breasts. She appeared very feminine except that she also had a fully developed penis and scrotum (Garfinkel 1967: 120–7). Agnes was seeking surgical intervention to remedy this apparent quirk of nature. After a period of extended consultation with various experts at UCLA, Agnes was diagnosed as suffering an endocrine abnormality and the prognosis was a castration operation. The surgery was performed in March 1959, the penis and testes were amputated and an artificial vagina and labia were constructed. It took less than six months for this process, from initial consultation to final surgery.

The medical professionals involved with Agnes were rightly concerned about their diagnosis prior to performing irreversible surgery. A great deal of conversation and formal interviewing had taken place with her to ensure this was a genuine case of sexual abnormality. Throughout the consultation period, Agnes was insistent that her body was a mistake; she was outside the norms for reasons beyond her control and it was the responsibility of medical science to alleviate her distress and give her a legitimate sexual status and identity.

Many years after receiving sex reassignment surgery, Agnes revealed to her physicians and consultant psychologists that she had deliberately duped them. She was born a boy, she knew she was a boy: she did not have a pathological endocrine imbalance. She had stolen her mother's hormone tablets over a long period of time and taken them to effect the physical changes in her appearance. She knew she needed to appear to have a rare abnormality or pathology in order to secure what she wanted, namely, gender reassignment. She knew how to invent herself, how to perform as a coy, sexually innocent, fun-loving, passive, receptive 'young thing' that every girl should be. She favoured feminine tasks: she elicited jealousy from other girls when boys were on the scene. She was completely dismissive of her sex organs and acted as if her penis was 'anaesthetized' (Garfinkel 1967: 123–30). Agnes, it turned out, was highly knowledgeable about the rules of self-invention and was able to deliver a thoroughly convincing performance that was sustained over many months in the face of probing professional examination. Agnes knew she was not as she outwardly appeared, but she also knew that most people trusted what they saw, and that all she needed was to perform successfully as a girl to be regarded as a girl.

Robert Stoller described the moment (October 1966) when Agnes confessed to him that she was not his famous case of rare testicular feminization syndrome as a well-constructed drama:

> … after having kept it from me for eight years, with the greatest casualness, in mid-sentence, and without giving the slightest warning it was coming, she revealed that she had never had a biological defect that had feminized her but that she had been taking estrogens since age 12.
>
> (Garfinkel 1967: 287–288)

Stoller was amazed but also amused that 'she could have pulled off this coup with such skill' (Garfinkel 1967: 287–288).

Such a performance might now be unlikely to succeed. Too much material is readily available on the lives of individuals who have successfully 'passed' and Garfinkel, Stoller and associates would be expected to know more about the field, and as a result be less vulnerable to a good performance (Garber 1992; Morris 1974; Smith-Rosenberg 1985).

In retrospect, contemporary analysts make the work of Garfinkel and Stoller seem quaint and naïve. Nonetheless, the episode is valuable for illustrating how difficult it can be to denaturalize the social world, to bring out its embedded assumptions and reveal the dominance of the visual. Agnes's success in deceiving her interlocutors reinforces the view that appearances are paramount and that social realities are often a tangle of perceptions and fleeting assessments. The variability of eyewitness reports of events (the Rashomon effect) further adds to the doubts we must recognize in constructing a sense of the world from the visual.

After all, seeing is believing; if looks can deceive and everyday conventions are sustained by skilful performances, what is it we think we know? We may understand there is no outside world that corresponds to the inner world of desire: we may know the value of a good costume, a measured performance, a well-rehearsed routine, and we may accept that the surface is there to be styled at our discretion. Yet, there is a reluctance to accept it. Even as we apply the tools of fabrication to go about our daily business, we are haunted by the anonymity that such self-invention delivers. John Banville sums up the puzzle in his novel about Anthony Blunt, one of the infamous Cambridge spies and the highly regarded Keeper of the Queen's art collection, '…. nothing, absolutely nothing is as it seems' (Banville 1997: 144). Blunt had appeared to be part of the English aristocracy for decades while all the time he was spying for Russia. He appeared so typical of his class that it was unimaginable that he could have been anyone else. Yet he was, and Banville's explanation is that he knew the importance of appearances, he understood how the obvious could be false, a fake, and this allowed him to live multiple lives.

At the end of these considerations we are left with the question of whether the emperors of fashion, like the master of disguise Anthony Blunt, know that appearances are unreliable. Fashions are displays: they are surfaces on which are written declarations of beauty, creative ingenuity and aesthetics. Fashions seek to stand outside the banal realm of the material everyday, to address the potential of the human form to look and act differently, to aspire to an as yet undefined desire. In this striving for something not yet realized, it is reasonable to question whether the emphasis that fashion brings to the surface is a form of resistance to a disciplining of the human form, or a clever mechanism of it. Fashions are expressions of some version of the world; they exist as living images of a viewpoint, an angle, and one take on an idea. As such, they join the rich history of the portrait as a tool for grasping the infinitely diverse ways in which we can conceptualize ourselves, play with how we might appear to others, and shape the social world in which we want to live.

References

Banville, J. (1997), *The Untouchable*, London: Picador.

Breton, A. (1924), *The Surrealist Manifesto*, http://www.seaboarcreations.com/sindex/manifestbreton. htm and www.surrealist.revolution@skymail.fr. Accessed 13 June 2010.

Cutler, R. J. (2009), *September Issue*, USA: A&E Indie Films.

Ekman, P. (1972), *Emotion in the Human Face*, London: Elsevier, see also Four Humours: http:// en.wikiversity.org/wiki/Personality/Types. Accessed 13 June 2010.

Garfinkel, H. (1967), *Studies in Ethnomethology*, New Jersey, Prentice Hall.

Hundert, E. J. (1997), 'The European Enlightenment and the History of the Self', in Roy Porter (ed.), *Rewriting the Self*, London: Routledge, pp. 72–83.

Jay, M. (1993), *Downcast Eyes: The Denigration of Vision in Twentieth Century French Thought*, Berkeley: University of California Press.

Magritte, R. http://onesurrealistaday.com/post/146305933/the-pretre-marie-the-married-priest-by-rene. Accessed 13 June 2010.

Prigent, Loic (2005), *The House of Chanel*, France, www.bbc.co.uk/bbcfour/documentaries/storyville/chanel-episodes.shtml. Accessed 13 June 2010.

Sennett, R. (1976), *The Fall of Public Man*, Cambridge: CUP.

Sharpe, K. and Zwicker, S. N. (eds) (2008), *Writing Lives: Biography and Textuality, Identity and Representation in Early Modern England*, Oxford: Oxford University Press.

Swift, G. (2003), *The Light of Day*, UK: Penguin.

Tyrnauer, M. (2008), *Valentino: The Last Emperor*, USA: Acolyte Films.

Wahrman, D. (2004), *The Making of the Modern Self: Identity and Culture in Eighteenth-Century England*, New Haven: Yale University Press.

Wilde, O. ([1890] 1973), *The Portrait of Dorian Gray*, Harmondsworth: Penguin.

Suggested citation

Finkelstein, J. (2010), 'Fashioned identity and the unreliable image', *Critical Studies in Fashion and Beauty* 1: 2, pp. 161–171, doi: 10.1386/csfb.1.2.161_1

Contributor details

Joanne Finkelstein is a sociologist trained in the 'Chicago School'. She has published six monographs including *Dining Out: a sociology of modern manners* (1989, Polity, Oxford); *The Fashioned Self* (1991, Polity, Oxford); *After a Fashion* (1994, Melbourne University Press); *The Sociological Bent: a study of metro culture* (2005, Thomson, Sydney); and *The Art of Self Invention* (2007, IB Tauris, London). She has undertaken research consultancies in the food, science, communications and insurance industries. She is currently Executive Dean of Humanities and Social Sciences at the University Greenwich.

Contact: School of Humanities and Social Sciences, King William Court, University of Greenwich, London, SE10 9LS.
E-mail: j.finkelstein@gre.ac.uk

CSFB 1 (2) pp. 173–180 Intellect Limited 2010

Critical Studies in Fashion and Beauty
Volume 1 Number 2

© 2010 Intellect Ltd Article. English language. doi: 10.1386/csfb.1.2.173_1

MICHAEL R. SOLOMON
Saint Joseph's University, USA, and Manchester School of Business, UK

Digital identity management: Old wine in new bottles?

Keywords

self-concept
body image
virtual worlds
avatars
impression
    management
digital identity

Abstract

Fashion and identity are inextricably linked. Consumers throughout the ages have strategically deployed apparel and other self-expressive products to signal real and aspirational personas and to pursue hedonic exploration and fantasy. Often these transformations are entrusted to aesthetic professionals such as clothing designers, cosmeticians and photographers.

Today, new technological platforms enable even the amateur to create a myriad of identities as she navigates the evolving virtual environment some call The Metaverse. *But this is by no means a one-way journey; in some cases cyber-spatial experiences also impact on real-world identity. This article explores the theoretical and practical ramifications of digital identity management as consumers – in the form of avatar representations – make the passage from the physical world to the virtual, and back again.*

A French legislator is raising quite a ruckus with her efforts to require fashion photos to carry a label that discloses if the models' images have been retouched. She argues that these digital distortions create false – and unattainable – expectations of beauty for girls; including her two daughters (Erlanger 2009). Her campaign is laudable, if a bit naïve (especially for a sophisticated Parisienne). And, she is not alone: the Liberal Democrats in the UK endorsed a similar labelling system as part of the party's official platform (Prince 2009). In Israel the Knesset is set to endorse a proposed bill that would force advertisers to issue a notice on each advertisement where models dimensions have been digitally altered (Lis 2010).

Let's put aside the rebuttal by industry insiders that this practice is so pervasive that such a law is highly impractical. Let's also sidestep the more abstract philosophical arguments about how we know that *anything* is real.

For our purposes, the debate more generally highlights our fundamental tendency to believe that what we see in the media is 'real' unless we are otherwise advised – and likewise our tendency to put more stock in what we *see* than in what we *know* (Benjamin [1936] 1973). The true reality: ignorance is bliss. Most of us are quite gullible and content to be so. We willingly 'suspend disbelief' any time we attend a live theatre production or watch a television sitcom. During these performances we enter into an unwritten compact with the show's creators to assume that what we see is really happening. Even the current craze for 'reality shows' belies the fact that there is very little that is real about them. Contestants are carefully screened, often coached, and sometimes willing to say or do whatever it takes to stand in the media spotlight (as President Obama's Secret Service recently learned after the embarrassing state dinner gatecrashing fiasco). And the shows' producers are willing conspirators in this illusion – specialists spray-paint the bodies of entrants on the American hit 'Dancing with the Stars' to deepen tans and even create the illusion of muscles where none really exist (Chozick 2009).

But wait – this is nothing new. Performances and marketing communications alike need to 'sell' to the receiver to achieve their objectives. Sophisticated digital technologies that remove cellulite or add higher cheekbones simply make the sales job a bit easier. Editing, whether roughshod or subtle, has been a fact of life for eons. As we will see, the real game-changers are new techniques that allow each of us to completely modify our appearance or even to invent a totally new visual identity as we interact with others in virtual realities. Digital identity management is the new order of the day.

You do not need to be a supermodel to 'manage' the way you appear to others. In fact we all do it every day. If we did not, we would have no need for mirrors. Fifty years ago, the sociologist Erving Goffman, among others, wrote extensively about the elaborate process of 'impression management'. Since that time, volumes of social psychological studies have empirically documented the preening process and the huge impact physical appearance exerts on our judgments of those around us ('beauty is only skin deep, but ugly is to the bone').

Furthermore, we know quite well that our perceptions of how we appear to others also profoundly influence feelings of *self-worth*. In this sense, the French legislator's concerns are well-placed: her daughters may well experience feelings of inadequacy when they see hundreds of images of impossibly beautiful women paraded in front of them week after week. Way back in 1902, the sociologist Charles Horton Cooley wrote about the *looking-glass self* that operates as a sort of psychological sonar: we take readings of our own identity when we 'bounce' signals off others and try to project their impression of us (Cooley 1902). Like the distorted mirrors in a fun-house, our appraisal of *who* we are depends on whose (imagined) perspectives we take. We also calibrate these sonar readings to the external standards we adopt: young women alter their perceptions of their own body shapes and sizes after they watch as little as thirty minutes of TV programming (Richins: 1991; Martin and Kennedy 1993).

But these standards have always been idealized. Throughout history, cultural elites and rulers have meticulously edited the impression they communicated to their peers and followers. It is hard to imagine that Julius Caesar, George Washington, or the British royal family (past and present) did not have strong opinions about which of their images would adorn currency or portraiture and the details that might appear (most likely with some embellishment) in official biographies. A prominent example of this strategic depiction is the famous Armada portrait of Britain's Queen Elizabeth I that George Gower painted in 1590. The queen skillfully and deliberately designed the portrait as a form of propaganda to stress the qualities she desired – including symbols she appropriated from biblical and mythological sources, such as pearls to depict virginity (Hill 2007). Today, of course, a massive public relations machine carefully crafts the images of modern royalty – we call these people celebrities.

Every society anoints certain men and women as aesthetic ideals, and motivates emulation of these ideals as it rewards attractive people (however defined) and makes life a bit more difficult for the rest of us. While there is legitimate cause for concern, the current discourse about the demoralizing impact of digitally altered photography is old wine in new bottles. Just as the victors in a war get to write its history, people with resources always get to manipulate the image they convey to others. Today they just have access to more powerful tools that enable them to do so.

However here is what *is* different now: mainstream consumers can play with the *same* tools, they too can carefully sculpt their public images. In the past only the elites had access to fashion designers or portrait artists. Today the masses purchase 'designer jeans' and luxury lipsticks. At the risk of stating the obvious, the entire cosmetics and apparel industrial complex owes its very existence to the desires of 'ordinary' consumers to manage their social identities.

Professional 'identity managers' assume many forms, from hairstylists and cosmetologists to wardrobe consultants and resume writers. In addition we have appropriated sophisticated medical techniques to pamper the well rather than heal the sick. Doctors perform nearly 860,000 cosmetic-surgery procedures in the US each year alone. In some circles nose jobs or breast implants are part of the rite-of-passage for teenage girls, and an increasing number of men opt for pectoral enlargements. The spate of popular books and seminars that encourage the eager job-seeker to regard herself as a 'personal brand' that needs to be packaged, positioned and promoted fuels the fire (mea culpa; I stress this approach in *Principles of Marketing* (Solomon, Marshall and Stuart 2009; Solomon and Richmond 2008; Peters 1999; Wilson and Blumenthal 2008; Montoya and Vendehev 2008)).

We may still need a trained surgeon to reshape a troublesome nose, but we can undertake other makeovers on our own. This is especially true when it comes to the identity we express on digital platforms. Professional editors (the bane of critics like our French legislator) have long been able to wield their airbrushes to give us advertising images of breathtakingly beautiful people who literally do not exist in the real world. Today, many techie teenagers can effortlessly produce the same results with PhotoShop. Millions of us manage – and embellish – our digital identities when we strategically populate a Facebook profile page or post a self-aggrandizing ad (perhaps with vintage photo from twenty years ago) on an online dating site. To repurpose an old joke, 'On the Internet nobody knows you're a dog.'

Many marketers do not seem to grasp the steady expansion of their customers' energies and even their very identities into online realms. Indeed, the firm line many of us draw between 'real world' and 'online' activities grows increasingly porous; the distinction will probably seem quaint to our grandchildren. Already many millions of consumers commute back and forth between their real and digital selves multiple times each day. It is unlikely that the ten million kids who visit a virtual world like *Habbo Hotel* for an hour or more each day would regard that aspect of their lives differently from the time they spend chasing each other on the playground.

Identity management is a fundamental social concern in our social and professional lives. It remains a concern no matter whether we network in an office building or at a virtual trade show, or flirt in a bar or on Facebook. The needs that relate to self-presentation in both domains yield three classes of opportunity for forward-looking companies:

1. *Offline to online*: The social media explosion means that we are what we post. Already we see a cottage industry emerging as consultants offer to customize Facebook profiles and help people generate a photo or avatar to represent their online identity. Other services, such as Reputation Defender, offer to digitally erase the inebriated photos we have already posted and now regret.

   As businesses continue to migrate their training, meeting and networking functions to virtual worlds the choice of an appropriate avatar will be more than a casual or aesthetic one. Indeed, the research firm Gartner predicts that within three years 70 per cent of businesses will maintain behaviour and dress-code policies for employees whose online avatars represent their organization. The so-called 'virtual goods' industry is booming (though still under the radar of most offline folks); in 2009 alone people who frolic in virtual worlds and MMOGs (massive multiplayer online games like *World of Warcraft*) shelled out over *$1 billion* for pixilated clothing, weapons, vehicles and furniture (Takahashi 2009). And, many entrepreneurs are migrating to virtual environments to peddle fashion goods. A consortium of 600 West End retailers in London is launching Near London, a digital version of high streets including Bond, Oxford and Regent (Gourlay 2008; near-global.com 2010). In the virtual world of *Second Life*, start-ups and established designers regularly exhibit their digital styles. Virtual London Fashion Week kicks off at the same time as the real thing and offers exhibitor space as well as runway shows (Bracken 2009).

2. *Online to offline*: Researchers are just starting to investigate how our experiences in online formats stay with us when we return to our corporeal selves. We know that when we assume an avatar identity, we transfer many of the interaction norms we use in the physical world. Just as in real life, male avatars in *Second Life* leave more space between them when they talk to other males than when they talk to virtual females, and they are less likely to maintain eye contact than are females. Work on so-called 'Proteus effects' demonstrates that the social feedback experimental subjects receive when they assume a virtual identity (such as being accepted or rejected by avatars of the opposite sex) lingers when they later interact with people in the real world. Rejection hurts, whether you receive it in an online format or as your physical self.

On a more optimistic note, the early evidence that our virtual encounters shape our 'real world' self-concepts present some promising therapeutic and marketing implications. Consider, for example, the potential to elevate the self-esteem of the thousands of disabled people who currently patronize *Second Life* gathering spots, where they can easily talk, flirt, and even dance. Or, think about the virtual branding experiences we accumulate during the course of our cyber-journeys; their lasting impact provides yet another reason to take emerging practices like 'advergaming' (where real-world products and logos are inserted into the storylines of fictionalized games) very seriously.

And, the fantasy identities people create online sometimes travel back with them: witness the growing global phenomenon of cosplay, where participants congregate at restaurants, clubs and conventions in full regalia as their avatars or other favourite characters from comic books and movies (www.cosplay.com 2010). We can expect this activity to influence fashion trends, licensing deals and perhaps the entertainment industry as social gamers and moviegoers increasingly import media characters into their daily lives. The proliferation of avatar-themed movies like *Surrogates, Tron Legacy, The Matrix* and of course the eponymous *Avatar* attests to this impact (*San Jose Mercury News* 2009).

3. *Offline merges with online*: We are about to be engulfed by a wave of *augmented reality* (AR), where a layer of virtual information embellishes the physical world. The new Layar browser that provides hybrid experiences like a real-world London city tour (where a superimposed image of the Beatles crosses Abbey Road) on your iPhone is just the tip of the iceberg (Eaton 2009). The fashion media are already salivating at the possibility of reviving the fortunes of print magazines on

the verge of extinction – *Esquire*'s December 2009 virtual reality cover was but the first salvo in the battle to champion a 3D experience for fashionistas. As these AR applications proliferate (and they will), the outmoded distinction between a real world and a virtual one will disappear. This process will bring us back full-circle to the task of identity management, regardless of whether the self we project is made of atoms or pixels.

Acknowledgements

The author thanks Professor Efrat Tseëlon for her helpful comments on the manuscript.

References

Benjamin, W. ([1936] 1973), 'The Work of Art in the Age of Mechanical Reproduction', in Hannah Arendt (ed.), *Illuminations*, London: NLB, pp. 217–242.

Bracken, J. (2009), 'Virtual London Fashion Week', *Prim Perfect: Second Life Style for Home and Garden*, 7 September, http://primperfectblog.wordpress.com/2009/09/07/virtual-london-fashion-week/. Accessed 10 March 2010.

Chozick, A. (2009), 'Rippling Muscles on TV Dance Shows Are a Pigment of Your Imagination', *The Wall Street Journal*, 23 November, http://online.wsj.com/article/SB125894440320760069.html. Accessed 10 March 2010.

Cooley, C. (1902), 'The Looking Glass Self', in *Human Nature and the Social Order*, New York: Scribner's, pp. 179–185, http://cosplay.com/. Accessed 10 March 2010. www.cosplay.com. Accessed 14 June 2010.

Eaton, K. (2009), 'Today's Vision of Tomorrow: Layar Takes Augmented Reality Everywhere', *Fast Company*, 3 December.

Erlanger, S. (2009), 'Point, Shoot, Retouch and Label?' *New York Times*, 2 December.

Gourlay, C. (2008), 'Virtual West End for Cyber Shoppers: Retailers to Offer 3-D Replicas of Top Stores', *The Times of London*, 28 December, http://business.timesonline.co.uk/tol/business/industry_sectors/retailing/article5404384.ece. Accessed 10 March 2010.

Hill, S. (2007), 'The Armada Portrait of Elizabeth I: A Perfectly Staged Tribute to the Queen', Suite101.com, 20 May, http://renaissance-art.suite101.com/article.cfm/the_armada_portrait_of_elizabeth_I. Accessed 10 March 2010.

Lis, J. (2010), ''Photoshop Law' will force advertisers to identify touched-up images', *Haaretz*, 14 June, http://www.haaretz.com/print-edition/news/photoshop-law-will-force-advertisers-to-identify-touched-up-images-1.295974 . Accessed 17 June 2010.

Martin, M. and Kennedy, P. (1993), 'Advertising and Social Comparison: Consequences for Female Preadolescents and Adolescents,' *Psychology & Marketing*, 10: 6, pp. 513–30.

Montoya, P. and Vendehev, T. (2008), *The Brand Called You: Make Your Business Stand Out in a Crowded Marketplace*, New York: McGraw-Hill. http://www.nearglobal.com/ (2010). Accessed 10 March 2010.

Peters, T. (1999), *The Brand You 50: Or: Fifty Ways to Transform Yourself from an 'Employee' into a Brand That Shouts Distinction, Commitment, and Passion!*, New York: Knopf.

Prince, R. (2009), 'Airbrushing of Photos Should be Banned, Liberal Democrats Say', *The London Telegraph*, 3 August, http://www.telegraph.co.uk/news/newstopics/politics/liberaldemocrats/5962358/Airbrushing-of-photos-should-be-banned-Liberal-Democrats-say.html. Accessed 10 March 2010.

Richins, M. (1991), 'Social Comparison and the Idealized Images of Advertising', *Journal of Consumer Research*, 18 June, pp. 71–83.

San Jose Mercury News (2009), 'Hollywood in *Second Life*', 5 October.

Solomon, M., Marshall, G. and Stuart, E. (2009), *Marketing: Real People, Real Choices* 6/e, Upper Saddle River, NJ: Prentice Hall.

Solomon, M., and Richmond, K. (2008), *Brand You for Marketing: Real People, Real Choices*, Upper Saddle River, NJ: Prentice Hall.

Takahashi, D. (2009), 'Virtual Goods Sales to Hit $1 Billion in 2009 as Social Games Pay Off Big,' *Games Beat*, 14 October, http://games.venturebeat.com/2009/10/14/virtual-goods-sales-to-hit-1-billion-in-2009-as-social-games-pay-off-big/. Accessed 10 March 2010.

Wilson, J. and Blumenthal, I. (2008), *Managing Brand You: 7 Steps to Creating Your Most Successful Self*, New York: AMACOM.

Suggested citation

Solomon, M. R. (2010), 'Digital identity management: Old wine in new bottles?', *Critical Studies in Fashion and Beauty* 1: 2, pp. 173–180, doi: 10.1386/csfb.1.2.173_1

Contributor details

Professor Solomon's primary research interests include consumer behaviour and lifestyle issues, branding strategy, the symbolic aspects of products, the psychology of fashion, marketing applications of virtual worlds and the development of visually-oriented online research methodologies. His

Michael R. Solomon

textbook, *Consumer Behavior: Buying, Having, and Being,* published by Prentice Hall, is widely used in universities throughout North America, Europe, and Australasia and is now in its ninth edition.

Contact: Department of Marketing, Haub School of Business, Saint Joseph's University, 5600 City Avenue, Philadelphia, PA 19131, USA.
E-mail: msolom01@sju.edu

CSFB 1 (2) pp. 181–202 Intellect Limited 2010

Critical Studies in Fashion and Beauty
Volume 1 Number 2
© 2010 Intellect Ltd Article. English language. doi: 10.1386/csfb.1.2.181_1

ALEXANDRA KOROTCHENKO AND LAURA HURD CLARKE
The University of British Columbia

Russian immigrant women and the negotiation of social class and feminine identity through fashion

Keywords

aging
immigration
beauty work
fashion
femininity
women

Abstract

Building on the growing body of literature that examines the consumption of fashion and the construction of identity through clothing, this article uses data from in-depth interviews with ten women aged 52 to 75 to examine Russian immigrant women's experiences of fashion. Specifically, we explore the ways in which Russian immigrant women's clothing choices and attitudes towards fashion are framed by their socialization within Russian cultural values (which privilege feminine appearance), their assimilation into Canadian culture, their resistance to Canadian views of beauty and femininity, and their feelings about their aging bodies. Our findings reveal that Russian immigrant women's doing of gender, age, social class, and immigrant status are shaped by culturally and historically situated conceptions of femininity as well as by decisions to either assimilate into North American culture or to 'other' the self as distinctively Russian.

Introduction

The socio-cultural literature has extensively theorized the production of fashion (Entwhistle 2006, Kaiser et al. 1991, Pannebacker 1997), fashion as a disciplinary mechanism (Bartky 1990, Bordo 1993) and the construction of identity through dress (Negrin 1999, Parkins 2008, Tseëlon 1992). Building on the theoretical literature, there is a growing body of research that examines women's everyday use of clothing and the effects of fashion on self-expression and self-perception (Colls 2006, Holland 2004, Klepp and Storm-Mathisen 2005, Kwon 1992, Kwon and Parham 1994, Lurie 1992, Morganroth Gullette 1999, Rudd and Lennon 2000, Trautmann et al. 2007, Tseëlon 1992). Additionally, there is increasing interest in the experiences of older women and the ways in which they navigate aging and ageist norms through clothing (Fairhurst 1998, Holland 2004, Hurd Clarke et al. 2009, Twigg 2007). This research reveals that older women's fashion choices are constrained by health issues, the desire to conceal the physical signs of aging, a lack of fashion choices for older women and narrow definitions of appropriate clothing choices in later life.

At the same time, relatively little research has studied the fashion experiences of immigrant women. As well as examining highly politicized practices such as veiling (Afshar 2008, Ahlberg et al. 2000, Ruby 2006), critical feminist discourse has explored the way fashion excludes non-white, middle-class women (McRobbie 1997) and produces difference through the cultural appropriation of 'othered' items of clothing and adornment (Puwar 2002). Largely focused on the experiences of visible minorities (Hondagneu-Sotelo 2003, Pedraza 1991), feminist scholarship has ignored white minority groups due to the apparent invisibility of their minority status and long-held understandings of whiteness as a marker of dominance and privilege (Davey et al. 2003). Researchers have suggested that Russian émigrés may have attracted little academic attention due to their rapid vocational and linguistic advancement (Chiswick 1993), their seemingly smooth transition into North American middle-class culture (Gold 1995) and their relatively low levels of political activism (Kishinevsky 2004).

In this article, we build on the extant research and investigate older Russian immigrant women's fashion experiences and choices pre- and post-immigration to Canada. Drawing on West and Zimmerman's (1987) concept of doing gender and using data from interviews with ten Russian immigrant women aged 52 to 75, we analyse how the 'interlocking categories of experience' (Anderson and Hill Collins 2001: xii) of gender, culture and age informed the women's styles of dressing. West and Zimmerman maintain that gender and femininity are accomplishments that are achieved through social interaction. Thus, we investigate how the women's cultural enactments of femininity through clothing were influenced by their socialization in Russian culture and the fiscal realities of life in the Union of Soviet Socialist Republics (USSR) as well as Canadian cultural norms and aesthetic ideals.

1. De-Stalinization refers to the time period in the 1950s and 1960s following Stalin's death, during which the Stalinist political system and cult of personality were gradually dismantled (Filtzer 2002).

Historical context

In order to fully comprehend Russian immigrant women's experiences and perceptions of fashion in North American culture, it is important to situate their clothing choices and preferences in a historical context. Prior to the collapse of the Soviet Union in 1991, Russia was a closed socialist state with limited exposure or access to western goods or media messages concerning femininity, fashion and beauty (Azhgikhina and Goscilo 1996). To reinforce its political strength and undermine the social foundations of pre-communist Russia, the Communist Party problematized Russian women's disenfranchisement within the family, labour market and society, and, beginning in the 1920s, instituted several policies that attempted to transform traditional gender relations (Ashwin 2000). These policies aimed to extend communism's influence on women by integrating them into the Russian work force and transferring their dependence from their formerly male-dominated households onto the state (Ashwin 2000).

Reflecting and bolstering the new gender order, the Communist Party valorized the unpainted face and short hair of the modestly dressed and self-effacing communist woman (Azhgikhina and Goscilo 1996). While western fashions were held in contempt for symbolizing bourgeois preoccupation with wealth and status, Russian women were compelled to wear simple, unadorned clothing that reflected the communist ideals of 'purposefulness and sanitized physical energy' (Azhgikhina and Goscilo 1996: 98). Notably, the moral meanings attached to the plain female face and body also masked the shortage of consumer goods in the newly formed Soviet state (Azhgikhina and Goscilo 1996). However, the government-dictated pressures and prohibitions only served to arouse Russian women's interest in the art of beauty, albeit in secret (Azhgikhina and Goscilo 1996).

The collapse of the Soviet Union in 1991 resulted in a reversion to the pre-communist gender order, the redefinition of work and motherhood as private responsibilities and the embracing of hyper-feminine notions of 'slim and sexy' beauty (Remennick 2007: 327, Ashwin 2000). De-Stalinization[1] and the slow introduction of western goods and media simultaneously allowed and encouraged Russian women to abandon the much-reviled communist beauty ideal of the unadorned, androgynous female body (Azhgikhina and Goscilo 1996). While the cultural acquiescence to an image of womanhood that identified femininity with fragility, beauty, overt sexuality and fashion was, in part, a rejection of the Soviet past, Kay (1997) found that Russian women additionally perceived it to be a mark of progress into a more civilized society.

At the same time, the country's subsequent social and economic instability instigated a large-scale emigration beginning in 1990 (Fassman and Munz 1994). Although research has examined Soviet immigrants' social, cultural and economic resettlement experiences (Aroian and Norris 2002, Miller and Chandler 2002, Remennick 2001, Shasha and Shron 2002, Vinokurov et al. 2000), to date, there has been relatively little research devoted to studying Russian immigrant women's beauty work practices. The few existing exceptions include the work of Kishinevsky (2004), whose study of Russian-American girls and women revealed that the longer former Soviet women had resided in the United States, the more they had internalized western beauty ideals. Similarly, Remennick (2007) found that Russian immigrant women living in the United States faced singular challenges stemming from cultural disparities in Russian and western definitions of femininity, feminine appearances and acceptance of traditional gender roles (Remennick 2007). For instance, most of the women were reluctant to soften their hyper-feminine dressing and make-up styles, and reminisced about their former lives in Russia, in which they recalled feeling more womanly and attractive. Some of the study participants also found sexual harassment policies in American workplaces to be stifling, as they were no longer complimented on their clothing, make-up and hairstyles.

Methods and sample

The data for this article is drawn from in-depth, semi-structured interviews with ten Russian immigrant women, aged 52 to 75, who were interviewed twice for a total of 19.8 interview hours. The women were asked about their beauty work regimens and clothing choices prior to and following their immigration to Canada. Although all of the participants had some knowledge of conversational English, most of the interviews were conducted in a mix of Russian and English by the first author. The interviews were later translated as they were being digitally transcribed in order to preserve the meaning and spirit of the women's narratives using the concepts of somatic and dialogic translation. Robinson defines somatic translation as 'an intuitive, gut-level sense of the "right" word or phrase' (Robinson 1991: 257) and dialogic translation as the varying, often unpredictable, interaction of the researcher/translator with the speaker and the audience.

Having immigrated to Canada between 1992 and 2004, the sample participants were diverse in terms of their ages, countries of origin, years in Canada and incomes (see Table 1). The women were relatively homogenous with respect to their educational attainment, marital status, physical ability and sexual orientation. Thus, most of the women were married and all were well-educated, able-bodied and self-identified as heterosexual. Although it is difficult to compare the Russian and Canadian education systems, all of the participants indicated that they had graduated from a post-secondary institution. Prior to immigrating, half of the women had been employed as engineers, while the other half had held various white collar jobs. At the time of the interview, three women were retired, three were unemployed, and four were currently working in professional positions.

The data was analysed using Strauss and Corbin's concepts of open and axial coding (1998). The transcribed interviews were read and re-read to produce an initial code book, which included fashion as an open code or broad analytic category. This open code was further examined to generate six axial or sub-codes, which included: 'Past and present clothing choices and habits', 'The importance

Age distribution	
50–55	3
56–60	3
61–65	1
66–70	2
71–57	1
Marital status	
Currently married	8
Divorced	2
Education	
College/University degree	10
Income	
Under $10,000	1
$10–20,000	2
$30–40,000	1
$40–50,000	3
$60,000+	2
Declined to say	1
Number of years in Canada	
5–10	3
11–16	6
17+	1
Country of origin (within the USSR)	
Russia	3
Ukraine	6
Belarus	1

Table 1: Sample characteristics (n = 10).

of fashion', 'Similarities and differences in Canadian and Russian attitudes towards fashion', 'Cost and availability of clothing in Canada and in Russia', 'Fashion and the body' and 'Familial and peer influences on fashion choices'.

Findings

Behind the Iron Curtain: Russian women and the construction of femininity through fashion

When asked to recall their fashion experiences in communist Russia, all of the women described how their clothing preferences and ideals were strongly influenced by their access to western European media images of beauty. Anna, aged 53, explained, 'There was this mentality – Europe was nearby, all the European news, magazines, television shows. And everyone wanted to imitate this. Russia has always respected foreigners and everything foreign, and has tried to emulate them.' Sofia, aged 75, spoke of the influence of foreign European films on Russian women's attitudes towards fashion:

> [Russia] was very insular, and when [women] saw pictures, or films, or magazines of foreign actresses, they thought that these women were so successful, and we wanted to be like them. And people thought that this was the way people abroad lived and that was how they dressed, so they thought, 'If I wear something similar, then I'll look so clever and rich, and all the boys will look at me.' And if you were older, then 'Everyone will tell me how beautiful I look.' And when the borders opened up, these sentiments still remained – that you had to look European, like a foreigner.

Katerina, aged 63, reflected on how watching foreign films and attempting to emulate the actresses' appearances were ways for Russian women to glimpse and enact an unknown world:

> When we watched a movie, I still remember that I was less concerned about the content […] I was mostly looking at the detail of their everyday life, because that life was closed to us […] We paid attention to small details: the furniture, the clothes, how they behaved.

All ten women recalled how the general scarcity of products in the former Soviet Union influenced their fashion choices. The women relayed particularly vivid recollections of the difficulties they had faced in acquiring clothing and how government stores were often empty and contained pricey, unattractive merchandise. Katerina had this to say: 'At our stores there was nothing. They were empty, or things were so ugly. Because mostly the budget of the whole country went to weapons in the Soviet Union, so there was nothing in the stores.' Daria, aged 70, recalled how women often wore the wrong

Figure 1: Gomel, Belarus, 1954: The first author's grandmother (centre) poses for a photograph with fellow classmates from the Gomel Pedagogical Institute.

size shoes: 'There were no shoes in the stores at all. So all Russian women, if you pay attention, their feet are all bent, because we bought not what fit us, but what was in stores […] It was a terrible time.' Oksana, aged 52, described the impact of having limited attractive clothing options in this way:

It was my birthday and we decided to go out to dinner in a really fancy restaurant […] and two weeks beforehand, I bought a really nice dress in the store, and when I came into this restaurant, I saw my friend coming in, in exactly the same dress. Because everything in every store was the same, right? If something fancy and nice came in, everybody started wearing the same thing.

The women also recalled having to stand in line for hours because of the shortage and resulting demand for clothing. For example, Valeria, aged 69, described having once stood in line for two hours in frigid weather for a pair of boots:

This one time, I was living in Moscow, and I had this one pair of boots, and winters are very cold there, and my boots had a big crack in them, right across the front […] I had money for new boots, but I couldn't find any boots anywhere. There just weren't any boots in the stores. And so one day I was walking around Moscow and I saw a line up of 50 or so people, maybe a 100, and when I came near I saw that they were selling boots. So we stood there bundled up. It was so cold! And when I was closer to the front, my heart was just beating, 'If only they'd have some left in my size!' And when I finally bought those boots, I was in heaven! Dry feet!

Additionally, the limited clothing available was often expensive and beyond the women's financial reach. Sofia remarked: 'People would save money all year to buy a fashionable pair of boots. You could save money for a year, because boots would cost a month's pay.' Consequently, many women resorted to making their own clothes or modifying garments that were already in their possession to keep up with the trends. Valeria remembered trying to look nice with very limited resources: 'I had this one black dress, and I made different collars for it so that it would look nicer, and […] at work the men always said that I was the best dressed … but in actuality, I only had two dresses.' Katerina recalled: 'I remember that I knitted very well and made myself lots of sweaters […] We all were trying to do something from nothing, otherwise, we wouldn't have anything.'

At the same time, clothes could be bought through *spekulanty,* or profiteers, who were able to import clothing from abroad and sell them on for large profit margins. Daria recalled this story:

It was very difficult to buy something in the shops, because there was just nothing to buy. And we over-paid *spekulanty* so that we could buy things. In Moscow, I fantasized about buying a fur coat […] but there weren't any in the stores. I earned fairly good money, I could allow

Figure 2: Otradny, USSR, 1965: The first author's grandmother (fourth from the left) with a group of students and teachers. The dress she is wearing was remade from a long skirt to approximate a fashionable dress style in the 1960s.

myself that purchase, but there weren't any for sale. And so, they brought me a Yugoslavian fur coat, the price was 600 roubles and they offered it to me for 1,500 – that is, more than twice the price. And I bought it because I really wanted it, and there weren't any for sale. We practically bought everything like that.

As a result of the difficulties that the women faced when attempting to buy clothing, Lydia, aged 58, said that Russian women treasured and preserved the garments in their closets: 'We didn't change clothes so often there. You bought things and you wore them for a very long time, because they were very expensive and you didn't throw things out. We wore things out. We really did.' Anna added: 'People had a completely different approach to clothing. Here in Canada, you can't wear the same thing twice in a row, but there people didn't [...] have that much money.'

Russian women's outward appearances quickly became reflective of their social classes and sense of individuality at a time of collective dispossession. Speculating that dressing up and fashioning their own clothes with limited resources had afforded Russian women a form of self-expression in a culture that encouraged conformity, Katerina had this to say: 'When I grew up, it was so difficult to find something better, something different than what other people wore [...][this is] why we all liked to be well-dressed.' Sofia added: '[The desire to look good] probably comes from being poor, because everyone there was poor. So to differentiate oneself somehow [...] you probably couldn't differentiate yourself in any other way. How else could a woman differentiate herself other than by her clothes?'

The reinforcement of social class through clothing was particularly evident in the work place. Sofia noted: 'Workers were dressed very badly because the pay was just meagre [...] they dressed very badly in anything at all [...] the women who dressed well were the more educated women [...] it was a segment of the population that could do it, not everyone.'

As middle-class, white-collar professionals, the women felt obligated to distinguish themselves through their fashion choices. For instance, Daria asserted: 'Where I worked, in the research technology institute [...] it was just absolutely necessary [to dress well]. They'd look at you like they'd look at a white crow if you came to work dressed unlike everybody else.' Similarly, Maria, aged 58, reminisced: 'We all tried to dress nicely, right? [...] And it was important, especially if you worked in the university, you couldn't come in shorts and a T-shirt. It wasn't a rule, but no one would come to work in jeans.'

Nevertheless, most of the women expressed ambivalence about the importance placed on fashion in the Russian workplace as well as in middle-class social circles and the concomitant financial burden they experienced. Polina, age 52, recalled grudgingly spending money on the stylish clothing she was expected to wear at work and when socializing with friends: 'You had to buy expensive clothes if you went to a party, or even to work, you would have to dress up and you had to spend money on it, even if you didn't have money for your kids.' Maria likewise remembered that she, like most women she knew, bought unnecessary items of clothing so as not to look inferior to other

Figure 3: Igarka, USSR, 1978: The first author's grandmother (second from the right) poses for a photograph with her fellow teachers at Igarka's School #1.

women: 'In my city, winter wasn't very cold, sometimes it could be minus fifteen, but only for a couple of days […] but maybe 30, 40 per cent of women had [fur coats] because most women didn't want to look worse off than other women.' Many of the women mentioned a Russian phrase that translated roughly to 'When you meet a man, you judge him by his clothes; when you leave, you judge him by his heart' to exemplify the importance Russians attributed to first impressions. Sofia elaborated by stating: 'There was this belief that if you looked good, you must be rich […] They used to say, 'Nobody sees an empty stomach, but everyone sees how well you're dressed.' So the first priority became looking good, and food became secondary.' Thus, Russian women quickly learned to adjust their outward appearances in order to increase their opportunities in life. Katerina remarked: 'If you looked well-dressed, you were treated better […] and if you didn't look good, you didn't command respect. So we were taught that if we looked good, we would be given preference.'

Assimilation and othering: Russian women's post-immigration use of clothing

When discussing their post-immigration attitudes towards and experiences of fashion, four of the women described themselves as having assimilated to North American styles of dress. Of these women, two were working, one was retired, and one was unemployed. These women described having relished their liberation from the obligations of Soviet beauty work expectations. The women expressed a strong desire to fit into their Canadian surroundings as well as an appreciation for the practicality and comfort of western clothing after spending years immersed in a culture that privileged a restrictive definition of femininity. For instance, Oksana, who was employed, asserted: 'I don't dress up here […] because I want to feel more comfortable and also, I want to be the same as other people […] I want to be like everybody else in my environment.' Sofia, who had retired, put it this way:

> Here they try to make clothing and everything suit their lifestyle. If it suits you to wear a low heel, wear it. If it suits you to wear a T-shirt, wear it and don't suffer. Back there, you'd board a bus, and you wouldn't be able to sit down in your skirt. You couldn't walk through the mud in your high heels […] but here you wear whatever suits your life.

Maria, who was unemployed, remarked: 'In Canada, people dress more simply, more casual […] they dress to feel comfortable.' The women additionally noted feeling less societal pressure to dress well and buy expensive clothing to denote their middle-class status. Polina, who was employed, asserted: '[Here], you can buy what you like and what you feel good in and you don't need to spend money or pretend that you like a certain style to fit in.'

At the same time, six women contended that irrespective of their employment and financial statuses, they maintained their former fashion habits and preferences in order to retain a distinct

Figure 4: Riga, Latvia, 1953: The first author's grandmother (far left), vacationing with friends in Riga, Latvia.

Russian identity. Of these six women, two were working, two were unemployed, and two were retired. The women stressed the superiority of European styles of dressing, and attempted to construct a fashionable look that echoed the fashions they had grown up emulating and imitating. For instance, Katerina, who was employed and had an upper-middle-class income, had this to say: 'It's a habit. It's my nature that I'm used to being dressed mostly like European women. So I have beautiful coats, I still like high heels […] and I hate wearing sweatpants.' Similarly, Valeria, who was retired and had a very limited income, stated: 'I grew up in a different culture, and I try to pick out clothing that looks elegant. For me, European style is still preferable, and I like it when women dress in a European manner.'

The women juxtaposed their distinct Russian identities and styles of dressing with Canadian fashion norms, which they openly scorned. Katerina asserted:

> Canadian women […] they're often dressing tastelessly, very often in things that don't match. They could be wearing a silk dress with sneakers […] I wouldn't do that. My feel will hurt, I'll hobble, but I'd wear proper shoes, you know? […] Canadian women look very, very plain. You can't even see them. They're like grey mice.

Valeria also had a negative view of Canadian style and stated that, compared to Russian women, 'the women here, they don't dress as nicely. Maybe when they're going out, they'll dress a little nicer, but as a rule, I don't see well-dressed women.'

As well as lacking fashion sense, the women perceived Canadians to be overly tolerant of obesity, which served to further undermine their ability to achieve an attractive appearance. Sofia stated:

> Here, [being overweight] is perfectly normal. These women, they're walking around, putting on whatever they like – even if it shows their flaws, they're perfectly content. They're taught that they are just like other girls and that's perfectly normal. But in Russia, they'd say, 'Oh, here comes a fat cow.'

The women expressed a strong dislike of the appearance of fatness as they made comments similar to those of Valeria who remarked: 'I don't like it when women who are chubby walk around in shorts. There's bulges sticking out here, out there […] But I think that in Canada there's a different understanding of [appropriate body weight].' While they perceived Canadian women to be too accepting of their figure flaws, the women esteemed Russian women who concealed their bodily imperfections with what were considered to be more appropriate clothing choices. Katerina asserted: 'Very often, Canadian women will wear things without understanding that maybe they shouldn't wear them. A big woman shouldn't be wearing shorts [...] it's just unpleasant to look at. A Russian woman just wouldn't allow herself to do that.'

Although the women disparaged obesity, their ability to achieve and maintain their preferred body weights and shapes were challenged by the physical realities of growing older. The majority of the women recalled being thin or of average weight in their youth and early adulthood, and expressed astonishment and dismay over the weight gain they had experienced after menopause. Articulating a strong sense of culpability, the women were deeply distressed by the changes that had occurred in their bodies and angered by their inability to maintain their formerly slim figures. For example, Maria contended the following:

The last couple of years, I have just gained weight, and gained more, and I just feel that I'm not fighting it [enough]. I have to think about dieting, because with the years [...] it is really easy to gain weight, and it's more difficult to lose weight. Before, if I wanted to lose five, seven kilos, I could do it easily, in two or three weeks. Right now, it is really difficult – it's difficult to change.

The women were particularly dissatisfied with the ways in which their increased weights had limited their ability to engage in fashion culture. Oksana put it this way:

I have fat everywhere, everywhere [...] I became puffy, and you know [...] when you're going to buy some clothes, and you look at the size, it's frustrating. Like, you look at the size and say, 'No! That cannot be my size.'

Nevertheless, the women maintained that fashion was an important means of strategically hiding what were perceived to be age-induced deviations from the slim, youthful, feminine ideal. Sofia tried to wear clothing that did not emphasize what she called her 'biggest flaws', saying: 'If you wear something with a low neckline, your skin is sagging [...] so it's better to wear something that would cover it up, all of those wrinkles [...] your stomach hangs out, so you wear something more covered up.' Anna similarly shared this advice:

There are many ways in which clothing can be used to [make a person] look younger or older [...] When you're older [...] you need to not reveal your décolletage, because your skin becomes different, you need to show less skin. If you feel like certain parts of your body still look good, you can show them off, but if you see that, for example, your chest isn't as firm anymore, you don't wear dresses with a revealing neckline [...] and you probably don't wear short skirts anymore or very tight pants. So clothing offers a lot of choices in terms of concealing what flaws you have and accentuating your best features.

However, the women's use of fashion to hide their perceived imperfections was constrained by notions of appropriate and inappropriate clothing choices for older women. Daria said that while she still enjoyed high heels and smart jackets, she no longer wore short skirts because 'there are some things old people should wear and some they shouldn't. And everybody can understand […] what's appropriate for older people.' Although the women endorsed the concept of age-appropriate clothing, they also indicated that adhering to these norms was often fraught with tensions. Daria put it this way: 'I'm trying to be fashionable […] but I'm trying to look not too young or like an old lady.'

Even as the women endeavoured to maintain a Russian, feminine identity through their clothing and despite the limitations of their aging bodies, they expressed ambivalence about their status and visibility as 'other' within Canadian society. Katerina had this to say: 'Sometimes I see Russian women and I can spot them from a distance. I don't like that sometimes they wear too much make-up, too much jewellery. Sometimes they're dressed up and they look out of place, you know?' However, Katerina continued to wear make-up and bright clothing, noting: 'It makes me feel like a woman […] I want to look at me in the mirror and I want to like myself. Then I feel more confident, my mood is going up, I go out and I feel like a woman.' Also struggling to find a balance, Anna, who was unemployed, attempted to maintain her individual sense of style while simultaneously blending into her surroundings:

I don't like being overdressed because I don't want to look different from everyone else. So I can't dress like I dressed in the Ukraine or it wouldn't look right […] I think that I could dress better. I mean, I'd like to dress better, but taking into account the Canadian attitude towards fashion, I try to adapt myself to this environment even if I don't subscribe to this attitude.

Finally, although Lydia, who was unemployed, spoke of not wanting to appear Canadian, she was also conscious that she looked out of place by virtue of the way she dressed:

I think that a woman is more confident if she looks better. But Canada is not very accommodating in that respect, because when you go outside, you feel like a white crow because next to someone else you're dressed very brightly […] but if I would dress like the locals here, I think that I would get very depressed, very quickly.

In this way, the women struggled to find a balance between assimilation and resistance in their clothing choices.

Discussion and conclusions

This article has examined the clothing choices of older Russian immigrant women and their construction and negotiation of femininity, cultural identity, social class and age through clothing. Our findings reveal that fashion is a means of doing gender (West and Zimmerman 1987) that is culturally and historically situated. Similar to western women, the Russian immigrant women we interviewed reflected their gender socialization and privileged the importance of appearance as a central defining marker of femininity. The import of female appearance in the former Soviet Union was further complicated by the social class connotations of clothing as well as financial hardships and the scarcity of goods that existed. Indeed, the women used fashion as a marker of their membership in the middle class, often despite extremely limited resources and sometimes at great personal cost. The women were painfully aware that their social opportunities were directly tied to their appearances and thus they learned to be resilient and resourceful in the face of harsh living conditions.

The women's translocation into Canadian culture required them to reconsider their understandings of feminine beauty and the concomitant implications for their clothing choices. Preferring the appearance norms of the former Soviet Union, the majority of the study participants perceived Canadian women to be less conscientious in their fashion and beauty efforts and, therefore, less attractive. However, the women responded to Canadian fashion culture in two disparate ways. To begin, some women considered clothing to be an important means of blending in and constructing themselves as Canadian citizens, thereby avoiding marginalization and being identified as immigrants. These women often expressed appreciation for their social and financial liberation from the disciplinary mechanisms of fashion (Bartky 1990, Bordo, 1993) that they had experienced in the former Soviet Union. Our findings are similar to those of Remennick (2007), who observed that some of the Russian-American immigrant women she interviewed felt that their feminine appearances were overly conspicuous among North American women, and attempted to alter their beauty work to fit with their new cultural surroundings.

At the same time, most of the women we spoke with resisted North American clothing norms, preferring to adhere to Russian fashion norms. Like the women in Remennick's (2007) study, these women were highly critical of what they perceived to be Canadian women's disregard for femininity. The women considered North American clothing culture to be an assault on and an affront to their identities. Reflecting on how their beauty work comprised an important part of their self-identities and an outward reflection of their internalized value systems, the women used fashion to pursue cultural capital, to shore up their self-esteem and to preserve their sense of selves as Russians.

Our findings are similar to those of Fairhurst (1998), Holland (2004), Hurd Clarke et al. (2009), and Twigg (2007) who found that the aging body was a considerable challenge to women's ability to engage in fashion and whose participants upheld and internalized restrictive clothing norms for the aged body. Our participants reflected on how their altered body shapes delimited their clothing options and choices even as they maintained that fashion was a means of disciplining the deviant, aging body by concealing the physical imperfections that arose over time. Like western women, the women in our study were displeased with their body weights and the weight they had gained following menopause. However, their strongly pejorative attitudes towards obesity (combined with their embracement of narrow definitions of femininity and fashion) served to further undermine the women's acceptance of their aging bodies.

A potential limitation for this study is its sample size and relative lack of diversity. Most of our participants were well educated and partnered. All of the participants were white and able-bodied, and none identified as lesbian. Therefore, the experiences and voices of less-educated, visible minority or lesbian Russian immigrant women are not represented by our data. In the future, it will be important to focus research on the experiences of a more diverse group of Russian immigrant women with respect to ability, age, education, ethnicity and income. It would also be important to explore the clothing and fashion experiences and perceptions of Russian immigrant men, as these will serve as an important point of comparison.

In conclusion, our findings demonstrate that clothing was an intrinsic aspect of the women's construction and negotiation of their identities and their cultural locations within Canada and the former Soviet Union. Our article elucidates how the accomplishment of normative conceptions of gender, age, immigrant status and femininity are influenced (though not determined) by an individual's access to material goods, the physical realities of growing older and cultural norms. Our findings suggest the importance of fashion and clothing in the everyday experiences of Russian women, both within the former Soviet Union and in Canada. Finally, our article highlights the centrality of clothing to a woman's story and experience of life before, after and through immigration.

Acknowledgements

The authors wish to thank the women who participated in the study and shared with us their stories, insights, and time.

References

Afshar, H. (2008), 'Can I see your hair? Choice, agency, and attitudes: the dilemma of faith and feminism for women who cover', *Ethnic and Racial Studies*, 31: 2, pp. 411–427.

Ahlberg, B. M., Njau, V. W., Kiiru, K. and Krantz, I. (2000), 'Gender masked or self-inflicted pain: female circumcision, eradication and persistence in central Kenya', *African Sociological Review*, 4: 1, pp. 35–54.

Anderson, M. and Hill Collins, P. (2001), *Race, class, and gender: an anthology*, Belmont, CA: Wadsworth.

Aroian, K. J. and Norris, A.E. (2002), 'Resilience, stress, and depression among Russian immigrants to Israel', *Western Journal of Nursing Research*, 22: 1, pp. 54–67.

Ashwin, S. (2000), *Gender, state, and society in Soviet and post-Soviet Russia*, New York: Routledge.

Azhgikhina, N. and Goscilo, H. (1996), 'Getting under their skin: the beauty salon in Russian women's lives', in H. Goscilo and B. Holmgren (eds), *Russia, women, culture*, Bloomington: Indiana University Press, pp. 94–123.

Bartky, S. L. (1990), *Femininity and domination: studies in the phenomenology of oppression*, New York: Routledge.

Bordo, S. (1993), *Unbearable weight: feminism, Western culture, and the body*, Berkley: University of California Press.

Chiswick, B. R. (1993), 'Soviet Jews in the United States: an analysis of their linguistic and economic adjustment', *International Migration Review*, 27: 2, pp. 260–285.

Colls, R. (2006), 'Outsize/outside: bodily bignesses and the emotional experiences of British women shopping for clothes', *Gender, Place and Culture*, 13: 5, pp. 529–545.

Davey, M., Eaker, D. G., Fish, L. S. and Klock, K. (2003), 'Ethnic identity in an American white minority group', *Identity: An International Journal of Theory and Research*, 3: 2, pp. 143–158.

Entwhistle, J. (2006), 'The cultural economy of fashion buying', *Current Sociology*, 54: 5, pp. 704–724.

Fairhurst, E. (1998), 'Growing old gracefully as opposed to mutton dressed as lamb: the social construction of recognizing older women', in S. Nettleton and J. Watson (eds), *The body in everyday life*, London: Routledge, pp. 257–274.

Fassman, H. and Munz, R. (1994), 'European east-west migration, 1945–1992', *International Migration Review*, 28: 3, pp. 520–538.

Filtzer, S. (2002), *Soviet workers and de-Stalinization: the consolidation of the modern system of Soviet production relations, 1953–1964*, Cambridge: Cambridge University Press.

Gold, S. (1995), *From workers state to the Golden State: Jews from the former Soviet Union in California*, Boston: Alwyn and Bacon.

Holland, S. (2004), *Alternative femininities: Body, age, and identity*, New York: Berg Publishing.

Hondagneu-Sotelo, P. (2003), *Gender and US immigration: contemporary trends*, Berkeley: University of California Press.

Hurd Clarke, L., Griffin, M., and Maliha, K. (2009), 'Bat wings, bunions, and turkey wattles: body transgressions and older women's strategic clothing choices', *Ageing & Society*, 29: 5, pp. 709–726.

Kaiser, S. B., Nagasawa, R. H., and Hutton, S. S. (1991), 'Construction of an SI theory of fashion: part I: ambivalence and change', *Clothing and Textiles Research Journal*, 13: 3, pp. 172–183.

Kay, R. (1997), 'Images of an ideal woman: perceptions of Russian womanhood through the media, education and women's own eyes', in M. Buckley (ed.), *Post- Soviet women: from the Baltic to Central Asia*, Cambridge: Cambridge University Press, pp. 77–98.

Kishinevsky, V. (2004), *Russian Immigrants in the United States: adapting to American Culture*, New York: LFB Scholarly Publishing LLC.

Klepp, I. G., and Storm-Mathisen, A. (2005), 'Reading fashion as age: teenage girls' and women's accounts of clothing as body and social status', *Fashion Theory*, 9: 3, pp. 323–342.

Kwon, Y. (1992), 'Body consciousness, self-consciousness, and women's attitudes toward clothing practices', *Social Behavior and Personality*, 20: 4, pp. 295–307.

Kwon, Y. and Parham, E. S. (1994), 'Effects of state of fatness perception on weight conscious women's clothing practices', *Clothing and Textiles Research Journal*, 12: 4, pp. 16–21.

Lurie, A. (1992), *The language of clothes*, Bloomsbury: London.

McRobbie, A. (1997), 'Bridging the gap: feminism, fashion, and consumption', *Feminist Review*, 55: 1, pp. 73–89.

Miller, A. M. and Chandler, P. J. (2002), 'Acculturation, resilience, and depression in midlife women from the former Soviet Union', *Nursing Research*, 51: 1, pp. 26–32.

Morganroth Gullette, M. (1999), 'The other end of the fashion cycle: practicing loss, learning decline', in K. Woodward (ed.), *Figuring age: women, bodies, generations*, Bloomington: Indiana University Press, pp. 34–59.

Negrin, L. (1999), 'The self as image: a critical appraisal of postmodern theories of fashion', *Theory, Culture, and Society*, 16: 3, pp. 99–118.

Parkins, I. (2008), 'Building a feminist theory of fashion: Karen Barad's agential realism', *Australian Feminist Studies*, 23: 58, pp. 501–515.

Pedraza, S. (1991), 'Women and migration: the social consequences of gender', *Annual Review of Sociology*, 17: 1, pp. 303–325.

Pannebacker, R.K. (1997), 'Fashioning theory: a critical discussion of the symbolic interactionist theory of fashion', *Clothing and Textiles Research Journal*, 15: 3, pp. 178–183.

Puwar, N. (2002), 'Multicultural fashion...stirrings of another sense of aesthetics and memory', *Feminist Review*, 71: 1, pp. 63–87.

Remennick, L. (2001), '"All my life is one big nursing home": Russian immigrant women in Israel speak about double caregiver stress', *Women's Studies International Forum*, 24: 6, pp. 685–700.

Remennick, L. (2007), '"Being a woman is different here": changing perceptions of femininity and gender relations among former Soviet women living in Greater Boston', *Women's Studies international Forum*, 30: 4, pp. 362–341.

Robinson, D. (1991), *The translator's turn*, Baltimore: The Johns Hopkins University Press.

Ruby, T. F. (2006), 'Listening to the voices of Hijab', *Women's Studies International forum*, 29: 1, pp. 54–66.

Rudd, N. A. and Lennon, S. J. (2000), 'Body image and appearance-management behaviours in college women', *Clothing and Textiles Research Journal*, 18: 3, pp. 152–62.

Shasha, D. and Shron, M. (2002), *Red blues: voices from the last wave of Russian immigrants*, New York: Holmes & Meier Publishers.

Strauss, A. and Corbin, J. (1998), *Basics of qualitative research: techniques and procedures for developing grounded theory*, second edition, Thousand Oaks, CA: Sage.

Trautmann, J., Worth, S. L. and Lokken, K. (2007), 'Body dissatisfaction, bulimic symptoms, and clothing practices among college women', *Journal of Psychology*, 141: 5, pp. 485–498.

Tseëlon, E. (1992), 'Self presentation through appearance: A manipulative vs. a dramaturgical approach', *Symbolic Interaction*, 15: 4, pp. 501–513.

Twigg, J. (2007), 'Clothing, age, and the body: a critical review', *Ageing and Society*, 27: 2, pp. 285–305.

Vinokurov, A. Birman, D., and Trickett, E. (2000), 'Psychological and acculturation correlates of work status among Soviet Jewish refugees in the United States', *International Migration Review*, 34: 2, pp. 538–59.

West, C., and Zimmerman, D. H. (1987), 'Doing gender', *Gender & Society*, 1: 2, pp. 125–151.

Suggested citation

Korotchenko, A. and Clarke, L. H. (2010), 'Russian immigrant women and the negotiation of social class and feminine identity through fashion', *Critical Studies in Fashion and Beauty* 1: 2, pp. 181–202, doi: 10.1386/csfb.1.2.181_1

Contributor details

Alexandra Korotchenko, MA, is a Ph.D. student in the School of Human Kinetics at the University of British Columbia, Vancouver, Canada.

Contact:
E-mail: a_korotchenko@yahoo.ca

Laura Hurd Clarke, MSW, Ph.D., is Associate Professor (Sociology of Health and Aging) in the School of Human Kinetics, The University of British Columbia, Vancouver, Canada.

Contact:
E-mail: laura.hurd.clarke@ubc.ca

CSFB 1 (2) pp. 203–215 Intellect Limited 2010

Critical Studies in Fashion and Beauty
Volume 1 Number 2

© 2010 Intellect Ltd Article. English language. doi: 10.1386/csfb.1.2.203_1

SIMONA SEGRE REINACH

Iuav University Venezia and Iulm University Milano

If you speak fashion you speak Italian:[1] Notes on present day Italian fashion identity[2]

Keywords

globalization
national identity
fashion
'made in Italy'
invention of tradition

Abstract

What is the meaning of national fashion in a globalized world? Having or not having a 'national fashion' upon which to rely seems to matter more and more for the success of brands operating in the contemporary market. This is so despite – and perhaps because of – production being increasingly transnational. The following article investigates how the project of a distinctive Italian fashion identity ('made in Italy') is produced through discursive formulations and industrial practices in China and in Italy. It explores the meaning of 'made in Italy' based on the perceived reproduction of historical or imagined traditions.

1. It is the claim of the
    2009 ICE (Istituto per il

'If you Chinese had skills, good taste and inventiveness, you would be the masters of the world', declared an Italian entrepreneur we interviewed[3] in 2007 when he was still the 50 per cent owner of a firm: the other half belonged to his former (Chinese) wife and partner, who, after years of marital and property fighting, now owns the business entirely. It was, of course, a private statement, though still revealing a certain cultural unconscious of taste, characteristic of global fashion and its Chino-Italian version in particular. That taste, considered as Bourdieu would have it – as socially and politically constructed – is often associated with a general, now very vague idea of Italianness.

In the romanticized narratives of the first entrepreneurs who reached China, the 'Italy of fashion' in China has played the part of David against Goliath. The slight figure of David, with his light, intangible attributes of style and good taste, the result of a cultural heritage constantly claimed through a precise, if not always concerted, communication – has been easily appropriated by the 'brute force' of Chinese production, as Italians would describe it, moulding, exploiting and shaping it. Lightness, together with aesthetics and astuteness, is seen to be superior to sheer size and labour force capacity.

Unlike the French, for example, who move strategically following their brands, the legends tell of Italian business people arriving in China in dribs and drabs, as pioneers in the late 1980s, and sometimes even earlier, in the late 1970s, for various reasons and motives. Back then 'made in Italy' as the concept we know today did not yet exist, and was at most only a manufacturing label. Anecdotes and curious stories tell of the heroic deeds and sacrifices of courageous men, and of exotic journeys into the remote, poverty-stricken countryside, where bonds of convenience and/or passion were forged with Chinese partners in remote geographic contexts by expatriates dreaming of Nutella, panettone and Parmesan cheese.

Here are some quotes in which the Chinese are described in the style of colonial narratives.

In Zheijiang. I took 8 hours to arrive. A peasant woman guided in the plane. Then 8 hours of dirt tracks. I looked for a hotel. There wasn't one. I found somewhere to sleep in a house… all dirty … damp … mosquitoes. My childhood experience helped me. There were barefoot children, as I had been in Friuli. The Chinese looked at me, they looked at the hair on my body, which they didn't have. They offered me what they had, I fell in love with those people. I fell in love with them. They brought me something to eat. I didn't eat anything. I couldn't eat that stuff. I didn't know what was in it. Rats everywhere.

(Pietro Ferrari,[4] 22 May 2007)

In Zhejiang where there are silkworms. I went there 20 years ago. I would ask: who knows how to do this, who knows how to do that? They would answer: 'everyone'. But they did everything badly. Or rather, they didn't do what we wanted. We were more advanced. They didn't have anything. We had to start everything from scratch. As a softener they used rice,

commercio estero) campaign to promote Italian fashion in the US. Sicilian model Eva Riccobono is photographed in a set of renown places in Rome such as Trinità dei Monti, Ara Pacis, Fontanone del Gianicolo.

2. A shorter version of this article was presented at the *Fashion & Materiality* conference at Stockholm University in October 2009.

3. This article is part of a broader project centred on the work relationships between Italians and Chinese and on the approaches to the training of a transnational class of workers. The research was conducted in Italy and China, between 2002 and 2009 jointly with Sylvia Yanagisako (Stanford University) and Lisa Rofel (University of California Santa Cruz).

4. Names of the interviewees have |been changed – for confidentiality reasons.

and also for the sizing. I learnt that from them. I got everything there. I know how to do my craft, I have learnt it on the job.

(Pietro Ferrari, 22 May 2007)

In April 1976, I went to China for the first time. Mao died in August. I found this strange planet, China, and I fell in love with it. In 1976 the factories were the Communes – everything was made by hand. Hundreds, thousands of workers. I remember one New Year (1978–79). The workers were given a little bone – maybe to make broth. That was their present, like Christmas panettone for us! Clothing they got every four years. The houses had broken windows, it was cold.

(Interview with Antonio Mancino, owner of joint venture, Rome, March 2007)

The Chino-Italian stories of the twenty-first century are less colourful and adventurous, but equally complex. We have entered that hard, unromantic terrain of competition which is brand management, the control of distribution and the conquest of new market segments; we are, that is, in joint-ventures marketing, and no longer in the prehistory of business. From the manufacturing of a product, achieved at a lower price but with just as much hard work – as I learnt – to the struggle between those most able to evoke desire and imagination with a logo.

The French do not need the 'made in France' connotation, probably because the 'made-in-France' element is somehow taken for granted. It was established centuries ago: in the seventeenth century Paris was already a 'capital' of fashion. Italian brands, on the other hand, need to promote themselves alongside the national image, which is constructed and reconstructed through an ongoing process. In contrast, 'made in Italy' is a recent concept, but it has rapidly become a sort of metaphor for modern fashion. It assumed its proper meaning during the 1980s, that is, since the invention of 'stilismo' (designers and industry collaborating in a fashion project), which set the standard of a post-bourgeois fashion practice. Post-bourgeois means the overtaking of a 'class taste' – as the late Gianni Versace clearly stated by declaring 'I hate good taste' – in favour of a language available to a much wider audience: the lifestyles communication. This was new and it was also considered 'democratic'. Italy played an important role in this shift towards 'modern fashion'. 'Made in Italy' is fuelled by the prestige and success of its brands, the result of individual entrepreneurial strategies. 'Pure Italian Expression', for instance, is the claim of one brand, Maurizio Baldassari, which has only become such in China, by Appointment to Her Majesty China – we might say.

I have been engaged in analysing how China had been seeking to affirm its identity in fashion, that is, the possibility of communicating a recognized Chinese aesthetics, emancipated from an exclusively manufacturing China (Finnane 2008, Wu Juan Juan 2009), and the negotiating for power within the joint ventures which are the subject of our study. In the course of my analysis it occurred to me that in the last few years, since 2005, the identity of Italian fashion (accepted abroad as stable, ancient and historicized) was in fact in a state of transition, both in Italy and in the rest of the world.

This is exemplified in the Altagamma project, 'which brings together Italian companies of international renown at the higher end of the market; companies that exude Italian culture and style in their company and product-management activities, and stand out for their innovation, quality, service, design and prestige' (from the 'Fondazione Altagamma' website). It goes on to confirm that even 'natural' heritage needs promotion:

> The Altagamma project will bring our 'Made in Italy' back to the top. Our great heritage of image accumulated in so many years thanks to 'Made in Italy' has spoilt us in some way. It has made us believe that that heritage would grow spontaneously, over the years, without needing to be promoted and supported with structural and constructive actions.
> (Declaration of Leonardo Ferragamo, President of Altagamma)

As Christopher Breward notes, modern fashion in particular is the outcome of a precarious marriage between the process of creative authorship, technological production and cultural dissemination (Breward 2003). However, the three-year plan of the Italian Fondazione Altagamma 'to affirm the Excellence of Altagamma member companies and promote, together, the primacy of the Italian lifestyle and culture in the world' – sounds more like a communiqué from the Chinese government, or a piece of imperialist propaganda, than the dissemination of a desire typical of the practices of contemporary consumption.

An analysis of the press in the last few months confirms the intensification of plans aimed at underscoring the prestige of Italian production: of 'made in Italy'.

During Pitti (men's fashion collection exhibition held in Florence, twice a year) in January 2009, men's socks were presented imprinted with the Italian national anthem, the story of Garibaldi and other cornerstones in the history of Italian national unity. The Lavazza Calendar for 2009 features episodes ranging from Roman history, with the Wolf and the Twins, Futurism, to *La dolce vita* (Fellini, 1960), through the Renaissance, still the most quoted reference when the words 'Italy', 'creativity' and 'fashion' are mentioned together. Futurism centenary (1909–2009) has also had an immediate impact on fashion communication. 'Since art and culture are in my DNA and in that of our country, I have devoted the collection I will be presenting at Pitti on Tuesday to the centenary of Futurism and Marinetti's manifesto' (statement made by designer Laura Biagiotti at the Pitti in January 2009, quoted by journalist Paola Pollo, *Corriere della Sera*, 10 January 2009). A few months later, in April 2009, during the Milan Furniture Fair, the artist Gaetano Pesce proposed a new Futurist manifesto entitled 'Avanti Tutta' (Full Steam Ahead), published in the *Corriere della Sera* on 22 April 2009:

Innovation, tradition and Italian style.
Need more?

Figure 1: Milano 2010, Wall advertising for Italian Shoes. Photo by author.

Italian designers and industrials have turned 'Made in Italy' into a value envied throughout the world. 'Avanti Tutta' signifies investing more in creativity – the only great natural resource Italy has. And in innovation to ensure that we overcome the recession as soon as possible.

In order to strengthen its brand, the Salvatore Ferragamo Fashion House has also focused on the relationship between history and Italian identity, celebrating the company's eightieth anniversary with an exhibition inaugurated in Shanghai (April 2008); this exhibition later moved to Milano at Triennale (October 2008). The central communicator of the Italianness of the brand, stemming from Renaissance workshops and craftsmanship, is the *Tableau Vivant*: a colourful reconstruction of a clean model workshop, full of leather scraps, hides and tools, in which two shoemakers make shoes by hand 'as they used to', wearing white aprons and spectacles perched on their noses. Ermenegildo Zegna adopted this same communication strategy for Milan Fashion's Night Out (September 2009). This company reconstructed a tailor's workshop in their main store in Milan.

Diego Della Valle Tod's brand sponsored a book titled *Italian Touch*, in which the 'Italian way of life' was presented. Here is what the website of the publisher of the book, Rizzoli, says:

> [the book] … includes more than 100 Italians of different ages photographed with their families, friends, children and an assortment of dogs in splendid historic palaces and the countryside, representing the Italian way of living and a certain 'style' that goes beyond fashion and time. They are all very elegant in jeans and moccasins, all 'testament' to a current but timeless style that is undeniably Italian and famous throughout the world.
>
> (www.Rizzoli.it).

The name of the sponsor Della Valle is not mentioned in the book – while many of the editorials underline the understatement of Diego Della Valle, the company is deliberately not mentioned except for a small Tod logo on the front cover. Some of the 'Italian Portraits' are now part of an advertising campaign for the brand centred on Italian style.

It is not on the authenticity of the *recapturing* of various images of Italian myths that I want to dwell, or on the veracity of 'made in Italy' – the word 'authentic' does not apply easily to fashion – which is always the result of many encounters and hybridization. Instead I am interested in the use of history in contemporary Italy communication strategy. History has a peculiar role in fashion, especially when applied to matters of national identity. 'For fashion, history is a sort of labyrinth', Caroline Evans writes, in that it makes it possible to juxtapose images from different periods. 'As the labyrinth doubles back on itself, what is more modern is revealed as also having a relation to what is more old', and what we take from the past may also be a key to reading the contradictions of the present. The initiatives and examples of the relaunch of Italian identity are too numerous to be

Figure 2: Milan 2009, Vogue Fashion Night. The 'Taylor's atelier' set in Ermenegildo Zegna shop in via Montenapoleone. Photo by the author.

considered only as a shared objective for many companies, a simple business matter; rather, they represent a cultural trend worth investigating.

In particular I am interested in elaborating on one aspect – that of the 'Renaissance artisan creativity' associated with 'made in Italy'. Ironically it is a considerable historical falsehood, since 'made in Italy' was born from abandoning artisan work for industrial fashion. In fact the 1980s model, on which 'made in Italy' made its name, was the first model of creative industrial fashion. After Florentine luxury prêt-à-porter (aristocratic couturiers with names such as Marchese Emilio Pucci and Donna Simonetta Colonna di Cesarò) made the first attack on French hegemony, Italian fashion left the aristocratic Florence, city of art, and moved the fashion shows to Milan, the city of commerce. The result was the birth of 'ready-to-wear', hallmarked by the so-called 'industrial aesthetics' of its 'Fab Four': Armani, Ferré, Missoni and Krizia (the creators of 'made in Italy'). The 7 June 1971 issue of the American journal *Women's Wear Daily*, entitled 'Putting It Together' attributed the 'total look' (coordinated garments and accessories) to Walter Albini. It is still a good metaphor for Italian prêt-à-porter. What was 'put together' was clothing design and beauty with the capacity for mass reproduction and the perfecting of the system of sizes which gave industrial production the accuracy it needed. In fact it is also a good metaphor for the synergy between Italian design and industry. A catalogue in a recent exhibition, *Off Series,* in the design museum La Triennale di Milano characterized this relationship as generating 'a high degree of productive flexibility and a continuing renewal of design's linguistic repertoire', which, in a globalized competitive market, 'constitute[s] an important aspect in the development of the Italian Design project universe'. (Triennale. Serie e fuori serie-Series off series 2009)

The industry-design collaboration was so successful internationally that it became a model for modern fashion, as economist Enrico Cietta explains:

> From the synthesis between the world of fashion and the world of industry came that complex system of production and service activities which is today described as the fashion industry, but which we may also call, due to its Italian origins, the model of fashion 'Made in Italy'.
>
> (Ricchetti and Cietta 2006: 25)

Thus the present relaunch of 'made in Italy' makes a 'creative' use of history as an epic, richly imaginative tale, but it leaves out the real history of fashion, i.e., the fact that 'made in Italy' is a recent phenomenon and a situated practice, and, above all, one which is no longer what it used to be. For economist Enrico Cietta, Italian fashion is in fact now in its fourth generation. The first generation (characterized by the collaboration between fashion design and industry) was industrial fashion arising in Milan in the 1980s. The second generation, in the 1990s, also integrated the distribution system: fashion design, industry and mono-brand stores. The third generation added

5. The title is a take on a song by musician and singer Gianna Nannini whose original title was 'Bello e impossibile', which refers to a boy who is difficult to reach. The current title refers to Italy and implies that it is beautiful but possible. The book can be read online at the Altagamma Website (www.Altagamma.it)

6. And French brand Louis Vuitton must have taken the same decision: a young woman artisan – depicted as in a Dutch portrait in the early seventeenth century – is manufacturing a different set of items, a purse, a handbag etc.

communication and marketing to the prolific relationship between fashion design, production and distribution. Lastly, the fourth generation, the current one as we know it, is the generation of fast fashion, which Cietta considers a hybrid between production and service in that its product is above all a container for information and fashion trends (Cietta 2009).

Italian fashion conjures up the myths of ancient history, but also those of its own history, equally glorious, *si parva licet componere magnis* (if one may compare small things with great), and of recent history. We might describe it as 'double vintage'. From the romanticization of a glorious remote past emerges the idea of craftsmanship and creative workshop, combined with a feeling of 'leadership in taste'. (Curiously enough China looks instead to the Beautiful Future, which is the name of a very recent joint venture between the Miroglio Group and Chinese Group, TBF! (The Beautiful Future).) The 1980s Italian fashion model, which enhanced the vertical production process from raw material to distribution, has been largely overcome today, or at least fragmented and diversified. All this is recast as the tale of Italian craftsmanship.

Falling back on craftsmanship also underlines the separation between those who boast the ideas and those who materially carry out the work; in the case of Chino-Italian joint ventures, this was perhaps the start of relations between Chinese manufacturers and Italian entrepreneurs. However, as the evolution of joint ventures clearly shows, it is no longer so, or at least not only so. Through the 'made in Italy' propaganda, the 'secrets' of relocated production to China are wholly or partially kept hidden. But this separation also helps to classify every piece of Italian fashion that is exported with the label 'Italian luxury', or 'made in Italy', as the work of skilful artisans outside globalization, standing still in a time bubble.

The Altagamma Foundation published a book *Bella e Possibile*[5] (2009), which aimed to relaunch the Italian image worldwide:

> We are living in an age that brings out all our uncertainties and fears – an age that obliges us to entirely reassess Italy as part of an increasingly close network of relationships in the modern world … This work thus examines the elements that create the identity of contemporary Italy, focusing on the best and suggesting the most effective ways of communicating them to the world.
>
> (from the preface to the book by Leonardo Ferragamo)

The book goes on to describe craftsmanship as one the main cornerstones to be used in relaunching the Italian image[6]:

> To achieve this level of excellence and mastery, crafts professions have deep roots in human values and in knowledge and skills which are brought to bear every day, in particular in striving

for perfection and constant innovation, curiosity and humility, to consolidate an ability to learn at all times, great passion for work, a deep understanding of everything that is involved in the work, an ability to create unique products and convey emotions to those who purchase them, a search primarily for patrons and not just customers. All this demands constant improvement in the person who unceasingly refines his or her own professional and creative skills. The transfer of the profession, skills, and secrets generally takes place between a master and an apprentice, and this requires continuity in the exercise of the profession and/or an organized system of transferring practical skills in order to create a new master craftsman.

(From *Bella e Possibile*, www.Altagamma. it)

Altagamma's high flown and carefully managed statements are sometimes contrasted with Freudian slips – those almost unconscious gestures which break the censure and reveal what one 'really' thinks of a matter. I am thinking about the many, sometimes involuntarily ironic, campaigns on 'Italian fashion' blossoming each day. The following examples of recent advertising give a flavour of this trend: – 'You Look Italian' together with the specification 'designed in Italy' clearly reveals the real preoccupation of the brand. Carlo Chionna's 'God save Made in Italy'; Lapo Elkann's 'Rock save Italy' and 'Italian Concept' (if nothing else the concept is Italian!); as well as 'Made in Italy autentico', 'Italymade' and '100% Made in Italy'. What these, and recent laws on textile labelling, all have in common is awareness of how slippery it is to find a common ground to describe Italian fashion. The paradox is that all the efforts to re-establish an idea of what 'Made in Italy is', and what it should be, end up confining it into a straightjacket. This restriction has the opposite effect of revealing that the 'Emperor today has No Clothes'. The chair of the young entrepreneurs in the footwear association (footwear being the sector that suffered most from international competition and especially from Chinese competition) said at a recent meeting, 'Talking about "Made in Italy" seems to be "out of date". We have to update our vocabulary' (Alessandra Iannello 2009).

The concept of 'made in Italy' is caught between propaganda and joking, and marketed through an increasingly obscure, vague concept of 'exclusiveness'. Many brands of Italian 'fast fashion' (the system of production that goes beyond the traditional seasonal presentation of new products) are included in this bracket, as most of them are really made in Italy (sometimes by Chinese factories in Italy) unlike global luxury brands.

We still have to discuss taste and the emerging forms of distinction to which fashion always refers. As Zygmunt Bauman (2009) reiterates, today's culture is made up of needs and desires, not rules. Similarly, fashion is disseminated through seduction, and not through regulations. And 'taste', as couturière Madeleine Vionnet once said, 'is the feeling that permits one to tell the difference between what is beautiful and what is merely spectacular' (Menkes 2009). Today we should probably read this interpretation of distinction and taste as anti-brand and anti-luxury. As Stefano Tonchi, the

7. A recent law about the label 'made in Italy' is under discussion (December 2009). It will be applied to products that can claim at least two phases of production in Italy. It is called Ddl 'Reguzzoni-Versace'.

editor of the *New York Times' T Magazine* states (regarding the current crisis of luxury in the UK, France and Italy:

> The key lies in a smooth transition from an economy of luxury to an economy of value. The aim is to redefine the value of labour in fashion and to perform the painful but necessary process of de-branding. The only brands that survive will be those with true value.
>
> (*Domus*, n. 924, April 2009)

De-branding is probably also applicable to 'made in Italy', which is rapidly becoming an empty void stereotype by which new Italian fashion designers might not like to be classified. 'Fashion' is partly an 'object' and partly an 'idea'; numerous examples of Italian fashion reveal that beyond the mythic paths of a Disneyfied past, lies instability, inconsistencies and irregularities, and a focus on creativity and product. Suzy Menkes has also recently spoken of a '"Made in Italy" Renaissance', but this is something diametrically opposed to what is usually conveyed by this term. She does not refer to resuscitating or reinventing Renaissance men, humanists, scientists, artisans, navigators and dreamers, and she refers even less to promulgating rules and regulations of 'Made in Italy'.[7] As the title of her article, 'Italy looks beyond its borders for Fashion talent', indicates, 'the search for new young talent in Italy has taken an intriguing twist: Look for creative designers who have moved to Italy to work with its craftspeople' (*The New York Times*, 20 June 2009). The article mentions Max Kibardin, a Russian designer specializing in accessories, particularly footwear. Kibardin also won recognition at the 2009 Florence Pitti 'Imagine Who's Next Awards', which are devoted to young talent. The awards set out to 'show a generation of designers from Eastern Europe the outcome of encounters with the extraordinary Italian production culture in fashion'. We could also add many others to this list – such as Indian born and New York based actor and fashion and jewellery designer Waris Ahluwalia, who has his products made in Bombay and Rome (houseofwaris.com). Is it therefore our turn to be 'Chinese'? Do foreign creatives come to Italy to 'exploit' our production capacities? It is an almost ironic twist the culture of foreign creatives exploiting the Chinese production capacities becomes the production base of foreign talent. In fact, Kibardin, a cosmopolitan designer as most of contemporary designers are, has moved to Milan, after studying in Russia and living in New York. In her book, provocatively entitled *Fatto in Italia* (in Italian means made in Italy, but labels usually carry the English 'made in Italy' and the concept , born for export, is usually expressed in English), fashion theorist Paola Colaiacomo questions precisely what culture existed in the Italian past (before 'made in Italy') and what fashion culture exists today. The shuttle of the loom is continuously thrown between present and past and it shows a process, not a structure; the meaning and the role of 'national identity' in fashion need to be researched. And the core idea of an 'Italian way' in fashion and design in a globalized world needs further investigation. What Kibardin – and many others – promote is not a return to craftsmanship, but a global and local fashion approach that represents, in Bourdieu's sense, 'a new form of distinction'. This distinction is at the junction between the materiality of the product and the individuality of the author (only in the last resort – is it a logo). The world of 'making' and the world of 'creating' no longer seem to be so separate. 'Artisan' products, as a practice and not as rhetoric, are thus present in a different way in many countries, according to traditions, but they are similar in each country and in Italy too. In part it is a by-product of the cultural dominance of industrial-financial fashion. But it is also positively marked by Italian culture, for example, in the capacity of Italian fashion to translate good ideas, wherever they come from, into business. As the catalogue of the *Off Series* exhibition in the Milan Triennale puts it 'ever since the beginning of the century, collaboration between the artistic avant-garde, artisan laboratories, and small and medium industries has allowed Italian designers …a high degree of productive flexibility … on account of their highly experimental and innovative charge' enabling them to experiment in visual languages and identify 'adequate interpretations' and 'practical applications' so as to adapt 'to different functional necessities and images'.

References

Bauman, Z. (2009), *Does Ethics Have a Chance in a World of Consumers?* Cambridge (Mass.): Harvard University Press.

Bourdieu, P. ([1979] 1984), *Distinctions. A Social Critique of the Judgment of Taste*, Cambridge (Mass.): Harvard University Press.

Breward, C. (2003), *Fashion*, Oxford: Oxford University Press.

Cietta, E. (2009), *La rivoluzione del fast fashion*, Milano: Franco Ageli.

Colaiacomo, P. (ed.) (2006), *Fatto in Italia*, Roma: Meltemi.

Finnane, A. (2008), *Changing Clothing in China. Fashion, History, Nation*, New York: Columbia University Press.

Iannello, A. (2009) 'Scommettere sull'Italia per rilanciare l'export', La Repubblica, Affari & Finanza, 20 July.

Menkes, S. (2009) 'Liberating Women's Bodies', IHT, 13 July.

Redini, V. (2008), *Frontiere del Made in Italy. Delocalizzazione produttiva e identità delle merci*, Verona: Ombre Corte.

Riello, G. (2009), 'Fashion and the Four Parts of the World', paper presented to the conference *Fusion Culture: Fashion Beyond Orientalism and Occidentalism*, Potsdam University, Potsdam 5–7 November.

Ricchetti, M. and Cietta E. (2006), *Il valore della moda*, Milano: Bruno Mondadori.

Segre Reinach, S. (2005), 'Fast Fashion versus Pret a Porter. Towards a New Culture of Fashion', *Fashion Theory*, 9: 1, pp. 43–56.

Segre Reinach, S. (2006), 'Milan, the city of prêt à porter', in C. Breward and D. Gilbert (ed.), *Fashion's World Cities*, Oxford: Berg.

Segre Reinach, S. (2009), 'From Made in China to made for China', paper presented to the conference *Fusion Culture: Fashion Beyond Orientalism and Occidentalism*, Università di Potsdam, 5–7 November.

Segre Reinach, S. (2010), 'Italian and Chinese agendas in the global fashion industry', in G. Riello and P. McNeill (eds), *The Fashion History Reader*, London and New York: Routledge.

Wu Juan Juan (2009), *Chinese Fashion. From Mao to now*, Oxford and New York: Berg.

Tonchi, S. (2009) 'A publishing parable in the cocktail of fashion and magazines', *Domus*, n. 924, April.

Suggested citation

Segre Reinach, S. (2010), 'If you speak fashion you speak Italian: Notes on present day Italian fashion identity', *Critical Studies in Fashion and Beauty* 1: 2, pp. 203–215, doi: 10.1386/csfb.1.2.203_1

Contributor details

Simona Segre Reinach, cultural anthropologist, is Contract Professor of Anthropology of Fashion at Iuav University (Venezia) and of Fashion and Turism at Iulm University (Milano). She has published several articles, 'China and Italy. Fast Fashion vs Pret à Porter. Towards a new Culture of Fashion' (*Fashion Theory*, 9: 1), 'Milan, the city of prêt à porter' (*Fashion's World Cities*, Berg, 2006), 'Italian and Chinese agendas in the global fashion industry' (*The Fashion History Reader*, Routledge, 2010) and three books: *Mode in Italy. Una lettura antropologica* (Guerini, 1999); *La Moda. Un'introduzione* (Laterza [2005] 2010); *Orientalismi. La moda nel mercato globale. Manuale di sociologia, comunicazione e cultura della moda* (Meltemi, 2006). She is currently undertaking research in China, collaborating with Professor Sylvia Yanagisako (Stanford University) and Professor Lisa Rofel (University of California Santa Cruz) on the project 'The New Silk Road'. She is on the Board of Advisors of *Fashion Theory: The Journal of Dress, Body & Culture*.

Contact: Via san Marco 46, 20121 Milano, Italy.
E-mail: simona.segre@gmail.com

CSFB 1 (2) pp. 217–231 Intellect Limited 2010

Critical Studies in Fashion and Beauty
Volume 1 Number 2
© 2010 Intellect Ltd Article. English language. doi: 10.1386/csfb.1.2.217_1

SHEILA CLIFFE
Jumonji Gakuen Women's University, Japan, and University of Leeds, UK

Revisioning the kimono

Keywords

kimono
fashion
orientalism
globalization
Internet
blog

Abstract

Whilst the kimonoed woman is an unchanging stereotype of Japanese beauty, this article suggests that due to the interaction of kimono with the processes of globalization (technological and in terms of communication), the kimono continues to metamorphose to meet the needs of its fashionable, urban, contemporary wearers.

Biographical introduction

It may be thought that everything that there is to say about the kimono – this iconic symbol of a gendered and traditional Japan – has already been said. It has long become a signifier of an exotic Oriental Other, often associated with the geisha, and as such, a part of an ossified tradition, not an item of living material culture. I want to propose a new way of looking at the kimono and what it tells us. My reading of the kimono is informed by inhabiting two cultures, both of the West and of Japan, and by a perspective that is both inside, as a kimono wearer, and outside, as a researching foreigner within the Japanese community.

When I first arrived in Japan from the UK, 25 years ago, my notion of Japan was limited to a series of stereotyped images of 'Japanicity': Mount Fuji, cherry blossom, and the kimonoed figure of a Japanese woman. In the days before Internet such ignorance could be forgiven, but now it seems almost embarrassing to admit. For me, what started out as a little flirtation with the beautiful, silk garment that was one of my first images of Japan, turned into a full-blown love affair. I was a regular browser at temple antique markets and in upmarket department stores, which have kimono sections, or floors, where one can be amazed at the incredible price tags on the lovely garments. Kimono shops are renowned for their hard-sell, and (another confession) while browsing, I fell for a sea-green, flowered kimono, was persuaded to get wrapped up in it, listened to the complimentary words of the surprised passers-by, and finally completed the purchase of the most expensive item I had ever bought in my life. Having agreed to buy it, I then learned that the price tag did not include either the lining or the sewing together, which almost doubled the price on the bill. I went away shaking, clutching a small white envelope that contained the receipt for the deposit and the order for the sewing, giving me three weeks to ready the money for this amazing purchase to which I had committed myself.

Only then I was to discover that there were about fifteen other items necessary to get dressed in a kimono, and that one learns how to get dressed by going on a training course. This is how I ended up, or rather started out, on a course of lessons that licensed me, after two years of evening classes, to wear various kinds of kimono, dress others and open a kimono class. At the same time as I embarked on this journey, I took up another one, *bingata* (Japanese stencil dyeing), which has also given me some insights into the production side of the garment. Thus, whilst I am going through the usual life stages of work (as a resident of Tokyo) and bringing up my three children, kimono has become a very big part of my life; it is something that I now study and collect, and also teach in dressing classes, make, exhibit and give presentations on. I am also pursuing a Ph.D. on the subject.

Kimono literature

The West holds a special fascination for its oriental 'Other' (see Edward Said's *Orientalism* 1978), and the kimono, especially when worn by geisha, is the epitome of this 'Othering'. There is a plethora of geisha and kimono books. There are histories, such as Minnich (1963), Liddell (1989), Kennedy (1990), Munsterberg (1996), and there are books on various textile techniques used in the making of kimono, such as tie-dyeing by Ito (1981). There is a 'how to wear it' book in English (Yamanaka 1987). I read kimono books in both English and Japanese. Lisa Dalby has written what has come to be regarded as the definitive book in English on the kimono, *Kimono* (1993), which includes some fascinating chapters on kimono fashion history, as well as an excellent description of

Only 1 or 2 cm of the collars showed, but women would spend more on their collars than on a whole kimono. This evidences a fashionable sense of the importance of detail, far ahead of the current craze for accessories in the West.

My fourth example is that according to Minami (also in Kondo), Mitsukoshi, one of the newly opened department stores, employed a team of artists and dyers in 1907 as proto 'trends researchers' (cool hunters) to find out what kimono consumers were wanting in order to establish Mitsukoshi as the centre of kimono fashion trends. This appears to predate 'cool hunting' in western trend research and forecasting.

Kimono in Japan Today

Having established kimono's fashionable history, I now turn my gaze to contemporary Japan. For a time kimono stores were just disappearing from the high street. This seemed to support the viewpoint of Dalby and Goldstein-Gidoni that kimono is no longer relevant. A white paper on the kimono industry produced by the Kansai Bureau of Economics, Trade and Industry also revealed some very negative data on the market. It shows that there has been a steady drop in kimono sales since the peak in the economic boom years of the 1980s. Since 1993, the drop has been sharp: from 1,299,200,000,000 yen down to 394,500,000,000 yen in 2008. This is a decline from 6–4 per cent of the overall garment market. However, according to the white paper, when interviewed, more than 80 per cent of women expressed an interest in kimono although they had not bought or worn one within the last year.

What accounts for this seeming contradiction between sales and the interest in kimono? Further reading of the white paper reveals that it is not the kimono that is outdated, but the traditional and rule-governed kimono industry, which has failed to move with the times, or understand the new market, and consumer behaviour. Traditionally families would be loyal to one kimono store, and stores did not have to compete. It was middle-aged women, who ran households and had a large budget that made up the kimono market. The traditional kimono stores have lost the pulse of the market and the trust of the customer. They have policed kimono, keeping away the less wealthy, younger customers, or those who are not sure of themselves, effectively preserving, even creating, the image of the traditional but dying kimono, available only to the special, wealthy few, and thus contributing to the stereotyped view to which Dalby and Goldstein-Gidoni refer. Customer demography and needs have changed, but the industry has failed to respond, leading to a decline in the market.

The winds of change are in the air, however. Today's consumer is a younger, professional, often single, computer savvy woman. She has far more available options, but her budget is lower than that of the middle-aged women who previously made up the market. She can choose from kimono shops, or can take lessons and buy through the kimono school's connection to one. Customers want kimono

Figure 1: Author wearing long sleeved kimono with coloured accessories and contemporary plastic earrings.

Figure 2: Author wearing casual kimono with flowered collar and a cotton obi with paper doll motif.

Figure 3: Author wearing taisho period kimono with obi, decorated by sewing on reindeer, lace and braid, for Christmas.

Figure 4: Author wearing punk styled kimono, with a black studded western belt. Kimono produced by rolling a bicycle tyre with acrylic paint on it, over the cloth. Coordinated with punk boots and spider earrings.

Figure 5: Author demonstrates the use of coloured collar with a formal kimono in addition to western earrings and Thai cashmere shawl.

stores to be easy to enter, like boutiques, and prêt-a-porter is increasingly popular as there is no waiting time. There are also many new routes available for the purchase of kimono. Whilst the overall market for kimono has been dropping off, the options of buying online or buying from a recycle store are becoming increasingly popular and have been doing brisk business, not only gaining a much larger share of the kimono market, but increasing their sales annually. (Flea markets have existed for hundreds of years, and are very popular too.) Successful companies are those that have a brand image, sell online, and/or have prêt-a-porter or polyester kimono or other reasonably priced lines that meet the needs of today's younger clientele.

Rental businesses for weddings and also for graduations and coming-of-age ceremonies are also a visible presence. About twenty years ago, about half of my university students graduated wearing the same suit that they wore to their entrance ceremony. Now almost 100 per cent of female students graduate from university in a kimono and *hakama* (split trousers), which most of them rent. Clearly kimono is alive and well for ceremonial wear, for certain groups as street wear, and for dedicated kimono lovers (e.g. the group 'Kimono de Ginza'). Rather like retail trends in other fashion markets, which Morace and the *Future Concept Lab* in Milan call 'consum-author' (2008), the consumer can contribute to the making of the object they are consuming. This is expressed in the growing liberation of traditional decorative motifs as well as kimono inspired garments that take 'shortcuts' into the kimono 'look' without all the details of etiquette.

Kimono goes global

The final signal of the contemporary revival of the kimono that I want to address is its new role as a 'social connector': as a way of building groups and relationships. The work of Assman (2008) examined this role of the kimono in different kinds of kimono groups. Traditional Japanese groups tend to stay together over long periods of time, with even aged people meeting together at reunions with friends from school. However, kimono-based groups as well as kimono markets are changing: the interaction of a 'traditional' cultural item with modern communication technology has opened up new ways of relatedness. Globalization, says Bauman, has undermined geographical communities but ushered in virtual ones. This has meant that we cannot only participate in local groups, but in national and international ones as well. Bauman says: 'Fun they may be, these virtual communities, but they create only an illusion of intimacy, a pretence of community' (Bauman 2004: 25).

Whilst online networks may not be a substitute for real life contact (they are not always designed to be), they sometimes do lead to real life contact. One member of such a community remarked how much better he had become at communicating because he practised it with far away kimono wearers, many of whom he ended up meeting and becoming friends with. Perhaps Bauman is considering social networking sites from the point of view of emotional involvement, but it can be seen that networking has great value as an educational tool, with kimono fans from many countries sharing information about books and websites that have helped them in their kimono-related practices.

Two main kinds of kimono activities can be found on the web. One of them is selling, and the other is blogging, or networking, a diary-type of activity. (There are also a few historical sites, particularly those concerned with geisha.) These two groups are not exclusive as many shops have their own blog, written by their staff members, which have a following amongst kimono fans. A glance at the web reveals that the traditional ways of buying a kimono from a local store, which one's family would patronize for generations, have changed vastly. There are two main shopping sites in Japan, similar to eBay. One is called Rakuten, and one is called Yahoo Auction. On any day there are about 30, 000 men's kimono, and 165,000 women's kimono for sale on Yahoo Auction. Of course, thousands of kimono stores have their own websites, too, meaning that the consumer has access not only to local stores, but stores all over Japan as well as the auction sites. Credit cards and efficient road parcel services ensure that goods are delivered within two or three days of purchase. What is the extent of kimono blogging? Accessing safari search engine and doing a Google search on *Kimono* (in Chinese characters) *buroggu* (blog in katakana script) on 12 December 2009 produced more than 4,410,000 hits. (One year ago, 26 October 2008, this produced only 2,820,000 hits.) A search in English produced 929,000 hits (compared to 885,000 on 26 October 2008). This amount of activity indicates that there are a lot of computer-savvy people who are interested in kimono, either for personal reasons, or for business. There are two main types of blogs. One type is of kimono stores, showing their wares through photographs, and these blogs sometimes include personal tips or coordination ideas from the staff. The second type of blog is the personal one, where ideas and dress are discussed, sometimes along with a diary-type record of events. These sometimes include anecdotal stories of how the writer had been embarrassed or had their kimono look tampered with by some well-meaning kimono expert on the street. In this way they discuss the rights and wrongs of kimono wearing and whether or not following the rules of kimono wearing was important or not. There is one site called Fashion blog *mura,* (village), which was accessed on 26 October 2008, and again on 12 December 2009. There has been a tremendous increase in blogging activity on this site, even over the past year. These are exclusively Japanese bloggers.

The total of 7,209 Japanese fashion blogs increased to 13,465. Whilst men or women may make the blogs for kimono stores, the majority of the personal bloggers are women. They are from a wide variety of ages and backgrounds. This suggests that the common misperception in Japan that only old women are interested in wearing kimono is incorrect. Although the number is very small, one can see a considerable growth of interest in men's kimono, too. Interestingly many of the English-language blogs are written by non-Japanese, who also discuss how to wear kimono, what they have bought and good kimono books (and sometimes reveal an obsession with geisha).

Facebook's kimono discussion page was started by Patrizia Crimi on 20 February 2009, and it can be accessed by all Facebook users by typing kimono into 'search'. I was introduced to the page and became

Categories of kimono blogs	No. of blogs 26 October 2008	No. of blogs 12 December 2009
Kimono, *wasou* (Japanese clothing)	438	655
Kitsuke (dressing)	27	115
Antique	20	109
Remake (western clothes made out of old kimono	5	37
Dansei kimono (men's)	5	28
Wasou-style fashion (Japanese style fashion)	5	66

Table 1: Showing blogging activity over time on the Japanese blogging website 'Fashion blog mura *[village]'.*

a fan in September. I first posted on 5 September. I started posting as there were not many good pictures on the site (including the main picture, which is a fake kimono), and I wanted to show what kimono is really like. Since the end of September I have posted new outfits each week with short explanations, and have answered questions and enjoyed a lot of positive feedback. The number of fans grows daily. When I first became a fan there were just over 400 fans, but the number passed 1,000 on 5 November, and on 22 November, 2010 at almost 3,900. Although this is a group in the very loosest sense of the word, no commitment, no need to post anything, or even to look at it, the speed of growth of the group is amazing, it has new fans from around the world everyday (about 50 per week), and it can be an interesting source of information. Whilst it may seem a very superficial base, 'I like kimono', I have found out from this group that there are people who have learnt to put on kimono without even coming to Japan, let alone going to kimono school. Through cruising blogs and kimono pages, they have learnt to put on the kimono themselves, and also to tie complicated *obi* bows. Kimono fans can easily purchase their kimono on eBay, Ichiroya or other online stores that ship outside Japan. What this means is that in a sense kimono really has gone global. There are numerous blogs in English by kimono fans outside Japan. The fact that Japanese can now learn kimono without going to kimono dressing school, and buy a kimono without stepping into a kimono shop, is very significant. It means that the hegemony of the kimono school is broken. It is even more significant when that begins to spread overseas. It is possible to follow an online guide to dressing, to post a question and get answers and help from all kinds of sources, and to learn completely independently of the official networks. This will inevitably lead to an increase in the variety of ways of dressing. In the sense that wearers are bypassing the official channels, it is a street level movement that is spreading through the use of cyberspace. In other words, wearers are reclaiming kimono from the official channels and deciding what to do with it themselves. The Internet is being used for developing social networks, but also for kimono education. It is entirely free and, in the sense that one can choose the sites one prefers, users can personalize their kimono learning to their own needs. Whilst an online community or network may not bring deep committed relationships, it is very egalitarian and can make available a whole range of educational options for those with the interest and the time to search them out. In this sense it is a very democratic phenomenon. A concern of the kimono schools is to teach the correct kimono knowledge '*tadashi kimono chishiki*' to the next generation. In a way the kimono schools are like the grammarians, or language teachers who are a conservative force, trying to deny change. Correct kimono knowledge is not actually kimono knowledge, but the teaching system that the schools themselves invented. If it is proved that the kimono schools are not necessary, then they will become irrelevant and will die out. The next generation of kimono wearers is choosing a more flexible approach and learning environment, and is selecting which knowledge sources, and which aspects of kimono knowledge, it wants to appropriate.

Some kimono businesses are doing well, and consumer surveys still indicate a high level of interest in kimono, as does the level of Internet activity. The number of blogs, homepages and activities in cyberspace indicate that kimono is a much discussed topic, and point to the fact that kimono itself still has an importance and a positive image in Japan, and that this image goes beyond the established and exported Japanese female image that is the conventional representation of kimono.

Conclusion

The conclusion that one can draw from this situation is that there is a gap between the traditional kimono industries and the way consumers wish to appropriate the product. This gap signals a fundamental shift in the power of purveyors of tradition. The result of the lack of trust in kimono shops, not to mention a changing group of consumers, is that kimono wearers have chosen to bypass the standard systems, the traditional kimono shop and also the kimono school. By using cyberspace networks they have begun to takeover, and, in a sense, reclaim kimono as a garment of the people. This is somewhat similar to the Edo period, when fashion leaders suddenly became the common people, traders and townspeople and their acting heroes, rather than the upper class and cultivated samurai class. The movement that was once spread by actors, courtesans, by flyers and posters, is now spread by bloggers and kimono fans, by cyberspace, and reaches not only to Japan, but also to the ends of the Internet-ed world. This reclamation of both physical kimono, and of kimono discourses and representations, outside the kimono school system has implications for the future. It seems likely that kimono schools will grow smaller, unless they can find a new niche, (perhaps teaching in schools), and that the high-end kimono market will continue to shrink, but will not disappear as ceremonies and rites of passage still require high quality kimono. Kimono stores will have to rethink their images and marketing strategy, and take notice of branding and labelling, or other means of making their goods attractive. They will have to improve their customer services and know their market better. Now that people are learning to wear kimono all over the world, through the Internet, the survival of kimono in some form is assured, though the regular kimono worn in the future will not necessarily be the traditionally represented, formal one that has become the standard image of a feminized and exotic Japan.

References

Assman, Stephanie (2008), 'Between Tradition and Innovation: The Reinvention of the Kimono in Japanese Consumer Culture', *Fashion Theory*, 12: 3, pp. 359–376.

Bauman, Zygmunt (2004), *Identity*, Cambridge, New Malden: Polity Press.

Breward, Christopher (2004), *Fashioning London*, Oxford: Berg.

Dalby, Lisa (1993), *Kimono*, New Haven and London: Yale University Press.

Entwistle, Joanne (2000), *The Fashioned Body*, Cambridge: Polity Press.

Flugel, John C. (1930), *The Psychology of Clothes*, London: Hogarth Press.

Goffman, Erving (1959), *The Presentation of Self in Everyday life*, New York: Random House.

Goldstein-Gidoni, Ofra (1999), 'Kimono and the construction of Gendered and cultural Identities', *Ethnology*, 38: 4, pp. 351–370.

Goldstein-Gidoni, Ofra (2001), 'The Making and Marking of the 'Japanese' and the 'Western' in Japanese Contemporary Material Culture', *Journal of Material Culture*, 6: 1, pp. 67–90.

Goldstein-Gidoni, Ofra (2005), 'The Production and Consumption of 'Japanese Culture' in the Global Culture Market', *Journal of Consumer Culture*, 5: 2, pp. 155–179.

Ito, Toshiko (1981), *Tsujigahana*, Tokyo, New York and San Francisco: Kodansha International Ltd.

Kansai Bureau of Economics, Trade and Industry (2008), http://www.kansai.meti.go.jp/35sangyo/kinuorimono/downloadfiles/2009_kinuorimono_honbun.pdf. Accessed 14 November 2009.

Kennedy, A. (1990), *Japanese Costume*, Paris: Adam Biro.

Kato, Manji (1980), *Taisho no Han Eri.*, Tokyo: Minzoku Ishou Bunka Fukyuu Kyoukai.

Kondo, Tomie (2002), *Fukusou de Tanoishimu Genji Monogatari*, Tokyo: PHP Bunkou.

Kroeber, Alfred. L. and Richardson, J. (1940), *Three Centuries of Women's Dress Fashion*, Univ. of California, Berkeley & Los Angeles.

Kuki, Shuzo (1997), *Reflections of Japanese Taste – The Structure of Iki* (trans. John Clark), Sydney: Power Publications.

Liddell, Jill (1989), *The Story of the Kimono*, New York: Dutton.

Lipovetsky, Gilles (1994), *The Empire of Fashion*, Princeton: Princeton University Press.

Minami, Hiroshi (1980), *Taisho Bunka no Honshitsu.*,Tokyo: Minzoku Ishou Bunka Fukyuu Kyoukai.

Minnich, Helen. B. (1963), *Japanese Costume*, Rutland: Charles E. Tuttle.

Morace, F. (2008), *Consum-Authors: the generations as creative enterprises*, Milano: Libri Scheiwiller.

Munsterberg, Hugo (1996), *The Japanese Kimono*, Hong Kong, Oxford and New York: Oxford University Press.

Murasaki Shikibu (1970), *The Tale of Genji* (trans. Arthur Waley), Tokyo: Charles E. Tuttle.

Said, Edward W. (1978), *Orientalism*, New York: Vintage Books.

Sei Shonagon (1967) *The Pillow Book of Sei Shonagon* (trans. I. Morris), London: Penguin.

Yamanaka, Norio (1987), *The Book of Kimono*, Tokyo, New York, London: Kodansha International.

Yoshida Mitsukuni, Tanaka I. and Sesoko T. (1986), *The Poeople's Culture*, Tokyo: Mazda Motor Corporation.

Young, Agnes. G. (1937), *Recurring Cycles of Fashion: 1760–1937*, New York: Harper & Brothers.

Suggested citation

Cliffe, S. (2010), 'Revisioning the kimono', *Critical Studies in Fashion and Beauty* 1: 2, pp. 217–231, doi: 10.1386/csfb.1.2.217_1

Contributor details

Sheila Cliffe is a graduate of Temple University of Japan and teaches English, kimono and fashion at Jumonji Gakuen Women's University in Japan. She is an avid kimono collector as well as a researcher and dyer of kimono. She is working towards a Ph.D. on this topic at the University of Leeds. She lives in Tokyo with her three children.

Contact:
E-mail: s-cliffe@jumonji-u.ac.jp
limegreen107@gmail.com

CSFB 1 (2) pp. 233–254 Intellect Limited 2010

Critical Studies in Fashion and Beauty
Volume 1 Number 2
© 2010 Intellect Ltd Article. English language. doi: 10.1386/csfb.1.2.233_1

DIRK GINDT
Ph.D., Stockholm University

Coming out of the cabinet: Fashioning the closet with Sweden's most famous diplomat

Keywords

the closet
fashion and
    homosexuality
cold war masculinity
Swedish sexual politics
Sverker Åström

Abstract

This article offers a critical analysis of the media discourse surrounding the Swedish diplomat Sverker Åström's coming out as a gay man at the age of 87. Particular interest is devoted to his striking fashion choice of wearing a pair of oddly coloured socks, which highlighted his contradictory masculinity as well as the many inherent paradoxes of the closet. Åström's red and green socks functioned as a means to express forbidden desires, to oppose normative expectations in a playful way and to grant the gay subject a presence in a world that is still very much structured by the logics of the closet. Moreover, his contradictory body language, coupled with his repeated affirmations that his coming out was a private issue, revealed a divided masculinity that was ideologically dependent on a pre-feminist understanding of gender and sexuality as private, that is to say non-political. The article argues that there was strong evidence to suggest that his coming out was in fact a tactical move in a political game, a move aimed to denounce and ridicule the

Swedish Security Police (SÄPO), who, after decades of surveillance, refused to grant the diplomat access to its classified files on him.

> Wiederholung! Dabei weiß ich: alles hängt davon ab, ob es gelingt, sein Leben nicht außerhalb der Wiederholung zu erwarten, sondern die Wiederholung, die ausweglose, aus freiem Willen (trotz Zwang) zu seinem Leben zu machen, indem man anerkennt: Das bin ich! …
>
> Max Frisch, *Stiller*[1]

Sunday, 14 September 2003 was the day of a national Swedish referendum. The referendum resulted in the population voting against introducing the Euro as their new currency and against joining the final stage of the European Monetary Union. The nation was also in mourning; shocked by the stabbing of foreign minister Anna Lindh in a Stockholm department store only three days before. On this particular Sunday, readers of *Svenska Dagbladet/The Swedish Daily Paper*, one of the country's largest morning papers, were confronted with a strange photograph on the cover of the cultural section. The larger part of the page depicted nothing more than the lower part of two human legs. The unidentified individual in the photograph was dressed in a perfectly ironed black pair of trousers and beige loafers, most likely new. Without looking very elegant, the shoes seemed to be very comfortable with their loosely tied shoelaces. Apart from the fact that the viewer could only see the lower part of the body, the most surprising aspect was the odd pair of socks that the person was wearing: the right one was bright green, while the left one was vibrant red. To whom did these socks belong? Had Pippi Longstocking been brought to life? The trousers and shoes could be identified as belonging to a man, but nothing in the picture disclosed his age. At the very bottom of the page, a small text in white letters read 'Nu kommer han ut'/'Now he's coming out' and referred the reader to pages 16 and 17, where it was revealed that the mysterious socks were owned by the former diplomat and under-secretary of state for foreign affairs, Sverker Åström, who, at the age of 87, publicly outed himself as a gay man:

> All my life, I lived a double life, but I have never been a security risk. In an exclusive interview with *Svenska Dagbladet's* [reporter] Karin Thunberg, the diplomat Sverker Åström, 87, tells the secret of his life: that he is gay. Only his bosses at the Department of State were informed. They shrugged their shoulders. – The only regret I have is that I never had any children. And I have probably lived a more lonely life than I would have as a heterosexual.
>
> (Thunberg 2003: 16)[2]

1. Repetition! Yet I know: everything depends on whether you succeed in not expecting your life outside of the repetition, but to turn the repetition, the hopeless one, out of your own free will (despite compulsion) into your life, by recognizing: This is who I am! (translation by the author).

2. All Swedish quotes have been translated by the author.

3. A word on the terminology: although the acronym LGBT might seem preferable at times because it is more inclusive and less male-centred, it would have been misleading to use it, since the article primarily concentrates on Åström and the implications of his coming out as a gay man. I have therefore decided to consistently use the terms gay and homosexual (a term which, despite its psycho-pathological connotations, is still widely used in the Swedish language).

4. After his coming out, Åström continued to be an opinionated social commentator who published debate articles on questions such as a possible Swedish membership in NATO and the EMU, the military invasion of Iraq, and the relationship of the former social democratic government to the United States of America under the Bush Jnr administration. He also translated Michelangelo's love sonnets into Swedish in 2005 and appeared on a number of TV programmes, including

The purpose of this article is to use fashion and queer studies as critical tools to offer an analysis of the media discourse surrounding Åström's late coming out and to detail what the case reveals about Swedish history and contemporary LGBT politics. By investigating the overlap between public/political manoeuvring and the private/personal game of sexual identity, I aim to complicate further the tense relationship between masculinity, male homosexuality and the Swedish state during the cold war. Throughout the article, particular interest will be devoted to the diplomat's odd pair of socks to tease out how this inconspicuous fashion choice highlighted his contradictory masculinity as well as the many paradoxes inherent in the closet. The case study, I argue, is significant not only for illustrating and analysing the conditions and politics of the closet in twenty-first century Sweden, but my interest and motivation also lies in querying some of the broader implications at stake, especially when it comes to the question of national security.[3]

Sweden's most famous diplomat

Born in Uppsala in 1915, at a young age Åström became an important figure in Swedish foreign politics. Following his post as a member of the Swedish delegation in Moscow during World War II (1940–1943), he had many positions with various Swedish government agencies: secretary of legislation at the embassy in Washington (1946–1948); head of division at the ministry for foreign affairs (1949–1953); councillor at the embassy in London (1953–1956); foreign affairs councillor (1956–1963); representative at the United Nations in New York (1964–1970); state secretary for foreign affairs (1972–1977); and ambassador to France in Paris (1978–1982). Working closely with key politicians such as foreign minister Östen Undén, diplomat and UN secretary-general Dag Hammarskjöld and Prime Minister Olof Palme, he had considerable influence on shaping Sweden's diplomacy during the cold war (a position of political neutrality between the two blocs). Two of his most important achievements were putting forward a resolution for the UN to become more active in environmental concerns (1968) and representing Sweden during the negotiations for the EEC treaty in 1970.[4] Interest was therefore high when he was about to release an updated edition of his biography *Ögonblick: Från ett halvsekel i UD-tjänst/ Moments: From half a century in the duty of the ministry for foreign affairs* in September 2003. The interview in *Svenska Dagbladet* was part of the promotional campaign for the book, which included a specially written afterword in which Åström acknowledged being gay and even expressed some slight regret about not having had the opportunity to be young in an era with a more progressive legislation that allowed for same-sex relationships: 'I have exclusively loved men. Some happy relationships I have had, but sporadically and short-lived. The relationships never developed into the legitimate partnership which I could have legalized with the new legislation' (Åström 2003a: 270).

At first it seemed astounding that a person of such an advanced age outed himself as a gay man. Moreover, given the development of Swedish sexual politics since the mid-1990s, the media impact which Åström's coming out generated was impressive. Aside from the possibility of registered partnership (1995), the institutionalization of an ombudsman to protect the rights of lesbians and gays, aptly titled HomO (1999), and a number of anti-discrimination laws (including protection from hate speech (2002)), several cultural events also contributed to the higher visibility of lesbians and gays from the mid-1990s onwards. The public debate around same-sex partnerships, for instance, was made easier by the coming out of several entertainers, followed by openly gay politicians in the early 2000s. In 1998, Stockholm hosted the Euro Pride festival. The same year Lukas Moodysson's movie *Fucking Åmål/Show me love* about two teenage girls falling in love with each other became a critically-hailed international success, and Elisabeth Ohlson Wallin's controversial photo exhibition *Ecce Homo*, depicting biblical situations to illustrate how the love of Jesus Christ embraces gays and persons with HIV/AIDS, caused reactions all the way to the Vatican. By that point, gay men and, to a lesser extent, lesbians had also been recognized as consumers and became the targets of large advertising campaigns by both national and transnational companies. This newly found social acceptance led one scholar to exclaim that the country had celebrated its own 'national coming out process' (Rosenberg 2002: 104). Unfortunately, while Sweden was busily affirming itself as a sexually liberated and tolerant state,[5] this did not involve a critical reassessment of the country's post-war history – something that became very clear in the media discourse surrounding Åström's coming out. Dismissing the importance of the diplomat's public coming out would belie what this unique case can reveal about Swedish gay history and the political dimension of the proverbial closet. In order to unpack the multiple issues at stake, I start by offering some reflections on the dramaturgical movement of an act of coming out.

The dramaturgy of a coming out

Ever since Stonewall and the ensuing gay liberation movement, coming out has been understood as not only a personal, but also a political statement, as a way to mark gay visibility and pride, to demand social rights and to shed off internalized oppression by developing group solidarity and a positive self-identification. Indeed, one of the first (short-lived) major publications by the Gay Liberation Front was called *Come Out!*, a magazine whose name also inspired the title of the Swedish Federation for Lesbian, Gay, Bisexual and Transgender Rights newspaper, *Kom ut!* Coming out continues to be a central concern for gay activists and academics, with a number of scholars conceptualizing it as a rite of passage. Jeffrey Weeks, for instance, describes it as a threefold stage designed to overcome self-oppression and mark gay pride: first, the individuals need to acknowledge their desires to themselves; thereafter, they attempt to approach other gay people and establish a

the infamous *Böglobbyn/The Gay Lobby* in 2006, from which he retired in protest after only a couple of episodes, claiming the show reproduced stereotypes of and prejudices against gay men.

5. For a discussion on how the perceived sexual liberalism in Sweden heavily regulates sexuality and channels it into hetero-normative patterns that only allow for morally 'good sex' sanctioned by the state and in coherence with a national identity built on the idea of a gender equality that continuously stresses the *differences* between women and men, see Kulick 2005.

social network or community; and finally they declare their sexuality to the rest of the world (Weeks [1977] 1990: 192). Volker Woltersdorff uses religious metaphors to explain a coming out and compares this act to the Christian genre of confession writings. He also describes it as a 'station drama' (or *Stationendrama*), that is, a series of smaller steps or scenes that a person lives through to develop a gay identity: from the first fantasies to the acknowledgment of difference and then on to the first sexual contacts and, finally, the integration into a subculture. The confession, the act of coming out, becomes the central turning point in such station dramas (Woltersdorff 2005: 37). While I do not question the centrality of the act of confession, any explanation of a coming out as a rite of passage is too linear and is, in effect, an incomplete description of reality as it does not take into consideration the fact that gay people never come out just once; they have to do so repeatedly.

In her seminal book *Epistemology of the Closet*, Eve Kosofsky Sedgwick (1990) identifies the closet as one of the fundamental structuring principles of modern western society: it is a social institution that permeates law, politics, religion, education, health care and popular culture. She further argues that the act of coming out is a continuous process. One cannot come out of the closet once and for all, as there is always somebody who does not know yet. Since a coming out has to be repeated over and over again, it is impossible to ever leave the closet behind. The closet therefore remains a particularly contradictory institution. Similarly, Judith Butler underlines the performative power of coming out and points out the divergent consequences. While it can be politically necessary to come out of the closet, not least in order to conduct political activism, such a step also means that one's identity (the so-called homosexual) is being locked in a position originally formulated by nineteenth-century pathology. At the same time Butler wonders what it means to be 'out' of the closet and if such a space can actually exist:

> For being 'out' always depends to some extent on being 'in': it gains meaning only within that polarity. Hence, being 'out' must produce the closet again and again in order to maintain itself as 'out'. In this sense, *outness* can only produce a new opacity; and *the closet* produces the promise of a disclosure that can, by definition, never come.
>
> (Butler [1990] 2004: 123, original emphasis)

Every time gay persons out themselves, or are outed, a social structure that defines them as different and deviant is reproduced. Rather than being a linear process, coming out becomes a spiral movement that makes it impossible to become liberated from the structure of the closet and encourages further repetitions to cement the socially abnormal identity. For Butler, the queer subject is constituted through this series of repetitions. However, since repetitions can differ from one another (a cornerstone in her theory of performativity), they also show the instability of the category and can therefore reveal the foundations of the closet and the insecurity of any sexual identity.

As Butler points out, 'paradoxically, it is precisely the *repetition* of that play that establishes as well the *instability* of the very category that it constitutes' (Butler [1990] 2004: 125, original emphasis).

This process of creating insecurity through repetition, I suggest, was illustrated by the diplomat's public confession and the ensuing media discourse. An analysis of this discourse allows for an identification of the many variations, inconsistencies and contradictions of Åström's coming out, with the potential to illustrate the very instability of the closet and the perpetually deferred disclosure of any coming out. For 87 years the diplomat seemed to have managed to escape the burden of classification, at least in public. Once he took the decisive step and published 'the truth' in his book, the machinery could not be stopped and the repetition of the statement was encouraged by outside forces. Within four weeks, he affirmed his homosexuality in at least six different public platforms: apart from the already quoted biography and the newspaper interview Åström did to promote the book, on 16 September he appeared on the news programme 'Efter tre'/'After three' on Swedish Radio, on 18 September he published a debate article in the newspaper *Dagens Nyheter/The Daily News* in which he severely criticized the Swedish Security Police for refusing him access to its archived files on him, on 4 October he made an appearance on the national TV 4 channel's programme 'TV 4 Nyhetsmorgon'/'TV 4 morning news' and finally met with an editor of the publication *QX* (*Queer Extra*). The material I base my arguments upon appeared within a very limited period of time, but covers an era that reaches back to World War II and the post-war decades.

Sartorial theatricality

In October 2003, Jon Voss, editor of *QX*, interviewed the retired diplomat for a long feature that was accompanied by a number of photographs by Ohlson Wallin. Åström stood against a black background in a dark suit and behind a large bouquet of white gladiolas resting on the floor. At first, the oddly coloured socks seemed to be missing, but a smaller picture below the editor's column revealed them; here, Åström was shown with his suit jacket unbuttoned, without shoes and with his feet on the couch table – allowing an unabashed look at his red and green socks. The possibility of him being colour blind should be ruled out as it had surely been a conscious choice. Furthermore, there was no evidence to suggest the colour of the socks was related to the 'gay hanky code' – the subcultural tradition of marking sexual preferences and positions with a handkerchief in the back pocket.

Apart from constituting a contradiction in themselves, the oddly paired socks also contrasted violently with the rest of Åström's outfit, which was very traditional, not to say conservative. The dour, dark, three-piece-suit that consists of a jacket, a vest and a pair of trousers made its entrance onto the British fashion stage under the rule of Charles II, as a reaction to a domestic political crisis at the Stuart court as well as to international tensions with France. It was introduced as a sartorial and political statement against the prevailing luxurious fashion consumption at the English court (inspired by French models), which was considered to be feminine and unpatriotic. Breaking the cycle of ever-changing styles and fashions amongst the nobility, the three-piece-suit was intended to mark 'a sartorial stability that would signal the restoration of political stability' and to 'permanently install modesty as a marker of elite masculinity' (Kuchta 2009: 45–48), which, in reality, would not happen until after the Glorious Revolution that overthrew James II in 1688. Moreover, the resulting need for English wool was a welcomed financial benefit. Thus the three-piece-suit became a fashion item where masculinity, power, morality, modesty, national politics and economics intertwined.

Although the dark suit has become a dominant uniform for urban middle-class men since the late eighteenth century, Christopher Breward points out the risks of oversimplifying and dismissing the development of men's fashion by stating that (heterosexual) men, unlike women, were not interested in fashion and did not pay attention to outer appearance. Such claims are historically incorrect, he insists, in as much as they divert attention from fashionable and alternative masculinities such as nineteenth-century aesthetes or dandies. Moreover, they also risk blinding scholars to the implications of masculine patterns of consumption and their impact on the formation of urban, bourgeois masculinities (Breward 1995: 170–178; 1999: 1–23). Significantly, Breward also reminds us of the importance of accessories to break the uniformity of the suit and create a more fashionable consumer identity. He identifies a tendency, which emerged in the last decades of the nineteenth century, to 'incorporate minor changes in the choice of hat, gloves, shirt or tie according to function or season, or a more obvious switching between garments to signify a knowledge of prevailing tastes' (Breward 1999: 39).

Another view on the evolution and spread of the suit is offered by John Carl Flügel, who saw one of the reasons for what he called 'the Great Masculine Renunciation' in the social upheavals of the French Revolution in 1789. During the resulting process of democratization, bright colours and elaborate ornaments disappeared and the suit abolished some of the more visible hierarchies among the social classes, between the rich and the poor. Thanks to its practicality and utility, the suit became a garment for the bourgeoisie to visibly distance itself from the perceived decadence and laziness of the aristocracy. Flügel regretted that men gave up any attempts at beauty and noted that 'modern man's clothing abounds in features which symbolize his devotion to the principles of duty, of renunciation, and of self-control' (Flügel [1930] 2004: 105). Clothes were thus supposed to serve as external markers of a number of characteristics for a bourgeois masculinity and work ethic. These attributes are very close to what David Savran identifies as 'the three cardinal masculine characteristics: achievement, responsibility, and authority' (Savran 1992: 36). Even today, these culturally celebrated virtues are visually expressed in the men's fashion of a social class. The dark bourgeois suit has become the norm for a particular type of masculinity, namely a cultural ideal of a stable, essential masculinity free from anything feminine or gay and independent of fashion trends. Savran summarizes the historical development that has promoted certain behaviours as masculine, while excluding and punishing others:

Since the sixteenth century […], the male subject's will to regulate others has been secretly subordinated to a silent injunction to self-discipline, to the policing of his own body and his own desires, an injunction accomplished at a crippling cost: the expense of permanent estrangement from the object that has been henceforth known as his own body.

(Savran 1992: 39)

Because of the need to supervise and control one's own flesh, it comes as no surprise then that the bourgeois suit established itself as the masculine garment par excellence. It not only covers the body, but also turns it into an unidentifiable and exchangeable unit. Moreover, it signals the body's boundaries and impenetrability. According to Richard Dyer, the straight male body is defined by its clear-cut boundaries against the outside world. It must not be penetrated under any circumstance and

a hard, contoured body does not look like it runs the risk of being merged into other bodies. A sense of separation and boundedness is important to the white male ego. […] Only a hard, visibly bounded body can resist being submerged into the horror of femininity and non-whiteness.

(Dyer 1997: 152f)

While Dyer makes these observations in relation to action movies and heroes, I would claim that the bourgeois suit works as a symbolic sartorial armour that gives the masculine body a sense of impregnability and protection, especially because this armour does not reveal any skin and therefore does not risk sexualizing the body or submitting it to the lustful, objectifying gaze of any gender.[6] Finally, the suit also demonstrates the intersections between gender, politics and economics. Raewyn Connell notes the social, political and economic power associated with the dark suit and points out that '[a]lmost every political leader in the world now wears the uniform of the Western business executive' (Connell 2000: 45). The masculine suit is thus one of the most discussed garments in fashion history; of particular interest to this article is the purported gender stability and the privileged socio-economic position that are connoted with it.

In his public appearances in the fall of 2003, Åström made sure to wear the standard attire of any politician, lawyer, diplomat, businessman, bank clerk, manager or any other man of a certain social and economic position – except for the socks. In the interview with *Svenska Dagbladet*, he himself offered the following explanation for this unusual fashion choice: 'I'm not a conceited man. But I am vain – and I cultivate my eccentricity' (Thunberg 2003: 16). The socks could thus be said to constitute a deliberate statement of his individuality, a contrast to the uniformity of the masculine suit. However, this choice of accessories was more than a charming act of a slightly eccentric, elderly gentleman. In light of Åström's recent coming out, the differently coloured socks functioned as a sign of deviancy; they

6. Anne Hollander puts forward a very different argument, suggesting that regardless of how streamlined the masculine suit might appear, it should not be misconstrued as devoid of any erotic appeal. On the contrary, the formal integrity of the suit represents 'the fantasy of modern form as the proper material vessel of both beauty and power, of positive sexuality' (Hollander 1995: 5). While the suit covers the entire body, it does not necessarily desexualize it; because it connotes social power it can be very attractive and does in fact 'continue to have its erotic appeal, in the confidently forceful mode. Suits are sexy, just like cars and planes' (Hollander 1995: 5). A man in a suit is therefore not necessarily free from an objectifying gaze.

7. Breward traces these assumptions back to the late eighteenth century, but also contests this somewhat simplified and stereotypical view because it disregards the complex patterns of male consumption. According to him, '[m]ale dress has undoubtedly been overlooked, subsumed by the assumption that a discourse of separate spheres, whilst constructing display and dress as innately feminine pursuits, enforced a model of masculinity in which overt interest in clothing and appearance automatically implied a tendency towards unmanliness and effeminacy' (Breward 1995: 170–1; see also Breward 1999).

undermined and destabilized cultural norms and expectations. They offered a subtle way of creating gender trouble, disturbing the normative facade of straight diplomatic masculinity and granting the queer subject a presence in a world that is still very much structured by the (il)logics of the closet.

The performance of normative gender is a traditional strategy for gays to secure the closet, and for this purpose clothing is of great importance. Until the sexual liberation started in the 1960s, mainstream society stereotypically identified gay men as displaying an effeminate appearance and behaviour. Considering these prejudices and ignorance, fitting in became easier for more 'straight-acting' gays. In order to be able to pass as straight, some gay men avoided any signs of flamboyancy and hid behind a facade of normative masculinity. Clothes and control over one's mannerisms were of great importance in these efforts to secure the closet. Concretely speaking, this meant that closeted gay men avoided any open display of a sense of fashion in order not to become conspicuous (Cole 2000: 59–60).

To clarify Åström's strategy of disturbing normative appearances and inviting queer interpretations, I propose to draw a comparison to a literary character who tries to maintain a masculine bourgeois appearance through a strategic use of fashion – the successful, yet doomed, businessman Thomas Buddenbrook in Thomas Mann's novel *Buddenbrooks* (1901), which describes the rise and fall of a nineteenth-century bourgeois family. Kekke Stadin (2007) offers an inspiring analysis of the significance of the suit as the compulsory fashion item for this bourgeois capitalist who harbours political ambitions. For Buddenbrook, the combination of jacket, vest and trousers signifies respect, honour and elegance. However, to invest in his elegance also means walking a thin line between effeminacy and stylish representation – after all, by the second half of the nineteenth century, fashion connoted femininity.[7] A man who was too concerned with his appearance was suspicious: 'Taking care of one's looks was and is just as necessary as it is forbidden for a successful businessman. In order to cope with this, he must create a secret room for the forbidden: vanity' (Stadin 2007: 233). The patriarch desperately struggles to uphold the image he has created of himself as a successful, driven and well-educated businessman. He becomes so obsessed with keeping up appearances that he changes his clothes several times a day and spends hours in the bathroom to freshen up before he can face the world, but he fails miserably. After a while his colleagues refuse to take him seriously and, eventually, the mask becomes too heavy to wear: he collapses in the middle of the street and dies soon after. What Stadin does not take into consideration, however, is that Buddenbrook also struggles with repressed desires, as he had to give up his love for the florist Lisa. The novel actually reveals many of the sexual norms of the German *Bildungsbürgertum*. In the last generation, the tendencies for masturbation and homoeroticism take over: in a brilliant use of a sexual metaphor, Thomas' son Hanno cannot resist the urge to 'play the piano' and develops an intensive relationship with his playmate Kai. Tragically, Hanno dies before reaching adulthood, thereby marking the end of the family line that once dominated trade in the Hanseatic city of Lübeck. The repression of secret desires, often homoerotic, functions as a leitmotiv throughout Mann's literary output. Without being a gay character, Thomas Buddenbrook pretends to be someone he clearly is not. His insecurities, his fear of failure and his forbidden love must literally be covered up by the dominant fashion of his class and gender.[8]

In the case of Åström, I suggest that while his self-proclaimed eccentricity was not particularly flamboyant or camp, he was still flaunting the closet with his socks. I would deem such a strategy *sartorial theatricality*, i.e., a way of using clothes and accessories to create a certain overflow, an excessive mark that disturbs an otherwise normative appearance. While theatricality is often used in a pejorative way, synonymous with inauthenticity, fakeness and hyperbole, for Sue-Ellen Case it works like a wave that breaks down borders: 'Theatricality exceeds theater as it exceeds traditional social boundaries. It marks the restrictions of the theatre by spilling over its boundaries as it spills over the boundaries of "good taste" or "proper comportment" in the social realm' (Case 2002: 187). In our case, the socks crossed the boundaries between the private wardrobe – the closet – and the public life of politics and diplomacy. Åström's bourgeois suit radiated authority and control (including control over his sexuality) and helped to secure the closet by guaranteeing a normative gender appearance, but the loud socks disrupted this facade from within by drawing attention to the otherwise taken-for-granted uniform of a social elite and revealing the three-piece-suit as a performative means to display a conservative masculinity. The socks were remnants of what Stadin identifies as 'a secret room for the forbidden' and they functioned as a playful accessory transferred from the private wardrobe and closet into the professional life, spilling over the boundaries between the secret inside and the public outside. More than a simple display of vanity or idiosyncrasy, they were a means to decorate the closet in order to make it a little more bearable.

A private and a public body language

Influenced by Butler's theory of performativity, Joanne Entwistle argues that clothes and dress are crucial mediums to perform social identities. However, merely concentrating on garments will only convey a limited amount of meaning and signification if one fails to take into consideration the bodies that wear them and how these bodies move and gesticulate. Entwistle therefore proposes studying dress and fashion as an 'embodied practice' (Entwistle 2000: 11) and demands a more consistent focus on bodies for an analysis of the relationship between dress, fashion and identities. In order to discuss further the significance of Åström's oddly coloured socks, a closer scrutiny of his body language is essential.

On 4 October 2003 Åström was a guest on the programme 'TV 4 Nyhetsmorgon'/'TV 4 morning news' of the national channel TV 4. The news show introduced him as 'Sweden's most well-known diplomat' and immediately said that, at the age of 87, he had just come out of the closet. Åström sat in the centre of a blue couch behind a wooden coffee table on which newspapers and apples lay, with the male journalist sitting on a sofa to his right side. An elegant grey suit and a grey waistcoat, a white shirt and a tasteful tie with black and blue stripes enhanced the serious and dignified impression created. The tie and a white handkerchief, which peeped stylishly out of the breast

8. Research on homoeroticism in Thomas Mann's work is rich. In this context, the aspect of homosexuality working as *the open secret* is the most relevant. See, for example, Detering 2002: esp. 273–322.

9. A similar observation was made by the journalist Karin Thunberg, who interviewed Åström for the article in *Svenska Dagbladet* on 14 September and compared the correct diplomat, with his dry voice and straight back, to the man who was prone to giggle and became reminiscent of a young, excited boy. This boyish masculinity proved a strong contrast to the severe and professional appearance of the retired diplomat (Thunberg 2003: 16).

pocket, were the only original, if discreet, accessories in an otherwise very traditional, anonymous outfit. Not long into the interview, however, the camera glided under the wooden table and viewers were given a prolonged glance at the by now famous socks.

At the start of the interview, Åström expressed his grief over the death of Lindh and shared some personal memories of the foreign minister. Thereafter, the subject immediately turned to his belated coming out. Throughout the conversation he leaned backwards on the sofa and his gesticulation was restricted and moderate. While his right elbow rested on the arm of the sofa, he sometimes made slight movements with his left hand to underline a certain thought. Only when he got excited, would he push his body forward and use both hands to emphasize a point. Not unlike the elegant, yet plain, suit, Åström's body language served as another illustration of Flügel's 'Great Masculine Renunciation'. After decades of experience the diplomat was adept at controlling his body to avoid conveying any hidden impulses. Just like a clever poker player, he had learned to monitor every movement, glance and facial expression. Not only did he appear as a well-articulated speaker with a rich and nuanced vocabulary, he was also skilful at deciding how much information to disclose and how much to keep to himself. He plainly refused, for example, to answer the reporter's (arguably silly) question about when Åström realized that he was gay. He was happy, however, to demonstrate his expertise of debating diplomacy and international relations, offering his opinion on the ongoing war in Iraq and condemning the military politics of the United States under the George W. Bush administration. During the programme, he gave the impression of an intelligent, warm and humorous gentleman who was not averse to a good laugh. Halfway through the interview, he relaxed a bit and began to talk of the many suspicions that the Swedish Security Police (SÄPO) held against him during his professional career. He explained that for a long time SÄPO had surveyed him and kept a record on his every action. Twenty years after his retirement, they continuously refused to grant him access to these files, arguing that these contained classified information. At this point in the interview his body language changed abruptly. Once Åström relaxed, he bent forward, the pitch of his voice changed noticeably and his gestures became much livelier. Now it was not only his clothing that was contradictory, but also his body language. When talking about the false suspicions of SÄPO, he was visibly and audibly amused. He chuckled, his voice went up into a falsetto register and he no longer sat with a straight back, but instead moved the upper part of his body to the rhythm of his laughter.[9] Depending on the nature of the subject, Åström presented a stiff, expert diplomat masculinity *or* a more relaxed attitude with an almost boyish charm. Ridiculing SÄPO for its suspicions, he offered a generous glimpse of his unguarded, hidden side.

Interestingly, he even claimed that the classified files were of no importance and only a matter of personal interest. When the reporter then reminded Åström that he did not come to the studio to discuss his personal life but to talk about politics, the retired diplomat readily agreed and claimed that he did not intend to 'nag' about his coming out. His being gay was thus presented not as a public and political issue, but as a matter of personal interest, just like the classified dossier of SÄPO. However, these claims were diametrically opposed to the radio interview ('Efter tre'/'After three') he gave on 16 September and the debate article he published in *Dagens Nyheter/The Daily News* two days later. On the air, he claimed that his homosexuality was *the decisive* reason for SÄPO to mistrust and survey him during the cold war. He even added that, as late as 2003, the security police might feel ashamed for these loosely based suspicions. In the debate article, Åström explicitly stated: 'The real reason for the suspicions against me was my homosexuality' (Åström 2003b: 4). While he was an active diplomat, he knew that he was at times being followed and that his phone was tapped. He even went so far as to claim that these misgivings led to unprofessional decisions and that because at times SÄPO kept him in the dark regarding certain political actions, 'the behaviour of the security police led at some occasions to severe damage to Sweden's national interests' (Åström 2003b: 4).[10]

How then could Åström claim on TV 4 that his being gay was purely a matter of personal interest, while he himself presented plenty of evidence that pointed to the opposite? One explanation I offer is that he was trapped in a 1950s, pre-feminist private/public binary ideology that did not conceptualize gender and sexuality as political concerns. His contradictory statements hinted at the political dimension of the private/public divide which has helped to shape the modern notion of bourgeois identity since the late eighteenth century. Åström represented a masculinity that was ideologically dependent on a discourse that strictly separated the public from the private. He understood homosexuality as a private, personal orientation or preference, while, at the same time, he would claim that, because of his homosexuality, SÄPO was particularly concerned about his diplomatic contacts (not least to the USSR). While this was an explicit way of drawing attention to the political side of homosexuality and the closet, he himself nevertheless refused to politicize sexual categories or to fathom the closet as an overarching social institution and structuring principle, as a 'curious space that is both internal and marginal to culture: centrally representative of its motivating passions and contradictions, even while marginalized by its orthodoxies' (Sedgwick 1990: 56). The dichotomies between centre and margin, between private and public, were mirrored in Åström's changing body language and gesticulations, and in his shifting voice modulations.

The alleged communist and his Russian cat

As a gay diplomat, Åström could not afford to become a victim of political blackmail. As a result, he was always careful to inform his bosses, that is, the Swedish prime ministers and ministers of foreign affairs, of his homosexuality. In a humble fashion he claimed to have 'served' (Thunberg 2003: 16) prime ministers Tage Erlander and Olof Palme, making them seem more like kings than democratically elected politicians. Apparently, they did not care about his sexuality and just 'shrugged their shoulders' (Thunberg 2003: 16). This further illustrates the contradictory relationship between

10. Åström was alluding here to Stig Wennerström, a colonel in the Swedish Air Force who was disclosed as a spy for the Soviet Union in 1964. SÄPO had kept Wennerström under close surveillance for a long time, but instead of informing Åström of their suspicions about the colonel, they kept the diplomat in the dark. Because of this, an unsuspecting Åström would hand highly confidential material to Wennerström, something that obviously added to SÄPO's suspicions against him.

11. For a detailed analysis of the relationship between cold war anxiety, masculinity and homosexuality in the US see: Clark 2000; Corber 1997; D'Emilio 1983; Johnson 2004; Savran 1992.

12. For an analysis of Swedish ideology and foreign politics during the cold war see: Bjereld et al. 2008, and Lödén 1999.

13. Swedish literature on this subject includes: Eliasson 2002; Hjort 2002; Flyghed and Gustafsson 2003.

Swedish national politics and the closet, as well as the centrality of both homosexuality and homophobia in the immediate post-war era. At the heart of cold war diplomacy was a gay man whose homosexuality posed an alleged security risk. A public acknowledgment would probably have ended his political career. However, to protect himself from blackmail, Åström told his superiors – *in order to secure his secret, he disclosed it himself*. Unlike a conservative politician who might keep clandestine desires hidden from party colleagues, the gay diplomat informed his social democratic bosses, who protected the secret homosexuality of one of their most valued associates while social discrimination was ongoing. For them, it was more important to retain the coherency of the homosocial political establishment than to expose the gay man at its core.

The West's paranoia regarding communist spies is often associated with the era of McCarthyism, when national anxiety and moral panic went hand in hand. The wave of anti-communism also led to a renewed homophobia, both in the US and in Europe. Apart from being perceived as a sexual threat, homosexuals in government positions were also seen as in danger of being blackmailed by communist spies. The perceived need for a strong, virile nation was conflated with the fear of homosexuality and, as a result, enhanced the social prescriptions of hetero-normative masculinity, both in political language and cultural representations.[11] Cold war popular imagination was thrilled by this possibility and the threat of queer communist spies such as Guy Burgess and the Cambridge group. Roy Cohn, the American lawyer who played a key role in the persecution of communists and gays during the McCarthy era, and who was only outed after his death of HIV/AIDS in 1986, also personifies gay closeted masculinity of that period. Unlike the monumentalized characters of Cohn and Burgess and their appeal in mainstream popular culture, Åström is a much less sensationalized and vilified example of a closeted cold war politician. He was neither a communist spy like Burgess nor a communist hunter like Cohn. Nevertheless, his experience of living a discreet existence while having a prominent political career bears upon Swedish and European gay history, especially given his significant mark on the political and diplomatic landscape of the nation. It is worth underlining Sweden's unique position in the West in the immediate post-war era, not least because it expanded the welfare state, but also because of its adopted policy of neutrality, for which Åström was a key representative.[12] Although Sweden chose not to become a member of NATO, the fear of communism was omnipresent during the cold war; hence the state's increased involvement in individual citizens' personal lives. For many decades, eavesdropping over telephones (among other tactical measures) was primarily how SÄPO registered people with purportedly deviant political opinions. Referring to interests of national security, they gathered information on diverse groups such as communists, peace activists, travellers to the former Eastern bloc countries, or subscribers to certain magazines.[13] The immediate post-war period was also marked by institutionalized homophobia through a combined attack from the government, media and medico-juridical establishments. The medical diagnosis list insisted on classifying homosexuality as an aberrant mental condition until as late as 1979, while social concerns were raised about whether the fact that young army recruits sometimes worked as prostitutes jeopardized national security. Newspapers attracted readers with gossipy reports about political scandals that involved 'homophile' men, giving their readers the impression of secret homosexual networks of men that were protecting each other's interests (Söderström 1999: esp. 485–501 and 522–629). It is fully understandable therefore that a man like Åström chose not to go public with his sexuality. In many ways, he personified this era and its intertwined fears of homosexuality and communism; the fact that he spent the early 1940s in the Soviet Union, spoke fluent Russian and was later in charge of diplomatic relations with the communist country, made him a convenient target for suspicion.[14] Åström was well aware that he needed to be careful and the motif of a double existence permeated his narratives when he came out in 2003. His biography, for example, included the intriguing observation:

> Being gay means to more or less live in two worlds. [...] Whenever I moved in either one of these worlds, the other one did not exist. At the same time, it is not without a certain satisfaction that I could state that the double existence allows for interesting experiences because you observe events, glances and coincidences that other people don't notice.
>
> (Åström 2003a: 271)

In the interview with *Svenska Dagbladet*, Åström further explained how his 'world was split into two existences. In my professional life, the gay world did not exist – privately, I have, all over the world, socialized with gay friends' (Thunberg 2003: 16). Some major ideas came forward in these lines. Because of the paranoid social climate that considered homosexuals as potential risks to national security, for a gay man to have a successful diplomatic career during the cold war era he had to lead a double, almost schizophrenic, existence. However, Åström also alluded to the advantages of his experience of duplicity. Maybe life in the closet was not all that different from being a diplomat during the cold war? Both conditions were based on secret codes, games, deceptions and fear of disclosure. Åström's statements also allowed the closet to be imagined as a privileged position from which the gay person observes the outside world, trying to learn the necessary codes in order to blend in.[15]

Regardless of any previous suspicions, Åström managed to display an ironic attitude towards cold war imagery. For example, the first chapter in his memoirs, *Ögonblick*, took the reader right to the Kremlin and the heart of European diplomacy during World War II. In December 1940, a young Åström accompanied his boss, diplomat Vilhelm Assarsson, to meet with foreign minister Vyacheslav Molotov to discuss the dangerous situation in Europe. The style of the narrative is reminiscent of a spy novel – was it Stalin himself whose steps and coughing Åström could hear behind the locked door during the meeting? In order to establish an authentic atmosphere, not even the vodka is missing in the biographical account. When German troops approached, Moscow was no longer safe, and the Swedish diplomats were evacuated. While waiting for the end of the war in the eastern part of the

14. As late as 1989, Åström's stay in Russia became an issue when *Dagens Nyheter* published a juicy news bill and revealed that SÄPO suspected Åström of being a communist spy.

15. David Halperin points out that such a position has the potential to produce knowledge and articulate social criticism, a Foucauldian *gai savoir* that allows the outsider to observe and analyse social reality (Halperin 1995: 56–62).

16. In his book Åström
confessed that he,
during some rare
pessimistic moments,
thought his cat to be
the only living creature
that loved him
unconditionally
(2003a: 271).

Soviet Union, Åström spent part of his time playing tennis. On TV 4, he reminisced about those years, and the programme even showed a picture of the young diplomat posing at a tennis court together with a colleague – under a large propaganda picture of Stalin holding a young girl, making it seem as if the two civil servants were followers of the Soviet dictator. Towards the end of the interview, Åström opened an animal cage he had brought with him and pulled out his cat, Dusjka, explaining that its name means 'little soul' in Russian.[16] He said he had chosen this particular cat because he liked the fur, which he described as rat-coloured. Further flaunting his eccentricity, he added that the cat itself got angry at this description – she preferred to be called lion-yellow. While the animal was obviously accustomed to lying on Åström's lap, the TV studio was an unknown environment and he held on to her firmly and petted her gently. Despite the shortness of this scene, which lasted for about ninety seconds, it remains of great interest because it subverts notions of cold war masculinity.

Let us recap. The viewer had just seen a photograph of a young Åström playing tennis in the Soviet Union with an over-sized picture of Stalin overlooking the court. The diplomat had also ridiculed SÄPO for suspecting him as a communist spy. Where upon, Åström proudly displayed his Russian named pet, holding it in his lap and stroking it in the best Bond-villain fashion, just like the character Ernst Stavro Blofeld, one of the most infamous scoundrels in Ian Fleming's Bond series and who appears in several of the movies. The iconic shots of the initially unseen character stroking his trademark Persian cat have been parodied countless times in popular culture. Needless to say, the Bond genre is rooted in the era of the cold war and the fear of Soviet communism as well as the perceived gay threat. On the TV-sofa, Åström performed a parody of this genre and its political and sexual connotations. Borrowing from Butler's terminology, his theatrical behaviour had the potential to be a subversive act and to question the stability of sexual classifications:

> Paradoxically, but also with great promise, the subject who is 'queered' into public discourse through homophobic interpellations of various kinds also *takes up* or *cites* that very term as the discursive basis for an opposition. This kind of citation will emerge as *theatrical* to the extent that it *mimes and renders hyperbolic* the discursive convention that it also *reverses*. The hyperbolic gesture is crucial to the exposure of the homophobic 'law' that can no longer control the terms of its own abjecting strategies.
>
> (Butler 1993: 232, original emphasis)

SÄPO had classified Åström as a secret homosexual and possibly a communist spy. While on TV, the diplomat offered an example of an excessive, theatrical behaviour, quoting and performing a classic cold war villain masculinity in a hyperbolic form, and thereby managing to parody that era's omnipresent fear of the evil communist and/or gay man. Just like the odd socks, the cat was one more accessory to make a spectacle of the closet, making it a bit more endurable.

A belated entertainment

At the end of the day, one question remained unanswered: given that Åström officially retired in 1982, at a time when demands for gay disclosure became more prominent, why did he wait until 2003 to finally reach the decision to publicly come out?[17] In the interview with *QX*, he himself admitted that his homosexuality had long been an open secret: 'My circle of friends and the media have known and I thought there wasn't much point to keeping it a secret any longer' (Voss 2003: 14). He had informed his bosses, the media had handled the issue discreetly, and in gay circles rumours had been floating around for a very long time.[18] However, the retired diplomat was carefully choosing his words and only revealing the partial truth of the matter. While he repeatedly described his coming out as a private issue – and revealed a divided masculinity that was ideologically dependent on a pre-feminist understanding of gender and sexuality as private, that is, non-political – there was strong evidence to suggest that this coming out was, in fact, a tactical move in a much larger political game. Regardless of the different variations, the thing that all six versions of Åström's public confessions had in common was a constant attack on SÄPO for not granting him access to his files. Even though the diplomat himself never acknowledged this, the main reason for coming out, I believe, was to launch this public and mediatized attack on SÄPO. In order to overtly denounce and ridicule them, he needed to come out of the closet first. Whereas this would have been a price too high to pay during his active years as a diplomat, he had little to lose in 2003. After decades of diplomatic experience he knew exactly how much information to disclose at the right moment in time. After all, he himself admitted that '[a] diplomat must never lie. There is no professional group for whom lies are as dangerous. But lying is one thing, not telling the entire truth is a different matter' (Thunberg 2003: 16). Once again revealing the similarities between a diplomat and a marginalized sexual identity, that last sentence certainly rings true for many gay people. However, since Åström never took the step to conceptualize homosexuality (his own or anybody else's) as political, he was caught up in a web of inconsistencies – making six media appearances to come out and at the same time claiming that being gay is not a big deal is contradictory (just like wearing a red and a green sock and just like the schizophrenic institution of the closet that never allows the queer subject to completely step outside of its logic).

The closet is more than a question of individual, undisclosed sexuality; it is intertwined with questions of power and knowledge. In the words of David Halperin:

> The closet is nothing, first of all, if not the product of complex relations of power. The only reason to be *in* the closet is to protect oneself from the many and virulent sorts of social disqualification that one would suffer were the discreditable fact of one's sexual orientation more widely known.
>
> (Halperin 1995: 29, original emphasis)

17. One can only speculate on why Åström was never outed against his will. Whether it was because of his powerful friends, the respectful attitude of journalists, his own cautiousness, the fact that he spent a large part of his political career abroad or the gay movement's lack of interest in outing someone who never promoted a homophobic political agenda, Åström had the rare privilege of regarding his coming out as a personal decision. For a study on the lively debates in the gay community about whether celebrities and closeted homophobic politicians should be outed, and the ethical consequences of such actions, see Gross 1993.

18. Sedgwick points to the centrality of gossip in the social life of gay people as a tool to make sense of the world and to disrupt hetero-normativity. According to her, 'the precious, devalued arts of gossip, immemorially associated in European thought with servants, with effeminate and gay men, with all women' is 'the refinement of necessary

skills for making,
testing, and using
unrationalized and
provisional hypotheses
about what *kinds of
people* there are to be
found in one's world'
(Sedgwick 1990: 23,
original emphasis).

19. To what extent the
closet has become a
question of
entertainment was
nowhere more obvious
than when the readers
of *QX* awarded Åström
the prestigious 'Gay
Person of the Year'
award in 2004. The
following year, a
celebrated musical
artist won the same
award for the same
reason, that is, for
having come out of the
closet. One might be
tempted to put forward
some sour comments
about the Swedish gay
community being
caught up in a
superficial world of
glitter and *schlager*
music, and choosing its
heroes according to
their entertainment
value while actual
activists are not being
recognized for their
efforts.

20. Swedish journalist
Johan Hilton (2005)
has investigated a
number of murders
motivated by
homophobia, murders
which never received a

The concrete social disqualification that gays (as well as lesbians, bisexuals and transgendered people) risk is verbal abuse, ridicule, legal and judicial discrimination, threats, acts of violence and hate speech. However, in the twenty-first century, the closet has also been turned into mediatized entertainment, at least when a famous gay person steps out of it that is. Once opened, the door of the celebrity closet leads directly to the TV couch and the gossip pages of the papers.[19] While such cases are often understood as a sign of the times that gay people are being embraced and accepted by mainstream society, the Åström example also clearly reveals how such spectacles are a convenient means to make homosexuality more unobjectionable by taming it. Epitomizing this process, the colourful socks contributed towards Åström's appearance as an eccentric, elderly and non-threatening gentleman. His advanced age mattered greatly in this context, because it helped to present him as asexual. In the different reports, his regret at not having had a long-term relationship was stressed, but no one ever raised the question of what life was like when he, as Sweden's UN representative, was living in New York in the 1970s, that is, at the height of sexual liberation. This taming of a once so scandalous and 'dangerous' homosexuality is a symptom of an ongoing normalization and assimilation that, conveniently, also keeps up the cultural stereotype of homosexuals as miserable and lonely. Moreover, nobody ever challenged Åström as to why he had not come out immediately after his retirement in 1982. Such a question would have directed attention to a time when the stakes for coming out were higher because of the media's sensationalized and homophobic reports on the HIV/AIDS crisis. The country's more recent homophobic politics would have been brought back into the light, and in 2003 neither Åström nor the media (both gay and straight) seemed to be interested in doing this. Instead, the public discourse around Åström's coming out produced the 1950s and the twenty-first century as dichotomies, with the immediate post-war period being labelled as the Dark Ages for gay people and the current period as the time of Enlightenment. Sweden was falsely constructed as a once homophobic country that no longer discriminated against gays in any way, and as a country in which the closet had become a redundant institution. The real dangers of living as a gay person in a hetero-normative society were disregarded, as was the fact that the closet continues to work as a murderous institution.[20] As a result, the media discourse sent out mixed signals: the green sock was a 'go' sign, the red sock a 'stop' sign. What good is coming out of the closet, if you are not allowed to clean it?

Final reflections

While gay people certainly have a right to live openly without facing the threat of discrimination, verbal harassment or physical violence, contemporary liberation also comes at a high price. One of the concessions that gay culture is making is to give up the right to critically revisit its own and, by extension, the country's history. As Sedgwick wisely points out, 'gay people […] have with difficulty and always belatedly to patch together from fragments a community, a usable heritage, a politics of survival or resistance […]' (Sedgwick 1990: 81). However, if mainstream society and gay culture collaborate in erasing this history, the result is a state of amnesia that badly prepares us for the challenges of the twenty-first century.

In an ambitious study on how the state has surveyed sexuality in the name of national security since the cold war, the Canadian scholars Gary Kinsman and Patrizia Gentile (2010: esp. 429–458) stress how the concept of national security has been redefined according to the needs of a neo-liberal economic system, where opposition to global capitalism (as is often manifested in large-scale protests against the World Trade Organization, the Group of Eight, the International Monetary Fund etc.) are understood to be the largest threats against western 'civilization'. They also reflect on how many of the stately means of regulation and surveillance still survive after the end of the cold war. Among the parallel practices used by intelligence services during the cold war and during the 'war against terrorism', they identify the following: different cells of the global justice movement are infiltrated by police spies; those arrested are being forced to name their colleagues; certain social groups are identified and made suspicious as subversive elements or as risks to national security; political regulations legally sanction attacks on these alleged subversive groups; twenty-first century terrorists are 'othered' in terms of race and religion, while queers in the cold war were 'othered' in terms of sexuality.[21]

One important dimension the authors do not specifically identify is the challenge of new technologies and the stately and military efforts to adapt to these in order to, once again, eavesdrop on so-called private citizens. What is very specific to Sweden, and what makes the Åström case still interesting after all these years, is how his stories about his phone being tapped were not a reminder of a time long gone, but had very direct parallels to our own contemporary moment. The unwillingness to critically investigate the country's history was exposed again a few years later, when, in the global paranoia caused by the 'war on terrorism', the Swedish parliament debated and, on 18 June 2008, ultimately ratified proposition 2006/07:63 which ruled that, as of 1 January 2009, the Swedish National Defence Radio Establishment has the right to control and save telephone calls, Internet traffic, e-mails, text messages and all other forms of electronic communication that pass the national border.[22] In light of this controversial law, known under the acronym FRA (*Försvarets radioanstalt/National Defence Radio Establishment*), it is worth pointing out that the country has a long history regarding the registration of people's political views and sexualities. Just how safe are gays, lesbians, bisexuals and transgendered people when the so-called 'war against terrorism' justifies the government supervising our activities on the phone or in cyberspace? How is a new generation to protect itself against stately surveillance if they are kept in the dark about history?

lot of media attention because they were not deemed to be newsworthy.

21. Kinsman and Gentile also stress that the current 'war on terrorism' has a pronounced gendered and sexualized dimension, as it promotes an aggressively heterosexual, white, military masculinity that claims to liberate women in the East and protect women in the West (Kinsman and Gentile 2010: 450–456).

22. The proposition was sanctioned by the Swedish parliament despite a broad popular resistance manifested in demonstrations and Internet forums. It was modified on 14 October 2009, with the promise to enhance personal integrity.

References

Åström, Sverker (2003a), *Ögonblick: Från ett halvsekel i UD-tjänst/Moments: From half a century in the duty of the ministry for foreign affairs*, Stockholm: Lind & Co.

Åström, Sverker (2003b), 'Därför såg Säpo mig som en säkerhetsrisk'/'This is why the Swedish Security Police saw me as a national security risk', *Dagens Nyheter/ The Daily News*, 18 September, p. 4.

Bjereld, Ulf, Johansson, Alf W., and Molin, Karl (2008), *Sveriges säkerhet och världens fred: Svensk utrikespolitik under kalla kriget/Sweden's security and world peace: Swedish foreign politics during the cold war*, Stockholm: Santérus.

Breward, Christopher (1995), *The Culture of Fashion: A New History of Fashionable Dress*, Manchester and New York: Manchester University Press.

Breward, Christopher (1999), *The Hidden Consumer: Masculinities, Fashion and City Life 1860–1914*, Manchester: Manchester University Press.

Butler, Judith P. (1993), *Bodies that Matter: On the Discursive Limits of 'Sex'*, London and New York: Routledge.

Butler, Judith P. (2004 [1990]), 'Imitation and Gender Subordination', in Sarah Salih and Judith Butler (eds), *The Judith Butler Reader*, Malden, Mass.: Blackwell Publishers, pp. 119–137.

Case, Sue-Ellen (2002), 'The Emperor's New Clothes: The Naked Body and Theories of Performance', *SubStance: A Review of Theory and Literary Criticism*, issue 98/99, 31: 2 &3, pp. 186–200.

Clark, Suzanne (2000), *Cold Warriors: Manliness on Trial in the Rhetoric of the West*, Carbondale: Southern Illinois University Press.

Cole, Shaun (2000), *'Don We Now Our Gay Apparel': Gay Men's Dress in the Twentieth Century*, Oxford and New York: Berg.

Connell, R. W. (2000), *The Men and the Boys*, Cambridge: Polity Press.

Corber, Robert J. (1997), *Homosexuality in Cold War America: Resistance and the Crisis of Masculinity*, Durham: Duke University Press.

D'Emilio, John (1983), *Sexual Politics, Sexual Communities: The Making of a Homosexual Minority in the United States, 1940–1970*, Chicago: University of Chicago Press.

Detering, Heinrich (2002), *Das offene Geheimnis: Zur literarischen Produktivität eines Tabus von Winckelmann bis zu Thomas Mann/The open secret: On the literary productivity of a taboo from Winckelmann to Thomas Mann*, Göttingen: Wallstein Verlag.

Dyer, Richard (1997), *White: Essays on Race and Culture*, London and New York: Routledge.

Eliasson, Ulf (2002), *Politisk övervakning och personalkontroll 1945–1969: Säkerhetspolisens medverkan i den politiska personalkontrollen/Political surveillance and personnel control 1945–1969: The participation of the security police in the political personnel control*, Stockholm: Swedish Government Official Reports SOU 88.

Entwistle, Joanne (2000), *The Fashioned Body: Fashion, Dress and Modern Social Theory*, Cambridge: Polity Press.

Flügel, John Carl (2004 [1930]), 'The Great Masculine Renunciation and Its Causes', in Daniel Leonhard Purdy (ed.), *The Rise of Fashion: A Reader*, Minneapolis: University of Minnesota Press, pp. 102–198.

Flyghed, Janne and Gustafsson, Kerstin (2003), 'Säposåpan'/'The Swedish Security Police Soap Opera', *Ordfront Magasin*, November, pp. 34–49.

Gross, Larry (1993), *Contested Closets: The Politics and Ethics of Outing*, Minneapolis & London: University of Minnesota Press.

Halperin, David M. (1995), *Saint Foucault: Towards a Gay Hagiography*, New York & Oxford: Oxford University Press.

Hilton, Johan (2005), *No Tears For Queers: Ett reportage om män, bögar och hatbrott/No Tears For Queers: A report on men, gays and hate crimes*, Stockholm: Atlas.

Hjort, Magnus (2002), *Hotet från vänster: Säkerhetstjänsternas övervakning av kommunister, anarkister m.m. 1965–2002/The threat from the left: The counterintelligence's surveillance of communists, anarchists a.o. 1965–2002*, Stockholm: Swedish Government Official Reports SOU 91.

Hollander, Anne (1995), *Sex and Suits: The Evolution of Modern Dress*, New York and London: Kodansha International.

Johnson, David K. (2004), *The Lavender Scare: The Cold War Persecution of Gays and Lesbians in the Federal Government*, Chicago: University of Chicago Press.

Kinsman, Gary and Patrizia Gentile (2010), *The Canadian War on Queers: National Security as Sexual Regulation*, Vancouver and Toronto: UBC Press.

Kuchta, David (2009), 'The Three-Piece-Suit', in Peter McNeil and Vicki Karaminas (eds), *The Men's Fashion Reader*, Oxford and New York: Berg, pp. 44–53.

Kulick, Don (2005), 'Four Hundred Thousand Swedish Perverts', *GLQ: A Journal of Lesbian and Gay Studies*, 11: 2, pp. 205–235.

Lodén, Hans (1999), *'För säkerhets skul': Ideologi och säkerhet i svensk aktiv utrikespolitik 1950–1975 /'For the sake of security': Ideology and security in active Swedish foreign politics 1950–1975*, Stockholm: Nerenius & Santérus, diss.

Rosenberg, Tiina (2002), *Queerfeministisk agenda/Queer feminist agenda*, Stockholm: Atlas.

Savran, David (1992), *Communists, Cowboys, and Queers: The Politics of Masculinity in the Work of Arthur Miller and Tennessee Williams*, Minneapolis: University of Minnesota Press.

Sedgwick, Eve Kosofsky (1990), *Epistemology of the Closet*, Berkeley: University of California Press.

Söderström, Göran (ed.) (1999), *Sympatiens hemlighetsfulla makt: Stockholms homosexuella 1860–1960/ The mysterious power of sympathy: Homosexuals in Stockholm 1860–1960*, Stockholm: Stockholmia.

Stadin, Kekke (2007), 'Iklädd borgerlighet – och utklädd: Stärkkrage, manlighet och borgerliga ideal i Buddenbrooks Lübeck'/'Dressed in bourgeoisie – and undressed: Stand-up collar, masculinity and bourgeois ideals in Buddenbrooks' Lübeck', in Lars Nilsson (ed.), *Stockholms Lilja: Stadshistoriska studier tillägnade professorn i Stockholms historia Sven Lilja 23 juli 2007/ The Lily Of Stockholm: Studies in urban history dedicated to the professor in Stockholm history Sven Lilja on 23 July 2007*, Stockholm: Stads- och kommunhistoriska institutet, pp. 205–237.

Thunberg, Karin (2003), 'Nu berättar han sanningen'/'Now he's telling the truth', *Svenska Dagbladet/ The Swedish Daily Paper*, Culture section, 14 September, pp. 1, 16–17.

Voss, Jon (2003), 'En gentleman kommer ut'/'A gentleman is coming out', *QX*, October, pp. 14–15.

Weeks, Jeffrey (1990 [1977]), *Coming Out: Homosexual Politics in Britain from the Nineteenth Century to the Present*, London and New York: Quartet Books.

Woltersdorff, Volker (2005), *Coming Out: Die Inszenierung schwuler Identitäten zwischen Auflehnung und Anpassung/Coming out: The performance of gay identities between rebellion and adaptation*, Frankfurt a. M.: Campus.

TV and radio broadcastings

'Efter tre'/'After three' (2003), P4, Sveriges Radio/Swedish Radio, 16 September.

'TV 4 Nyhetsmorgon'/'TV 4 morning news' (2003), TV 4, 4 October.

Suggested citation

Gindt, D. (2010), 'Coming out of the cabinet: Fashioning the closet with Sweden's most famous diplomat', *Critical Studies in Fashion and Beauty* 1: 2, pp. 233–254, doi: 10.1386/csfb.1.2.233_1

Contributor details

Dirk Gindt holds a Ph.D. in Performance Studies and has worked as an Assistant Professor at the Centre for Fashion Studies at Stockholm University, where, in autumn 2009, he was awarded a two-year

Dirk Gindt

research position as a Postdoctoral Associate. Gindt is co-editor of *Fashion: An Interdisciplinary Reflection* (Raster, 2009). He has published in *Nordic Theatre Studies*, *The Tennessee Williams Annual Review* and has a forthcoming article in *Fashion Theory*. He is also the editor-in-chief of *lambda nordica* for which he has edited a special issue on masculinities (13: 4) and a double issue on queer fashion (14: 3–4). His current research projects investigate the original Swedish stage productions of Tennessee Williams' plays in the 1950s and the collaboration between fashion designers and performance artists.

Contact:
E-mail: dirk.gindt@yahoo.ca

CSFB 1 (2) pp. 255–269 Intellect Limited 2010

Critical Studies in Fashion and Beauty
Volume 1 Number 2
© 2010 Intellect Ltd Exhibition Review. English language. doi: 10.1386/csfb.1.2.255_7

EXHIBITION REVIEW

The return of the absent body in the fashion museum: 'Dressing the body' exhibition
DHUB Museu Tèxtil i d'Indumentària, Barcelona, permanent exhibition

Curators: Teresa Bastardes and Sílvia Ventosa

Teresa Bastardes, Head of collections, Disseny Hub Barcelona (DHUB)
Dr Patrícia Soley-Beltran, Honorary Fellow, University of Edinburgh
Helena Tatay, Curator and art critic (www.blablart.com)
Dr. Sílvia Ventosa, Chief curator, DHUB Museu Tèxtil i d'Indumentària de Barcelona
Anne Zazzo, Conservateur en chef du Patrimoine/Chief Curator of Heritage, Musée de la mode de la Ville de Paris

The mannequins as a person substitute

Ever since Marie Vernet (wife of Charles Worth and the first known fashion model) successfully increased sales of the crinolines designed by her husband in the mid-nineteenth century, the importance of mannequins' bodies as a strategy of fashion marketing has not been lost on the fashion industry. Nevertheless, until very recently, as the exhibition 'Dressing the Body' exemplifies (Ventosa and Bastardes, DHUB Barcelona 2008), the body's presence has been silenced in fashion exhibitions (Soley Beltran & Tatay 2009).

The first challenge for fashion museums is to present clothing without the living bodies that give them movement, volume, seduction, shape and character. To compensate for the absence of a real body, bodies are recreated through the shape of the garment, which is enhanced with the help 'silhouettes cheaters' such as covered prostheses, casts, dressmakers' dummies with stitched shapes stuffed with cotton (which gives them hips or chest), busts made of cardboard, and small pillows sketching the arms. Even paper curls hairstyles are used as a reminder of heads – when they are not left strangely bald. When wigs are realistic, stylized abstract faces with blind eyes and a cadaverous complexion highlight the artifice (Zazzo 2009).

Inventing the missing body

Since the 1980s, the museums of fashion and costume have specialized in inventing the missing bodies under the aegis of scenography textile conservators, curators and some designers. Museums like the Costume Institute at the Metropolitan Museum of Art in New York, or the Victoria & Albert Museum in London, now ask designers to create hairstyles and makeup for museum models in the same way that they would for catwalk shows. In the spectacular exhibition 'The Model as Muse: Embodying Fashion' by Harold Koda (Costume Institute, Metropolitan Museum, May–August 2009) in one room some models were hung vertically, as if they'd jumped in the air and were suspended by their hair, glued to the ceiling. Elsewhere, the artificial hair was curved like in paintings and outrageous makeup reminiscent of the mask-like faces of catwalk stars was used (Zazzo 2009).

Echoes of the repressed body

The exhibition, however, is far from the fever of the catwalk podium: invincible artificial stiffness freezes the conventional grand dolls – always inadequate to present clothing. Ventosa and Bastardes (2009) distinguish the *consumer* from the *curator*. The museum space maintains a dialogue between the visitor, who is accustomed to being a consumer who touches the products and feels them before acquiring them, and the curator, who uses the language of museography and turns mannequins into a showcase of style in a display cabinet. The fashion display at the museum becomes a silent impression that recalls the absence of a body and its sensations, and evidences the missing wardrobe in the dark museum's showcases.

The shop's space is glittering in the spotlight or lit from the street; outfits and accessories are awaiting a buyer to try them on, imagining multiple scenarios and stories of possible use. In contrast, at the museum the garment still tells stories and feelings, but by proxy. I, the visitor, am not part of the memory and the imagination of museum garments. For the clothes in the clothing museum are never just material objects. They are simultaneously a 'textile object' and an 'image'.

The museum body is an absent presence. It is banned by the principle of the textile museum. Textile heritage conservation does not tolerate fat, moisture or acidity of the skin, and fibres suffer from every tension or manipulation. The museum body is a repressed body. We are now witnessing a new trend of the 'return of the repressed' body in museum exhibitions (Zazzo 2009).

Which absent body returns to the museum space?

Every period contemplates the body – through the filter of its own moral values and standards of tastes – as a cultural object of style, position, conduct, identity and clothing. In his classic book *The Nude: A Study in Ideal Form* ([1956] 1972) Kenneth Clark distinguishes the *naked* from the *nude*. In contrast to the naked body, which is without clothes, the nude as a conceptual and artistic category always involves the notion of 'an ideal' abstracted from the reality we confront in our everyday lives. Anne Hollander adapted this insight specifically to fashion when she argued, in *Seeing Through Clothes* ([1975] 1993), that in every period depictions of the nude in art and sculpture correspond to the dominant fashions of the day. In other words, the nude is never simply 'naked' but represents the contemporary conventions of dress. Thus 'the body of fashion' is not the body as 'nature' but the body as 'art'.

It is not enough for the fashion museum to chronicle the fashioned body as art. In *The Fashioned Body* (2001), Joanne Entwistle reminds us that it is necessary to transcend the argument of fashion as pure aesthetics, since fashion is also product of a chain of industrial, economic and cultural activities (Ventosa and Bastardes 2009).

Several exhibitions explored the differences between art and fashion, setting both at the same level, among them 'Dysfashional. Adventures in Post-Style' (Luca Marchetti and Emanuele Quinz, MUDAC, Laussane, 2007) and 'Looking at Fashion' (Germanic Celant, Luigi Settembrini and Ingrid Sischy, Biennale of Florence, 1996). 'Dysfashional' reacts against the notion of fashion as a simple collection of clothes and accessories, and argues for the 'subjectification of the object', alongside a notion of 'the garment as a subject [that] makes us, even defines us' (Soley Beltran and Tatay 2009).

Dress presented in a museum is usually like a fetishized object displayed outside its historical and social context. However, the function of a fashion museum is not merely descriptive; museums describe canons of beauty, tastes and style, and the materials and techniques of various periods. Above all they need to provide a critical or polemical interpretations of the social problems that are linked to fashion. Fashion is more than a meaning system. And as Kamawura says in *Fashion-ology* (2005), it is a system, not an isolated phenomenon, in which creators, publicists, companies of production and distribution, journalists, consumers, and other museums interact (Ventosa and Bastardes 2009).

A conceptual approach to fashion display

Artists and designers from the 1960s until the present day have shared an interest in embodiment. However, as a result of embodiment's current social importance, and the academic emphasis on the body as key site for the definition of identity, it has recently appeared as a new museographic perspective that looks at 'fashion bodies' (Soley Beltran and Tatay 2009).

Anne Zazzo (2009) identifies two groups of fashion displays: sensorial (*passer d'abord par la sensation*) which focuses on visual and tactile qualities, and conceptual (*passer d'abord par l'esprit*) which focuses on abstractions, ideas and the relations between garments and body.

The permanent exhibition 'Dressing the Body', which opened in December 2008 at the Museu Tèxtil i d'Indumentària in Barcelona, belongs to the second group and it constitutes a quiet revolution in scenography but a revolution nonetheless.

The relationship between fashion and the artificial body from the sixteenth century to the present day was the theme that guided the curators of 'Dressing the Body'. The exhibition is designed to show that it was the **dress** that **created** the outline of a **historicized body**. The forerunners of this exhibition were two earlier exhibitions. In 1999 the Kyoto Costume Institute showed an exhibition 'Visions of the Body', which explored fashion as a history of the fictitious body on a visible surface, and as a social structure that supports human relations. In 2001, the Metropolitan Museum of Art, New York, opened the 'Extreme Beauty' exhibition by Harold Koda, which divided the body horizontally and conducted a comparative analysis between the devices used to compress or to extend bodies, in western fashion and globally (Ventosa and Bastardes 2009).

'Dressing the body'

Amongst the exhibitions that adopt the body as a perspective 'Dressing the Body' is the most innovative. The exhibition's starting point is a notion of the body as a hybrid artefact caught between culture and nature. From here, a history of fashion is put forward that renews its meaningfulness by attending to the ways in which fashion design modifies the body. The show effectively establishes the incorporation of the changing anatomical canon by means of interventions that reveal the aesthetic modification of the body in an engaging and entertaining manner.

The exhibition runs chronologically and thematically: each theme is represented by a large display cabinet, where clothes are arranged so they can be reflected upon from many points of view – sometimes with the aid of reflecting mirrors.

The design of the space, by the architect Julia Schulz-Dornburg, presents two parallel narratives. On one side the dresses of the collection are on display, and on the other the textual timeline contextualizes the periodic styles that underlie the concept. This is not a 'staged presentation', but a conceptual dialogue where the characters relate to each other through contrasts or similarities.

The narrative thread of the exhibition explores how the dress modifies the form of the body throughout history by operating on the body in a number of ways: *reduction, extension, elongation, outlining, revealing*. This endless variation underlies the essence of fashion and its arbitrariness: it does not respond to anything other than itself, located in a given social context (Ventosa and Bastardes 2009) (see pages from the exhibition catalogue below).

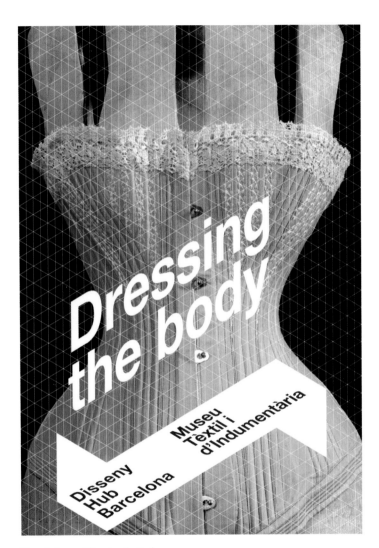

Figure 1: Image of Dressing the Body.

Dress changes body proportions, modifies a person's relation to space and to other people with some **actions**: increase, reduce, lengthen, define and reveal.

1. Increase: creates volume by added structures, stiff fabrics or tailoring that separate the garment from the body. The figure is widened: guardainfantes, hooped petticoats, crinolines, bustles and capes.

Figure 1a: Crinoline, c.1858.

2. Reduce: minimizes the body's natural shape, in particular the thorax and waist. The torso is squeezed: corsets, bodices, brassieres and belts.

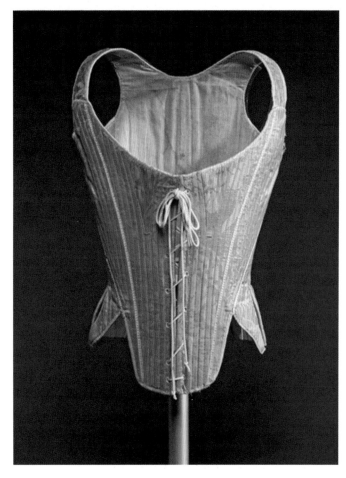

Figure 1b: Stays, 1750–1800.

3. Lengthen: stylizes the body so that it seems taller. Lengthens the body: high heels and platform shoes, hairstyles, hats and coat tails.

Figure 1c: Dress, end of the eighteenth century-beginning of the nineteenth century.

4. Define: adapts the body shape without changing it. The outline is highlighted: stockings, gloves, body stockings and stretchy t-shirts.

Figure 1d: Mariano Fortuny, Delphos tunic, 1909.

5. Reveal: suggests the body's shape, uncovers arms and legs, and shows skin. The body is exposed: transparent fabrics, sleeveless, low-cut, short dresses.

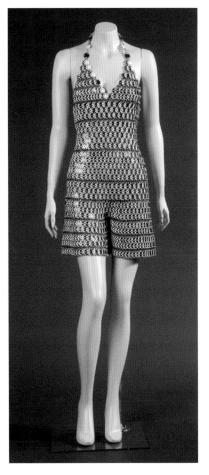

Figure 1e: Paco Rabanne, 1965.

The presentation of the dresses themselves is novel. It is done with the dress that best portrays the real body 'of the period'. This ruled out a standard mannequin of the kind used in shop windows. Each museum model is 'naked' in line with the conventions of body shape of its time.

For simplicity, the presentation method breaks down each set of display cabinets into the best five objects, illustrating the most important concepts in the field with some examples along the following lines (each one addresses a different question (figure 2 from right to left)):

1. How? Anatomical modifications: anatomical mannequins with joints highlight the body parts that are modified by clothing.
2. With what element? The prosthesis – the silhouettes are changed on a partial mannequin made of cardboard.
3. Which example? The prototype garment that best represents the standard shape of a period.
4. Like who? Reference to a garment from another period 'that does not fit' which reminds us of the cyclical nature of fashion.
5. What context? Finally, the representation (in the background) helps us understand the clothed person in their period, with accessories, hairstyles, etc.

The contemporary significance of the analysis presented by 'Dressing the Body' is related to a self-evident social phenomenon – namely how current body ideals imply aesthetic interventions that transcend clothing, thus realizing Elsa Schiaparelli's tenth commandment: 'never adapt the dress to the body, but train the body to adapt to the dress' – a peculiar inversion of priorities that – it is actually only the tip of the iceberg in a complex ordering of subjectivity. The exhibition invites continuing necessary and deeper consideration – from both academic and activist domains, as well as from art and even the fashion system – in order to confer meaningfulness to creative rebellion: a rebellion that should count on a 'delirious museum' (Storrie 2006) as a continuation of the city, the place where the body and lifestyle become the main site for identity construction (Soley Beltran & Tatay 2009).

Figure 2a: Luxury and movement, 1670–1789 at Dressing the Body, *DHUB, Barcelona.*

Figure 2b: Clothing and revolution: the liberated body, 1789–1825 at Dressing the Body, *DHUB, Barcelona.*